The Complete Idiot's
Quick MP3 Refe
MP3 Web Resour

Sources For MP3 Rec

URL	Contents
www.peoplesound.com	Find Free MP3s in your chosen musical style
www.vitaminic.co.uk	Free MP3s from signed and unsigned artists
www.mp3.com	Huge library of free, legal music MP3s
www.crunch.co.uk	Underground labels sell MP3s individually or as albums
www.toryumon.co.uk	Dance industry site featuring free downloads
www.getoutthere.bt.com	British Telecom site featuring free downloads
www.audible.com/mp3	Spoken word MP3s
www.amp3.com	Quality, free, legal MP3s with brief ads
www.emusic.com	MP3s by known artists for sale
www.rioport.com	Small but quality list of MP3s
www.betalounge.com	Weekly new music forum with old shows in MP3
www.blindfrog.com	Cutting-edge new bands
www.getsigned.com	Unsigned band MP3s, plus info for musicians
www.ihearyou.com	Friendly free MP3 site
www.layer3recordings.com	Small-but-growing MP3 site
www.mammoth.com	Indy label with free MP3 samples
www.mjuice.com	MP3s for sale
www.wiredplanet.com	Shockwave-powered music site
www.heartsongs.org	Christian music
www.jazzpromo.com	Jazz, cool and hot
www.bluesrevue.com	Magazine site with blues MP3s
www.pghblueswomen.com	Women from Pittsburgh sing the blues
mp3.songs.com	New bands screened for recording quality
www.epitonic.com	Reviewed and selected MP3 music
www.worldwidebands.com	Unsigned bands
www.resortrecords.com	Label-supported free MP3s

MP3 Reference Sites

URL	Content
www.narcopop.com	Guide to legal MP3 sites
www.mp3now.com	MP3 links and info
drogo.cselt.stet.it/mpeg/	The MPEG organization
www.mpeg.org	FAQs and links
www.soundbyting.com	Site on the stances of MP3-foe RIAA
www.iis.fhg.de/amm/	Fraunhofer, developer of the MP3 format

MP3 Player And Encoder Software

URL	Player
www.sonique.com	Sonique player for Windows
www.winamp.com	Winamp player for Windows
www.xingtech/mp3/player/	XingMP3 player for Windows
www.macamp.com	MacAmp player for Mac
www.audioactive.com/player/	AudioActive player for Windows
www.freeamp.org	FreeAmp player for Windows and Linux
www.xmms.org	Xmms player for Unix
www.musicmatch.com	MusicMatch player/encoder for Windows
www.RealJukebox.com	RealJukebox player/encoder for Windows
www.audiocatalyst.com	AudioCatalyst encoder for Mac and Windows
www.audioactive.com/MP3/	MP3Production Studio encoder for Windows

MP3 Hardware Player Manufacturers

URL	Hardware
www.RioPort.com	Diamond Rio portable player
www.saehan.com	MPMan portable players
www.thomson-lyra.com	Thomson Multimedia's Lyra portable player
www.lge.co.kr	LG Electronics portable players
www.mpress3.com	Mpress3 portable player
www.sem.samsung.com	Samsung Yepp portable players
www.jazpiper.nl	JazPiper portable player
www.casio.com/hpc/	Cassiopeia PDA and MP3 player
www.empeg.com	Empeg car player
www.audiorequest.com	AudioRequest home MP3 player

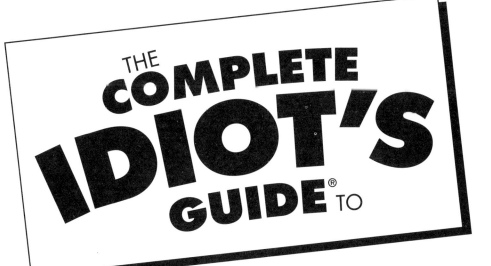

MP3 UK

Music on the

Internet

Roger Brown
Rod Underhill
Nat Gertler

que®

A Division of MacMillan Computer Publishing
201 W. 103rd St., Indianapolis, IN 46290 USA

PEARSON EDUCATION LIMITED

Head Office:
Edinburgh Gate
Harlow CM20 2JE
Tel: +44 (0)1279 623623
Fax: +44 (0)1279 431059

London Office:
128 Long Acre
London WC2E 9AN
Tel: +44 (0)20 7447 2000
Fax: +44 (0)20 7204 5771

First published in Great Britain in 2000 by Pearson Education Limited

Authorized adaptation from the English language edition published by Que Corporation Copyright © 2000
Adaptation published by Pearson Education Limited
© Pearson Education Limited 2000

The rights of Roger Brown, Rod Underhill and Nat Gertler to be identified as Authors of this Work have been asserted by them in accordance with the Copyright, Designs and Patents Act 1988.

ISBN 0-13-087921-5

British Library Cataloguing in Publication Data
A CIP catalogue record for this book can be obtained from the British Library.

10 9 8 7 6 5 4 3 2 1

Typeset by Land & Unwin (Data Sciences) Ltd

Printed and bound in Great Britain by
Redwood Books Ltd, Trowbridge.

The Publishers' policy is to use paper manufactured from sustainable forests.

Contents At A Glance

Contents

Afterword   245

Glossary   251

Index   257

Foreword By Judge Jules

The rise of MP3 and online music is a natural progression for music in these computer-obsessed times and one that is helping bring control of music back to where it belongs – with the people. For dance music in particular the democratisation of the music industry is a very positive thing. Dance doesn't need the heavy production of other genres, and great tunes can often be made by a couple of people in a home studio. With MP3 these same people can now get their stuff out to the public, and do their own publishing, marketing and even sales. The possibilities for the future are staggering, and can only be good for music.

– Judge Jules

About The Authors

Roger Brown is a new media manager, currently working in the exciting new field of interactive television. A music programmer who cites the computer keyboard as his first instrument, Roger is the author of *Electronica Dance Music Programming Secrets* (available from the same publisher) and collaborator on numerous electronica and Internet projects.

Rod Underhill is a musician, composer, songwriter, attorney and director of music for mp3.com. He will keep singing songs and putting them on the Internet until somebody stops him.

The closest Nat Gertler has ever come to musical coolness was when the indescribable Canadian band Moxy Früvous seriously considered naming its second album after him. Nat is a computer-book-writing son-of-a-gun, having penned such popular tomes as *Easy PCs* and *The Complete Idiot's Guide to PowerPoint 2000*. He unleashes his personal creativity through comic books, having worked on well-known titles such as *The Flintstones* and *Blood Syndicate*, as well as on his own creations, *Mister U.S.* and *The Factor*. His ultimate goal is global domination but he's taking his own sweet time getting around to it.

Dedications

To my mother, for showing me how to find the beat in music, to my father for showing me how to find the melody and to Mr Karmu, my music teacher, who showed me that it was all mathematics.

– Roger Brown

To my mother, Edith Estelle Underhill.

– Rod Underhill

To Lara Hughes and everyone else who keeps my world filled with music.

– Nat Gertler

Introduction

The electronic music phenomenon known as MP3 is stirring up a lot of interest and not a little controversy. By making quality recorded music files small enough to download, MP3 has turned the Internet into a plentiful and practical source of music. This has created vast opportunities for the musician who wants to spread his music around. It has also created vast headaches for the musicians and record companies that don't want their music spread around without getting paid for it.

You may wonder just what the MP3 phenomenon is and how it all works. You might be familiar with the technology and wonder where you can find some great music online. You probably want to know what choices you have in terms of software or even portable players. You may even be a music maker wanting to record and distribute your music over the Internet.

Regardless of the origins of your interest in MP3 music, this book is your guide. It has information that will help you, history that will inform you and insights that will enlighten you. It also has a CD-ROM laden with software that will let you listen to and make MP3s, and contains MP3 files filled with hours of music and more.

Conventions Used In This Book

To get the most out of this book, we've used some standard methods of referring to the items you see on screen and the things you should type. We've tried to put things together in such a way as to make reading the book both rewarding and fun. So, here's what to do when you see any of the following:

➤ Web page addresses (URLs) are presented in a `computer monospace font`. When you're being told to click a link on a Web page, the link is presented in **bold**. Click the link (or enter the URL into your browser's address field) to proceed.

➤ Anything you need to type on your computer's keyboard is presented in a `computer monospace font`. Key combinations are presented using a plus sign (+), such as **Shift+J**. For this combination, you hold down the **Shift** key and press **J**.

➤ New terms are presented in *italicised text*; pay close attention to these terms.

Extras

To pack as much information as possible into *The Complete Idiot's Guide to MP3: Music on the Internet,* we'll present a lot of additional tips and advice as you read the book. These elements enhance your knowledge or point out important pitfalls to avoid. Along the way, you'll find the following elements:

Check This Out!

These boxes contain warnings, notes and other information you'll find useful when using MP3.

Techno Talk

These boxes contain high-tech, in-depth information about the matter at hand. They'll define the sometimes arcane terminology used by musicians and computer programmers.

On Another Note

In these boxes, you'll find personal insights and handy tips from the authors of this book.

Part 1
What Is MP3?

You've probably heard a lot about MP3 in the press recently. How it will change the world of music, bring down the big record companies and enable anyone who makes music to make a fortune. It's technological; it's digital; it's creative! Everybody who is anybody is talking about it, as are lots of people who aren't anybody but want to be.

But what is it and where did it come from? In this part of the book, we ask the musical question: Say, what is MP3 anyway?

Chapter 1

Compressed Music: What Is It?

In This Chapter

➤ What is digital music?

➤ What is compressed digital music?

➤ What is MP3 and what can it do for you?

The Internet is huge but, until recently, it's been better known for sex than music. It's been a great way to get text and a pretty good way to get pictures but it was terrible at sending music. Our ears hear sounds very precisely and pick up lots of subtleties and we can tell if those subtleties aren't right. In order to fool our ears a recording needs to hold a lot of information about the original sound.

Information, in computer terms, takes up space. A clearly recorded tune takes up a lot of space on a computer's hard drive. Sending that much information over the Internet takes a lot of time. Sending an hour of CD-quality music recording over the Internet using a fast modem generally takes about a day and a half. It also takes up a lot of space – you could probably only store a few CDs on your hard disk before you'd filled it up.

MP3 Makes It Happen

All these limitations of online recorded music were true until someone devised a way of using a lot less information to re-create the sound. People now use a format called MP3 (we'll explain the acronym later) to keep that clear, crisp recording sound – a format that uses about one-twelfth as much disk space. Now you have room to keep lots of music on your disk and downloading a tune takes only minutes. The Internet is suddenly useful to music fans and music makers.

So What Can MP3 Do For Me Now?

All this talk about the wonders of compression and sharing your music with the world makes it sound like something from the 1930 World's Fair, telling you how nuclear-powered flying cars will make life a breeze in 1965. Plenty of people are predicting that MP3 is the future but it's easy to overlook all the wonderful things it can do in the present.

Music Wants To Be Free

There are already tens of thousands of songs legally available for download on the Internet, free of charge. More are being added all the time. These songs range from ambient to electronica, hip hop to rock and 'world' music. They aren't hard to find, either; there are a number of popular sites that offer large music catalogues.

Much of the free, legal music that's out there is from new and unknown bands, which means that much of it might be considered rather overpriced at 'free'. However, there are some high-quality discoveries to be made. In addition, more and more established artists are distributing free MP3s to drum up publicity and fan response.

Shell Out For Some Sounds

There are also sites that let you download popular songs by well-known musicians for a small fee. This fee is much lower than the cost of a CD-single, if that song were even available as a single at the time you went to buy it; the fee is also cheaper than buying an entire CD for the one song you like.

At this point, the number of songs available for commercial download is fairly small – at least when compared to the amount of songs available on CD. However, it has been growing and is likely to continue to do so as the music business works out ways to make selling downloadable songs profitable.

Make Your Sounds Heard Around The World

If you're a music maker, the MP3 revolution is your chance to get your music to the people. It used to be that to get your music heard you either had to travel around and perform publicly or find a way to get your music on the radio. If you turn your song into an MP3 file, however, you can put it on to the Internet, where thousands of people a day can download and listen to it.

Turning your recordings into MP3s is easy. Once you've done that, you can upload it to major MP3 Web sites, where others can download it. Not only do the sites not charge for this service, some will also provide free Web space to promote your band, or even help you sell a CD of the recordings you've made.

Even if you're just looking to send the music to one person, emailing your MP3 files means that your music will arrive quickly and sound clear as a bell when received.

Turn Your PC Into A Digital Jukebox

If your PC is equipped with the proper sort of CD-ROM drive (and most modern PCs are), you can take tracks from your favourite CDs, compress them into MP3 files and store them on your hard drive along with all your downloaded MP3s. You'll be able to listen to those through your PC speakers or you could connect the sound out from your PC to your home stereo system.

'So what? If I wanted to hear the songs on that CD, I'd just play that CD,' you mutter. The difference? When that CD is over, you have to go and put on another, and then another and then another. You also have to suffer through the songs you don't like. Even if you have one of those big CD jukeboxes with a randomise setting, you end up hearing all the wrong music at all the wrong times. It's good, but it's not ideal.

If you have all those songs on your hard disk, there's no need to switch CDs! Better still, you can easily make and store separate playlists (lists of songs you want to hear) for different moods. You can have one playlist that tells your MP3-playing software to play only upbeat tunes (to pull you out of a bad mood) and another playlist full of nasty and harsh songs (if you want to really wallow in misery).

Portable Player Power

Those MP3 songs don't have to stay on your computer. There are portable MP3 players that let you bring the music with you and they can do things for you that your CD player never could.

With an all-electronic MP3 player, you can download an hour or so of your favourite music from your PC and carry it with you. These players have no moving parts, which gives them three big advantages over portable CD and cassette players:

➤ They go through fewer batteries. A good MP3 player will use one battery in the same time that a CD player uses four.

7

➤ They're lighter, which is important if you jog.

➤ They're immune to the problems caused by shaking and jostling. Shake a CD player and the music will skip. Shake a cassette player and the music will tend to screech. Shake an all-electronic MP3 player and your arm will eventually grow tired.

If your PC has a CD-R (CD recorder) drive, you're ready to take advantage of a different sort of MP3 player. A CD-based MP3 player looks like a standard portable CD player; in fact, it will play standard CDs. The player can also read MP3-compressed songs from CD-ROMs. Those CD-ROMs can store around 12 hours of music, whereas standard CDs store about 74 minutes. By making your own MP3 CD-ROMs, you can carry around your entire Beatles collection on a single disk, your entire Wu-Tang Clan collection on another.

But I Heard That MP3s Were Evil!

There have been a lot of negative stories in the media lately about MP3. The record industry has publicly attacked this format. However, if it's just a simple and high-quality way to compress music, what's all the fuss about?

The problem (as the record companies see it) is that it's too simple and too high quality. A lot of people have been purchasing CDs, making MP3s out of the songs and illegally sharing those files online with people who have not paid for the music. The record industry fears that people who would otherwise have bought the CDs are instead listening to these illegal MP3 copies. Performers don't make any money from the illegal copies. Worse yet (in record industry eyes at least), the record companies don't make any money.

Of course, illegally duplicating music is nothing new. The record industry hasn't just been going after the illegal copiers, however. They've been going after MP3 altogether, through attacks in the media and in the courtroom.

Later in this book we'll discuss the legal and ethical implications of MP3s and talk about how you can use them legally.

What Is Digitally Compressed Music, Anyway?

Music For Mathematicians

Deep inside, computers only really deal with numbers. If you want to find a way for a computer to deal with a word, a picture, or anything else, you have to find a way to convert that thing into a series of numbers. For example, when a computer is dealing with words, it's using a special code, in which the letter a is 32, the letter b is 33 and so on.

Sound is not naturally made up of numbers. Sound is actually a very small vibrating motion (called a sound wave) that is carried through the air. When that sound wave reaches and shakes your eardrum your brain interprets the vibration as sound. A microphone is just a device that turns air bounce into an electrical vibration that heads down the microphone cord. Speakers work the other way, turning vibrating electricity into vibrating air. The figure below shows a sound wave.

This is a drawing of a sound wave. How quickly does sound bounce? This sound lasts about 1/200th of a second.

Turning sound into numbers is called digitising. A computer keeps checking that sound, repeatedly measuring how high the bounce is. By stringing together these measurements (called samples) the computer records the path of that bounce. How exact the re-creation of the vibration is depends on how precise each measurement is and how frequently the measurement is taken. For example, sound measurement on a CD (which was the first popular form of digitally recorded sound) takes over 44 000 samples per second – each sample can be any of 65 536 different heights. As if that isn't enough, it's doing that all twice, by recording separate sounds for the left and right ears and thus making stereo. The figure on the next page shows a digitised soundwave.

When the recording is stored on a CD or as an uncompressed computer recording (called a WAV – pronounced wave – file), the file just has a list of the value of each sample. You can easily understand how all those thousands of samples add up to a lot of information very quickly.

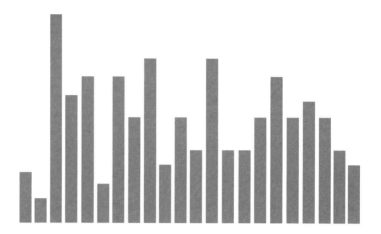

The same sound digitised. Each column is a single sample, measuring the height of the wave at a single moment.

Compressing Sound

Your ears are amazing things. In addition to stopping your sunglasses from sliding down your nose, they can also hear precisely enough to ensure that they don't get fooled easily. Thousands of sound samples per second are needed to fool the ear. At least, that's true for part of the sound.

For other parts of the sound, though, the ear is not so precise. It doesn't recognise all of the information that's in an uncompressed file. If that information isn't being used, why bother saving it? That's where a lot of the compression takes place: getting rid of sound information you can't hear.

Another aspect of MP3 compression is that the vibration of sound goes up and down in certain shapes. Just as you can't step down 100 feet with one step and then up 100 feet with the next, a series of samples can't bounce quickly between the highest and lowest possible measurement. Instead, the sound moves smoothly from level to level. The compression can record the shape of the sound more efficiently than recording the height of every single point along the curve.

Stereo offers another place to use less information. An uncompressed digital recording stores separate full recordings for each ear. The two recordings are very similar. MP3 uses less information space by keeping one main recording and then keeping track of how the sound differs from ear to ear.

Finally, MP3 saves space by keeping track of repeating information. If the same number is repeated 10 000 times in a row in an uncompressed file, all that information is stored on the disk. It's like telling someone to get to a shop by saying 'Walk one block north, then another block north, then another block north, then another block north...' When the MP3 compressor sees repeated information, it counts the repetitions and stores the information, as well as how many times it repeats ('walk 10 blocks north').

Less Means Lossy!

Because the MP3 format doesn't store all of the information that's in the uncompressed sound file, it's considered a 'lossy' format. In the rate of compression usually used with MP3, that loss makes no difference to what you can hear. Once you have an MP3 file, you can copy and recopy it and the sound never gets any worse, which makes it much better than a cassette tape. Every time you copy one cassette to another you end up losing sound quality but MP3 copies losslessly.

MP3 High Fidelity Details

The foregoing description of MP3 compression is obviously not very detailed. It's probably more than you'll ever need to know, unless you're going to design your own MP3 recorder or player. If you're an audio-theory buff and not afraid of advanced maths and a lot of techno babble, however, you can find more detailed descriptions of the compression scheme at `http://www.iocon.com/mp3/coding.html` on the Web.

Compressing Sound To Death

When we say that compressed MP3 music sounds are as good as uncompressed music, we're talking about the best qualities of MP3 compression. You can use MP3 to compress by different amounts. Even if you have a complex sound specifically chosen so that the ear could detect any loss in sound quality, you can compress that sound to one-sixth of its original size and still have a re-creation so perfect that your ears can't tell the difference. With standard music, you can compress down to one-tenth the space and it will sound like CD-quality to most people (although they might be able to tell the difference if they carefully compare the compressed version to the uncompressed version).

Things get a little trickier if you want to compress a sound even further than that. Compressing it that much will lose some of the information and there will be an audible difference in quality. It's sort of like how they take coffee and turn it into instant coffee – when you add hot water, it still looks and smells and tastes a bit like coffee. It just doesn't look and taste and smell like real coffee.

That's because, in order to save space, the compressing program starts throwing away some of the vital information of the sound. The notes just won't sound as crisp or as clear. It will sound less like a CD and more like listening to the same music over an FM radio. Compress it more and it sounds like an AM radio. Compress it even more and it sounds like it's coming out of an old Look and Speak toy. Still, highly compressed sound can be good for things that don't need high-quality recording, such as books on tape or audio letters from your aunt.

The Least You Need To Know

➤ Digital music is music that is stored as a series of numbers. Computers can only handle digital music.

➤ Compressed digital music is digital music that has been stored in a way that takes up a lot less space, without compromising sound quality. MP3 is a popular format for compressed digital music.

➤ There is plenty of music available for free on the Internet in the MP3 format. You can also take music from CDs you own and convert it into the MP3 format.

➤ You can play MP3 format music on your computer and on special portable MP3 players.

Chapter 2

MP3: A Compressed History

In This Chapter

➤ What does MP3 mean?

➤ Where did MP3 come from?

➤ How did MP3 become so big?

The MP3 file format didn't just spring up out of nowhere. All that compression, that controversy, that potential – it all came from somewhere. Even that cryptic name – MP3 – doesn't give away any clues. Perhaps you will be able to better understand where MP3 came from if you know what the MP stands for.

Well, the MP stands for moving pictures.

No, that doesn't help. It doesn't even make sense.

MPEG: Many Professional Engineers Gather

Most file formats come from companies. A company coming out with a word processor creates a file format to store word processing documents, or a company (say, MicroCat) with a cat-folding program comes up with a document to store cat-folding designs. If another company (DataCat) wants to put out its own cat-folding program, it comes up with its own file format. You may not be able to move a cat-folding design easily from one program to another but it's not often that you'd need to.

If you need to be able to use the same file with various programs, there are two ways to go. One is to pick the format already used by a popular program and have everyone design their programs to use that format. The problem with this option is that MicroCat's format, while well designed for MicroCat's programs, may not be able to hold the information that other programs need. Plus, any time that MicroCat puts out a new program, it can change how the file format works and cause problems for everyone else.

The other way is for everyone to work together, creating a team of engineers from various companies and from academia and have them work on the format. By doing it that way, you make a format that is useful for everyone and that isn't owned by any one company. Standards organisations exist not only to design file formats but to design all sorts of standards for physical and electronic items, so that, for example, light bulbs made by one manufacturer fit into sockets made by another.

ISO: Is Surely Official

The big boy of standards organisations is the International Standards Organization, better known as ISO. The people at ISO saw that digital TV was on the way and that, in order to save information space, they would need a standard method of compression to handle digital video. In January of 1988, they gathered together 25 experts in the field and called them the Moving Pictures Expert Group, or MPEG.

MPEG set about inventing a codec (short for compressor/decompressor) standard for video. Its first standard, MPEG-1, came out in July of 1989. MPEG-1 was designed for video stored and played on computers. When you buy a video CD, you don't just have a very shiny coaster, you also have MPEG-1!

Three Layers Of Sound

Early moving pictures had no sound and people liked it that way. Nowadays, we expect sound with our movies, so it was important that MPEG-1 have a format for compressed sound to mix with the compressed video.

Those MPEG geniuses didn't come up with a way by themselves. They basically got the German company Fraunhofer-IIS to come up with a way. Actually, they came up with three ways, calling them layers:

➤ Layer 1 uses only a few of the compression tricks. The drawback to this is that it doesn't compress very well. On the other hand, decompression doesn't take a very powerful computer.

➤ Layer 2 uses more of the compression tricks. It compresses okay but needs a more powerful computer to decompress it.

➤ Layer 3 uses the whole bag of tricks but it needs a very powerful personal computer to decompress it. Very powerful, that is, by 1989 standards. A decade later and just about any computer you can get will be more than adequate.

What's In A Name?

Now there's this great method of compressing sound in a video file and some smart engineer says 'If I want just music in the file, why don't I use this method?' Thus, the compression method is separated from the video usage and a new file format is born. The engineer needs to create a file extension for this format. A file extension is a dot followed by up to three characters at the end of a filename; the extension identifies what type of file it is. Four characters are often used outside the Windows world but you have to stick with three if you want Windows to understand it.

Other MPEG Formats

The efforts of the Moving Picture Experts Group did not end with MPEG-1. The group not only continued to work but also grew, going from 25 experts to 350. They followed up MPEG-1 with MPEG-2, which was a standard for full-digital television compression. The future of TV is very much tied to MPEG-2, with its usage in HDTV. In fact, it's a growing part of the present, as DVD uses MPEG-2 video.

MPEG-2 also included some improvements for Layer 3 audio, including the capability to handle all the channels of sound needed for today's home theatre systems. Oddly enough, DVD doesn't use MPEG audio compression. Instead, it includes another form of compression developed by Dolby, building that into the MPEG-2 compressed video. The group later added a standard for somewhat improved sound compression to MPEG-2. This standard is Advanced Audio Compression (AAC), but some people just refer to it as MP4.

The MPEG-4 standard goes beyond defining just a single stream of sounds and pictures in a fixed order. Instead, it's designed around setting up an audio–video scene, which can be used for interactive purposes. Expect to encounter MPEG-4 in ATMs, interactive advertising and video Whack-a-Celebrity games.

Work is zooming along on MPEG-7, a standardised manner for describing multimedia content. Eventually, MPEG-7 will make it easier for you to search the Web for national anthems sung by house pets, for example.

To learn more about the Moving Pictures Expert Group, surf on over to `http://drogo.cselt.stet.it/mpeg/` on the Web.

And so the file extension .mp3 was created, standing for **MPEG**-1 Audio Layer **3**. People saw this and simply began referring to them as MP3 files. Thus, the name was born.

MP3 Goes To School

Once you have a compressed music standard in place and software available to compress and play this music, it's all ready to take off. All you need are the right conditions to get it started. You need some place with a lot of people who are into music, people with computers and a good understanding of those computers, lots of data storage and some high-speed data connections to make it all quick and easy.

In other words, you need a college – a wonderful place for playing with computers, listening to music and all sorts of things that let you avoid starting that report on the economics of South-East Asia that isn't due for a whole three hours yet.

Repositories of thousands of songs have begun popping up on college hard disks. Students from various schools exchange songs via the Internet. Leaving your computer running in the background playing the latest tunes is now common. The students are quite happy; even those dressed in black.

The record companies aren't so happy, though. They love it when a student shells out £12.99 for a CD. When that student converts all the songs on the album into MP3s and puts them on a network where everyone can get them, the record companies are less than happy. Suddenly, it is not only cheaper but actually easier for thousands of students to get the album over the Internet rather than buying the album or having a friend tape it. This illegal distribution worries the record companies because it looks like an indication of the way music will be distributed in the future.

Little Bit Legal

Not all MP3s were illegal, even in the early days. Techno-savvy music composers started distributing their creations in MIDI format via computer long before there were MP3s; those composers quickly expanded to show off their work via MP3s. Musicians only needed one computer enthusiast among their members or fans to get themselves compressed.

These weren't generally bands anyone had heard of and MP3 seemed like a good way to spread their sound around. Since it was their own music, it was perfectly legal for the bands to spread it around in that format. In terms of showing off the band at its best, this high-quality electronic reproduction worked a lot better than encouraging fans to make tapes for their friends, with each generation of tapes sounding worse than the last.

What's This MIDI Stuff?

MIDI stands for Musical Instrument Digital Interface. If an MP3 file is the computer version of a CD, then a MIDI file is the computer equivalent of sheet music. The MIDI file contains a list of what instruments are supposed to be heard and what notes each instrument is supposed to play. MIDI files are often used to control electronic instruments. People downloading them from the Internet can listen to the music on their PC, which synthesises the sound of the instruments. When your PC synthesises a glockenspiel, for example, it may sound very different to how the composer's PC synthesises a glockenspiel. What you're hearing may not be what was intended and the file has no efficient way to include vocal recordings.

The MOD file is a cousin of the MIDI file. As well as the note information it can also include a digital sample of each instrument. The PC playing the MOD file can use this sample to create the same sound as the composer intended.

One advantage to MIDI files is their small size. They're typically less than 20 KB, compared to several megabytes for an MP3 file.

Most of these legal MP3s were overlooked in the past, however, in the vast stream of illegal tracks from well-known names. When you're trying to find Public Enemy or Sheryl Crow, it's easy to ignore Bouncing Joe and His Almost All-Girl Band.

Dotcomming The Format

At first, the MP3 craze was largely an invisible movement. You could look around the World Wide Web and see no mention of it if you weren't looking specifically for it – but people were looking for it. They had heard about this stuff. Some were searching for large sites full of illegal MP3 tracks or for the software needed to make and play MP3s.

The people in the Web business noticed and began setting up sites for the MP3 fans. People like Michael Robertson, for example, a guy who wasn't a particularly fervent music buff, who didn't even know what MP3 was. But Michael had a Web site called filez.com, which was a popular search engine for finding downloadable files. As a good businessman, he kept an eye on what it was that people were searching for and he noticed that two words kept popping up: sex and MP3.

Michael already knew what sex was. In fact, he'd heard good things about it. He also knew that there were already plenty of Web sites offering sex (or at least as close to sex as anyone can put out on the Internet).

Master Of His Domain

A little research told Michael not only what MP3 was but also that there really wasn't a major Web site feeding this lust for MP3 files. Someone had already bought the rights to the Web site name mp3.com, paying $100 for the name. Michael offered a full $1000 for the site name – a 900% mark-up.

In November 1997, Michael took that name and opened a Web site that offered thousands of free downloadable MP3 files. You could also download from mp3.com all the necessary MP3 software and instructions on how to use it. mp3.com is currently worth more than $10 million.

It took more than just the name to get there. Michael didn't just discover the MP3 format; he fell in love with it. He quickly grew to be one of its most visible champions, speaking out for and defending MP3 at all opportunities and employing other MP3 enthusiasts such as Rod Underhill, one of the American authors of this book.

Legal And Legitimate

The folks at mp3.com worked to make sure that the MP3 files on their site were legal. Some of them are from well-known acts but the vast majority are from those who are struggling to succeed or those who have no particular designs toward big-time record contracts.

Because the people who find sites like mp3.com aren't finding a lot of pirated music, they're eagerly downloading what they do find. Someone downloads a song by an unknown band millions of times per month. It's really the free and legal sites that are spearheading MP3 as a way for fresh young bands (and refreshing old ones) to reach a new audience.

MP3 Without A PC

The time is March 1998. The location is an electronics trade show in Hanover, Germany. The event is the unveiling of the very first portable MP3 player. The MPMan F10, manufactured by the Korean company Saehan Information Systems, Inc., grabs a lot of acclaim at the show.

The mainstream media doesn't pay much attention to MP3 until the release of a competing product. Diamond Multimedia, best known for its powerful PC video cards, tries to compete with the MPMan with its own unit, the Rio. The product gets good reviews but it also gets negative reaction from some very powerful folks: the Recording Industry Association of America (RIAA). RIAA exists to represent the needs and desires of the big CD publishers.

RIAA Versus Rio

The RIAA is against MP3, having seen how it can be used to pirate millions of dollars worth of music. The Rio, with its capability to carry MP3 music beyond the constraints of the PC, seems to scare them. They raised a legal fuss over the Rio, trying to prevent its release.

Do they stop it from coming out? No. In fact, it backfires on them. They draw press attention to the product. This publicity generates a large demand for the Rio. (For more on the details of this lawsuit, see Chapter 12, 'Music Pirates'.)

Meanwhile, the recording industry has formed the Secured Digital Music Initiative (SDMI), its attempt to provide a piracy-proof alternative to MP3. The SDMI works with various manufacturers trying to come up with a format that would let the recording industry sell music online while preventing people from distributing the files. (Of course, they could sell MP3 files but then one buyer could distribute the file to all his or her friends or post them on a Web page.) Several different formats exist but so far there is little consumer interest in them. They rely on encryption, electronic scrambling of the music. Only the purchaser can decode and play the song clip.

And here we are today: a popular yet controversial file format; Web sites with thousands of legal songs; portable players; one annoyed recording industry; and millions of MP3 fans.

The Least You Need To Know

➤ The Moving Pictures Expert Group devised the MPEG audio/video compression format.

➤ The format known as MP3 is actually Audio Layer 3 of the MPEG-1 standard.

➤ MP3 first gained popularity as a separate audio format on highly computer-connected college campuses.

➤ MP3 has generated controversy due to the ease with which music can be pirated and consequently the recording industry attempts to suppress MP3 products.

Part 2
Getting And Playing MP3s

So far we've talked mainly about the compressed part of compressed music. In this part of the book, we talk about the music. Specifically, we tell you where you can download music from the Web as well as how to set up software to play MP3s. We even take a look at the new and upcoming MP3-playing hardware, so you can listen to your tunes on the go.

Chapter 3

Installing And Using MP3 Software

In This Chapter

➤ How do you *install* MP3 software from the CD-ROM?

➤ How do you play music?

➤ How do you set up your Web browser to work with your MP3 player?

As far as your computer is concerned, an MP3 *file* is just a string of ones and zeros. That's not much good unless you have a way to convert it back into sound. To do that, you'll need a computer with speakers and you'll need an MP3 *player*, a program that reads the file and sends the sound to the speakers.

The Windows Media Player

If you have a recent copy of Windows 98, you may already have an MP3 player. Windows 95 and 98 come with the Windows Media Player, a program that can interpret a number of sound and video formats. Although earlier versions of this program don't play MP3s, newer versions do. Microsoft got hassled by the recording industry for including MP3 compatibility. Between that and the fact that Microsoft is now promoting its own alternative to MP3, don't be surprised if future versions of Windows don't include that feature. (Finding out whether your version of Media Player supports MP3s is easy: try following the instructions here for playing MP3s. If they don't work, you don't have a compatible version!)

If you use the Web-based Windows Update feature in Windows 98 (click the **Start** button, choose **Settings** and then choose **Windows Update**), your system can automatically check to see if you have the latest version and recommend that you download the new one if you don't. If you're using Windows 95, you can just point your Web browser to `http://www.microsoft.com/windows/mediaplayer/` and download the current version.

Playing Songs With The Windows Media Player

You can start Windows Media Player and select a song in several ways. If you haven't installed any other MP3 players, Windows knows that the Media Player will work with your MP3 files. Find an icon for an MP3 file (using Windows Explorer, or by double-clicking the **My Computer** icon on your desktop and finding it there). Double-click the **MP3** file icon and the Windows Media Player starts up and starts playing that song.

Finding The Song Files On The CD-ROM

To locate the free music tracks included on the CD-ROM that came with this book, put the CD-ROM into your CD-ROM drive. Double-click the **My Computer** icon on your desktop. In the resulting window, right-click on the icon for your CD-ROM drive and choose **Explore**. The contents of the CD-ROM will appear. Double-click the folder marked **Music** and you will see folders containing all the song files, broken down by musical genre. Double-click the folder of your choice and double-click one of the songs to begin playing it.

You can also start the Windows Media Player by clicking the **Start** button and selecting **Programs**, **Accessories**, **Entertainment**, **Windows Media Player**. This sequence starts the program but it doesn't begin playing a song. You can play a song by choosing **File**, **Open**, clicking the **Browse** button, selecting a song file by navigating to it in the Open dialogue box and then clicking **OK**.

Controlling Windows Media Player

The Windows Media Player interface for MP3 files is fairly simple. That's because it really can't do much more than loading and playing one song. The following are the controls (see the following figure for locations of these controls):

Stop
Seek bar
Play
Pause

Volume control
Mute

The Windows Media Player appears like this when playing audio formats. It may appear different when first opened because it's set up a bit differently when it expects to play a video file.

➤ The Play button starts a song playing after it has been stopped or paused.

➤ The Pause button stops the song. After pausing, the Play button restarts the song exactly where it left off.

➤ The Stop button stops the song. After stopping, the Play button restarts the song at the beginning.

➤ Dragging the slider box across the Seek bar changes what section of the song is playing. The left end of the bar represents the beginning of the song; the right represents the tune's end.

➤ Dragging the Volume control bar left decreases the volume; going right increases it. (You'll probably find it easier to leave this control on high and use your speaker's volume control instead.)

➤ Click the Mute button to silence the song quickly. The song keeps on playing; you just can't hear it. Yes, this is rather stupid. It makes a lot more sense if you're using the Windows Media Player to view a video. Click it a second time to resume hearing the song.

Check This Out

Drag And Drop Is Not A Drag

Most MP3 players support drag and drop. This means that after you've started the program, you can drag the icon for an MP3 file from a Windows Explorer window, from the desktop, or from any other file icon display, into the program window to play the song. Drag and drop is an easy way to handle things; just leave a window open displaying your song files.

Better yet, if the player program puts an icon on the desktop (and most do), you don't even have to start the program first. Instead, just drag the song's icon over the program icon and release the mouse button.

25

Licence Agreements

Licence agreements are long, boring, often badly written legal documents. A lot of people just skip reading them. But it is something you're agreeing to legally, so you really may want to look it over.

Other Media Player Features

The Media Player is a basic, no-frills viewer for a wide range of audio and video formats. It can play CD audio tracks, MIDI files, WAV files and videos in MPEG, QuickTime and AVI formats, among others. You can open those files in the same way that you open MP3 files.

Winamp For Windows

Winamp is an MP3 player program manufactured by Nullsoft (http://www.winamp.com), a small company that has been bought out by online mega-corporation AOL. The program is a player only; it can't encode MP3s, or burn CD-ROMs. It will play MP3 files, CD tracks and a number of other formats. It's a colourful and feature-laden player and a lot of people are creating cool customisations for it.

Winamp Requirements

Winamp requires Windows 95 or 98, or Windows NT 4 or higher. It will run on a very fast 486 but you're better off if you have a processor of Pentium-or-better power.

How Do They Do That?

Many players can automatically identify the musician and the title of songs. This recognition isn't some magic trick; it's due to ID3, a standard for embedding track information into an MP3 file. It's up to the person who encodes the file to include this information and many people don't remember to do it, so there's a lot of MP3s out there without this information.

Upgrades On The Web

The various programs that come on the CD-ROM were the newest versions we could put out with the book. However, MP3 is a rapidly growing field and newer versions of these programs are being released frequently. When you decide which program you like, check out the company's Web site. You'll probably find a more recent version of the program on there, with new features, improved old features and old bugs replaced with new ones.

Installing Winamp

To install Winamp, first insert the CD-ROM that accompanies this book. Close any running programs. Next, double-click the **My Computer** icon on your Windows desktop. In the resulting window, right-click the icon for your CD-ROM drive and choose **Explore** to view its contents. Double-click the **Programs** folder and when it opens, double-click the **winamp223** icon. A dialogue box opens suggesting a folder to store the program files in. Click **Next**.

Winamp Is Shareware

Shareware is a system where sharing your software files with others is encouraged (as opposed to software you buy in a store, where sharing it is generally illegal). Anyone can try out a copy of Winamp for 14 days at no cost. If you like the software and want to keep using it on your machine, then you pay for it. The price is just $10 for personal use, or $25 for commercial use. If you have a credit card, you can pay for it at Nullsoft's Web site (http://www.winamp.com). Otherwise, just mail your payment to: Nullsoft Inc., 60 Palisades Drive North, Sedona, Arizona 86336, USA.

A dialogue box appears with a checklist of options (see the figure below):

➤ **Autoplay audio CDs** Whenever you put a CD into your CD-ROM drive, Winamp launches and starts playing the CD.

➤ **Make Winamp the default audio player** Whenever you double-click an icon for an MP3 or other sound file, Winamp automatically starts. If you don't select this option, you can still use Winamp to play your sound files. You'll just have to start Winamp first and then tell it to play the file.

➤ **Add group to Start Menu** Creates a new Winamp group in the Programs section of your Start menu.

➤ **Add icon to desktop** Puts a Winamp icon on your desktop.

➤ **Add icon to quick launch bar** Puts a Winamp icon on your quick launch bar, which most Windows 98 or Windows NT users will find just to the right of the Start button.

➤ **An Internet connection-style drop-down list** Choose the type of Internet connection you use.

➤ **Check for new versions of Winamp** Checks over the Internet from time to time and tells you when a new version of Winamp is available.

You can choose to let Winamp practically take over your system!

Make your selections and click **Next** again. A window opens displaying the contents of the new Winamp program group. You may have to close this window to see the dialogue box that asks you for personal information. If you don't want to bother with this step, you can click **Later**. Otherwise, fill it out and click **Next**. (They do ask some personal information, like age and gender, but they swear that it's just for statistical purposes. Be sure to keep the **Please send me Winamp announcements** check box clear if you worry about getting too much email.) After you fill in the information, Winamp connects to the Internet. (You may need to click the **Connect** button on your Dial-Up Connection dialogue box for the connection to go through.)

After you're done, a dialogue box offers you a link to run a Winamp Flash Walkthrough, a quick tutorial session. You'll need the Macromedia Flash plug-in for your browser for this tutorial to work. Click the link to do that, or just click the **Run Winamp** button to get started.

Starting Winamp Playing

There are a lot of ways to start Winamp playing an individual song. If Winamp isn't already playing, you can double-click the icon for any song file (if you chose to set up Winamp as your default audio file player) or drag and drop the icon on to the Winamp logo on your desktop.

Browser

Equalizer

Playlist

Player

*The Winamp window has four sections, each of which can be separated or closed by clicking on its own small Close (**X**) button.*

After you've started Winamp running (either by one of the methods we just mentioned, by using the Start menu, by double-clicking the Winamp icon, or by clicking on the Winamp button on the quick launch bar), you'll see that the Winamp display has four sections, as shown in the figure above:

➤ Player

➤ Equalizer

➤ Playlist

➤ Browser

You can start a song by dragging and dropping a song icon on to the player section. You can open up a file browser to choose a song file to play by using one of several methods:

➤ Clicking the **Eject** button on the player.

➤ Pressing **L**.

➤ Clicking the upper-left corner of the player portion and selecting **Play File**.

➤ Right-clicking an unmarked area of the player portion and selecting **Play File**.

In other words, there are few things you can do in this world that *won't* start Winamp playing a song.

29

Winamp Playing Controls

The player display has the standard VCR-style controls to skip ahead or back a track and to start, pause, or stop the song (see the figure below). It has a slider to adjust where within the track is playing, another slider to adjust the volume and a third to adjust the balance between the left and right speakers.

The Winamp song-playing controls.

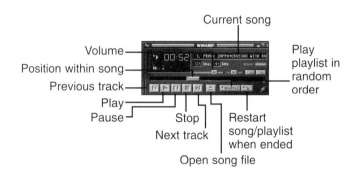

The equalizer window (shown in the figure below) lets you adjust the way the music sounds. You can crank up the bass to set the whole room shaking (or, if you have typical under-powered computer speakers, vibrate them annoyingly on your desktop).

The Winamp equalizer doesn't make your music equal, it makes it better!

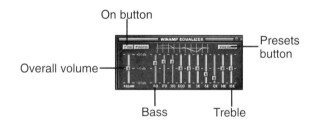

To take advantage of the equalizer, you first have to turn it on by clicking the **On** button. You can see that it's on by the little green light that appears on the button. The slider on the far left adjusts the pre-amp level, adjusting the overall volume; slide it up for more volume, down for less. The rest of the sliders adjust the level of individual portions of the sound. The leftmost sliders adjust the lowest (*bass*) sounds, while the rightmost adjust the highest (*treble*) sounds.

Different music sounds good with different equalizer settings. After you find a combination that you like, you can save it by clicking the **Presets** button, selecting **Save**, **Preset** from the resulting menu and then entering a name for the combination. You can load an equalizer setting by clicking the **Preset** button, selecting **Load**, **Preset** from the menu and then double-clicking the name of the setting you want.

Stuttering Sounds?

If your music starts sounding choppy or has little stutters in it, it means that your player is having problems keeping up with the music. Usually, this happens if you're running some other program that is using up processor and hard disk time, or if you're using a computer that's too slow. However, Windows performance tends to decay after it has been running a while, so if it starts happening later in the day, your best bet may be to close all your programs and reboot your system. To reboot, click **Start** and select **Shut Down**. In the dialogue box that appears, choose the **Restart** option and then click **OK**.

Playing With Winamp's Playlist

Winamp's playlist window (shown in the next figure) may look too small for viewing and working with a large list but you can enlarge it by dragging the lower-right corner.

To add a song to the current playlist, you can just drag the song's icon into the playlist window. You can also click the **Add File** button and select the file using a file browser. Right-clicking the **Add File** button gives you a menu that lets you add an entire directory of song files (shortcut: **Shift+L**) or, for those of you lucky enough to have high-speed connections, the URL of a file on the Web (shortcut: **Ctrl+L**).

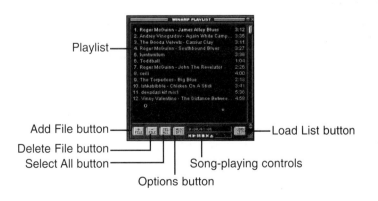

The Winamp playlist controls.

31

Don't Add CD-ROM Tracks To The Playlist!

We're not saying the great MP3 music on this book's CD-ROM isn't worth putting on playlists. Instead, when you find songs you like, copy them from the CD-ROM to your hard disk. Otherwise, you'll have to have that CD-ROM in the drive each time you play that playlist.

To work with the songs already on the playlist, you need to be able to select the songs to work with. Click any one song to select it. To select a range of songs, click the first song in the range, then hold down **Shift** and click the last song. To select a bunch of songs that aren't in a row, hold down **Ctrl** while clicking the songs. Select all the songs by clicking the **Select All** button.

After you have the songs selected, you can drag them to a new position on the list. You can also delete them by right-clicking the selection and choosing **Delete** from the pop-up menu.

To save the playlist, right-click the **Load List** button and select **Save Playlist** from the pop-up menu. Use the file navigator to select a name and directory for the playlist and then click **Save**. To open a saved playlist, click the **Load List** button, find the playlist with the file navigator and double-click it.

To view or edit the information on a song in the playlist, right-click it and select **File Info** *(shortcut:* **Alt+3***).*

Nifty Winamp Features

The Winamp minibrowser is a simple little Web browser. This may not seem to be important (after all, you probably already have a far better Web browser) but if all you're using your computer for is playing MP3s, it's a quick and handy way to get MP3s off the Web. (If you've closed the minibrowser, press **Alt+T** to make it reappear.)

The minibrowser is also good if you want to pick up SHOUTcast broadcasts. SHOUTcast is a system developed by the Winamp people to enable someone to broadcast a continuous stream of audio over the Internet. To view a list of SHOUTcast channels click the up-arrow button on the bottom of the minibrowser and select **Shoutcast Top 50** from the menu that appears.

Winamp also supports *skins* and *plug-ins*. A *skin* is just a different visual design for Winamp, making it look like a car radio, a space design, or any of literally thousands of other appearances. A *plug-in* is an add-on program that expands Winamp's capabilities. Some plug-ins allow Winamp to play additional music formats, ranging from old Commodore 64 formats to next-generation compressed music formats. Others add special effects to the sound output. Most of them, however, just add nifty-looking moving visual effects to accompany the music, ranging from psychedelic patterns to dancing-stick figures.

Head on over to `http://www.winamp.com` to find a selection of over 100 plug-ins and more than 3000 skins to pep up your Winamp experience.

MusicMatch Jukebox For Windows

MusicMatch is another all-in-one audio file player, encoder and CD player. The free version included on the CD-ROM has almost all the features you're likely to want. About all that's missing from the free version is the capability to encode MP3s at the highest-quality rates but if you upgrade the software for $29.99 at MusicMatch's Web site (`http://www.musicmatch.com`), you can quickly give it the capability to do even that.

MusicMatch Requirements

MusicMatch requires a multimedia PC with Windows 95 or newer and 30 MB of hard disk space. Theoretically, it will run in 16 MB of RAM but things will go smoother if you have at least 32 MB, as well as a 166 MHz or faster processor.

Installing MusicMatch Jukebox

To install the Jukebox, first insert the CD-ROM that accompanies this book. Close any running programs and double-click the **My Computer** icon on your Windows desktop. In the resulting window, right-click the icon for your CD-ROM drive then choose **Explore** to view its contents. Double-click the **Programs** folder and then double-click the **mmjb4161** icon. An on-screen meter shows the progress of the installation program. After everything is in place, the installation program begins.

On the Welcome screen, click **Next**. The license agreement appears. (It's a long one but it includes some guidelines on what is legal to convert to MP3s.) If you agree to the license agreement, click **Yes**. (If you disagree with it, click **No** and then go and do something else, because you're not going to get the software installed until you choose Yes.)

The installation program suggests a folder to install the software in. Click **Next** to accept the default. This is followed by a suggestion of a folder in which to store the music you encode; again, click **Next** to accept this suggestion. It then suggests a new Start menu folder for the software. You can accept that suggestion, or you can click on one from a list of your existing Start menu folders. Click **Next** after you've made your selection and the installation takes place.

A dialogue box asks you if you want MusicMatch Jukebox to be your default CD player. Choose **Yes** or **No**. After you make that decision, the installation is complete. Click **Finish**.

Put A Disc In The Jukebox And Start It Playing

Before you start MusicMatch for the first time, put a standard audio CD into each of your CD-ROM drives. MusicMatch is going to need those there because it will run a test on your CD-ROM drives. This test gives it information it will need when you start encoding MP3s (as described in Chapter 8).

Because MusicMatch Jukebox makes itself your default MP3 player, you can start it up by double-clicking any MP3 file icon. Additionally, you can start it using the Start menu, by double-clicking the **MusicMatch** icon on your desktop, or by dragging and dropping an MP3 file icon on to the MusicMatch icon. MusicMatch opens two windows: a window with the song-playing controls and a playlist, plus a help window.

After you have the program going, you can play a song by dragging and dropping the program file on to the player window. When you do so, the song title or filename appears in the playlist window at the right end of the MusicMatch panel. What MusicMatch really wants you to do, however, is to enter your songs into its music library. That way, it knows where all your songs are and all you have to do is click the song name on the library list to hear it.

Where's The Music Library?

To see the Music Library, click the tiny button with the picture of a musical note. The Music Library window opens (see the figure below), with a list of all the songs in the library. The surprising thing is that there actually is a song there the first time you open it up. Jukebox comes with a song (actually, a short song segment), which is handy for testing it out if you don't have any MP3 files yet.

MusicMatch Jukebox has a Music Library system and you don't even need a library card to use it.

To add songs to the library, click **Add**. A file navigator opens that looks different to the standard file navigator you see in many Open dialogue boxes. Icons for your drives and your desktop appear in the left panel. Click the plus sign next to **Drives** to see a list of all your drives, each with a plus sign next to them. Click the plus sign next to any drive to see a list of folders in that drive and on the plus sign next to any folder to see the folders in that folder.

Click on any folder icon and the right panel displays a list of all the MP3 files in that folder. When you find the song you want to add, click that song to select it. If you want to add all the songs in that folder, click the **Select All** button. After you select the songs you want to add, click **OK** and they are added to the music library.

If no songs are playing, you can start any song in the music library by clicking the song title and then clicking the > that appears next to the song.

MusicMatch Jukebox Playlist

At any time you can add any song to the current playlist by double-clicking the song title in the music library, or by dragging and dropping it (either from the song's icon or from its entry in the music library) into the playlist.

To save a playlist, click the **Save** button. A dialogue box appears, explaining saving and loading playlists. Click **OK** and another dialogue box appears. Type a name for the playlist and press **Enter**.

To load a playlist, click the right-arrow button next to the AutoDJ button. The playlist area expands to include a list of saved playlists. Double-click any playlist name to load that playlist. You can shrink the playlist area back to its usual size by clicking the left-arrow button.

Controlling The Play

The player portion of the window contains the standard VCR-style controls, with buttons for Previous Song, Play, Pause, Stop and Next Song (see the figure below). There is one control that most of the other players don't have: a Record button, which you'll use when converting audio CD tracks to MP3. (You'll learn more about that process in Chapter 8.) It also has a left–right slider to control where in the track you're playing and an up–down slider for the volume.

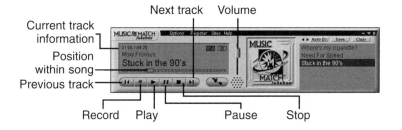

Like other players, MusicMatch uses VCR-style controls. Considering how many people have trouble using their VCRs, this may not be wise...

AutoDJ: Fast Automatic Playlists

Click the **AutoDJ** button above the playlist and you can take advantage of a feature that automatically plays songs out of your music library based on criteria you select. You can listen to songs by specific artists, or specific tempos, genres, moods, or other criteria. There's one major problem: MusicMatch can't really tell by itself the tempo, mood and so on, of each song. It relies on that information being embedded in the song itself and many of the songs you download won't have that info.

The dialogue box that appears when you click the button has everything you need to set your criteria (see the next figure). First, enter the number of hours you want the AutoDJ to play. Next, select the category of criteria from the first criteria option button list. After you select the category (for example, **by Artist**), a list of all the possible entries within that category appears next to it. Click the check boxes for all the entries that are acceptable to you.

The AutoDJ feature lets you select just to listen to your favourite types of music, or just your least favourites, if you want.

First, select the number of criteria.

For each criteria, select the category…

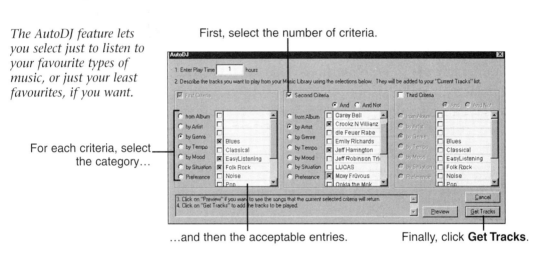

…and then the acceptable entries.

Finally, click **Get Tracks**.

If you want to set more than one criteria (if, for example, you only want to listen to upbeat songs by the Shoe Gazers), click the **Second Criteria** check box before setting up your first criterion. Doing so reveals a second list of option buttons and a list of possible entries for whatever you select. If you want a third criterion, click the **Third Criteria** check box immediately after clicking the **Second Criteria** button. Three's the limit. The second and third criteria also have an **And Not** option; click this to exclude songs based on that criteria.

After you've set all your criteria, click **Get Tracks**. The program searches the music Data base and reports how many songs meet your criteria, as well as their total playtime. Click **OK** to let it know that you've seen the information (or that you didn't see it and just don't care.) The songs it found are added to the playlist.

As we noted, this only works if the song files have the information in them. Luckily, this chapter does have a section on how to add song information using MusicMatch.

How To Add Song Information Using MusicMatch

Adding information is easy. Right-click the song in the music library list and select **Edit Track Tag** from the pop-up menu. A dialogue box appears, with fields for the track title, the lead artist and the album name (see the next figure). Just type in that information.

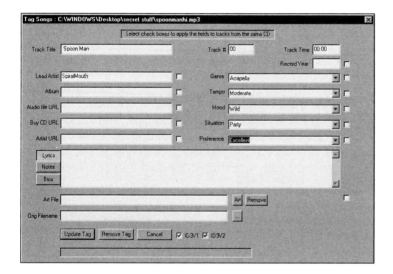

MusicMatch can read and change tags – information about the song hidden in the MP3 file itself.

Then it's time to *describe* the music. Use the Genre drop-down list to choose any music style ranging from *acapella* to *vocal*. The Tempo drop-down list lets you indicate the speed of the song's rhythm. The Mood drop-down list lets you define the song as anything from wild to comatose. The Situation drop-down list lets you align the song with situations where you might want the accompaniment to be anything from background to seasonal music. And using the Preference drop-down list, you can keep track of whether the music is very good or just plain bad taste. With any of these settings except Genre, you can also type your own description into the field instead of using the drop-down list.

After adding all this information, click **Update Tag** and the information is added directly into the music file.

What Are All Other Fields for?

The Tag dialogue box has a number of fields that you're not likely to use when adding information to a single file. Some of the fields are more for when you're encoding an entire CD, and others are for when you're encoding your own song for distribution to others. As such, those fields are covered in more appropriate chapters of this book.

Closing And Shrinking Windows

The MusicMatch windows may not look like standard Windows windows but they do still have Close (**X**) buttons in the upper-right corner of each window. You can use these to close the help window or the Music Library window. If you click the one on the player/playlist window, it closes the whole program, stopping your music from playing.

To the left of the Close (**X**) button on the player/playlist window is a down-arrow button. Click this and the window shrinks. All you'll have is a little window (shown in the figure below) with the VCR-style controls and a small readout about the current track. After you have your playlist going, this minimised panel is all you need to control playing your songs. Plus, it's small enough that the boss may not notice it when walking by. (Of course, the fact that your speakers are blaring out *That's What I Call Dance Music, Volume 2000* might be a clue that not all your attention is focused on your work.)

When you reduce MusicMatch, it shrinks enough so that it won't get in the way of your all-important game of solitaire.

Enlarge button

Next to the Close (**X**) button on this window is a small up-arrow; click this to get the full-sized window again.

Giving MusicMatch A Second, Third, Or Fourth Look

You can choose from different visual themes for your MusicMatch windows (see the figure below). Themes are different designs for different appearances. To choose a theme, click the **Options** button on the player window and choose **View**, **Change Theme**. A dialogue box appears listing the different visual themes. Double-click any theme name to apply the theme. After finding one you like, click **OK**.

MusicMatch's Other Tricks

MusicMatch has a number of other capabilities beyond playing MP3s. It can encode MP3s, which is covered in Chapter 8. MusicMatch also plays audio CDs and encodes into RealAudio format.

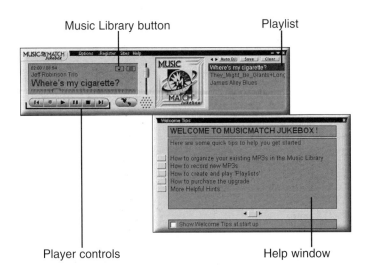

Music Library button   Playlist

Player controls   Help window

MusicMatch Jukebox has different visual themes. On some themes, the buttons may be in slightly different places.

Sonique For Windows

Sonique is an MP3 player program put out by Mediascience (`http://www.sonique.com`). The program is a player only; it can't encode MP3s, burn CD-ROMs, or make your clothes whiter and brighter. It will play MP3 files, CD tracks and a number of other audio formats. It's yours to use, for free.

Sonique has a number of nifty built-in special effects, both audio and visual. Because it's such a unique-looking program, getting used to its controls can take a little time but it's definitely a fun player to try.

Soniquirements

To run Sonique, you'll need to be running Windows 95 or newer on a computer with a Pentium 100 or faster processor. You will also need at least 16 MB of RAM and a sound card, of course. Oh, and speakers. And ears to listen with.

Installing Sonique

To install Sonique, insert the CD-ROM that accompanies this book. Close any running programs. Next, double-click the **My Computer** icon on your Windows desktop. In the resulting window, right-click the icon for your CD-ROM drive, then choose **Explore** to view its contents. Double-click the **Programs** folder and when that opens, double-click the **s100wma** icon. A dialogue box tells you that you are about to install Sonique and asks if you want to continue. Click **Yes**. An on-screen meter shows the progress of the installation program. After everything is in place, the installation program begins.

A Welcome dialogue box appears. Click **Next**. The licensing agreement for the software appears. If you agree to this, click **Yes**. (If you don't agree to it, then it's not really a licensing agreement, is it? More of a licensing disagreement. But if you disagree, you don't get to use the software.)

The program gives its expectation of a proper destination location for program installation. To continue installation click **Next**.

Then the installer will suggest creating a new program folder called Sonique on your Start menu. You can accept this folder by clicking **Next**, or you can select one of the existing folders from a list and then click **Next**. You are then shown all the settings you accepted during this installation. Click **Next** again. (You are now an official next-clicking expert.)

A dialogue box appears, listing different audio file types you can put Sonique in charge of:

➤ MPEG files (including not only MP3 but the lower compression schemes *MP1* and *MP2*, short for *MPEG-1 Layer 1* and *MPEG-1 Layer 2*, respectively).

➤ *Modules*, which are various formats of sheet-music-style song files.

➤ *Waveform audio files*, which are uncompressed digital audio files such as WAV.

➤ Audio CDs.

Select the check boxes for the audio types for which you want Sonique to be your main player and then click **Next** (of course). Another dialogue box asks you what sort of Internet connection you use. Select the appropriate option button, click **Next** and the actual installation takes place. Finally, the installer tells you that the setup is complete and that you have to restart Windows before you can use Sonique. Close all other programs you have open and then click **Finish**. Windows will close down, restart and Sonique will be ready to use.

Getting Musique Out Of Sonique

You can start Sonique using the Start menu, or by double-clicking the **Sonique** icon on your desktop. You can also drag and drop music files on to that desktop icon.

The first time you start Sonique, a dialogue box pops up asking for your name and email address so that your free copy can be registered. (It also has a check box for putting you on Sonique's emailing list and that defaults as checked, so you might want to clear it if you don't like getting corporate email.) Click **Register Now** and your information will be sent via the Internet (or just click **Register Later** to skip the whole thing).

Sonique's Unique Displays

Sonique doesn't just have the full-sized player and the miniaturised player that other players have. Instead, it has four different sizes, each of which looks very different and each of which has different uses.

Use medium display   Hide display

Use small display   Close Sonique

Previous track

Next track

Pause/unpause

Start/stop

Click for other controls

Volume

Track information

Select shuffle mode

Open files   Select repeat mode

Open/close equalizer

The large Sonique display is needed if you want to edit playlists or set options.

The Sonique buttons work a little differently from the buttons on other players. If you click **Pause**, for example, you have to click the same button again to restart, rather than clicking the Play button. In fact, there isn't a dedicated Play button; when you click it to start the track playing, it turns into the Stop button. And when you click **Stop** to halt the music, it turns into the Play button. To open a song, you can either drag and drop the song's icon on to the player, or click the **Open Files** button and select the file using the file navigator. (This navigator also has a place for a URL, for playing songs directly from a high-speed Web connection.)

Click **Visual Mode** to see the main display area replaced with full track information and a *vis*, a nifty little light show that accompanies the music. You can use the big grey up-arrow and down-arrow buttons to choose from several different vis styles.

The name of the vis appears above the vis display. To the right of the vis name are two little buttons. Click the second one and the Sonique goes into *full-screen vis mode*, Sonique's largest mode (shown in the previous figure).

Full-screen vis mode turns your entire display into a psychedelic light show. While Sonique is in this mode, there are no on-screen controls. You'll have to use Sonique's keyboard controls:

41

➤ Press **X** to start or stop playing a song.

➤ Press the right-arrow key to move through your playlist.

➤ Use the up- and down-arrow keys to change the volume.

➤ Press • to change which vis is playing, **[** (left bracket) or **]** (right bracket) to change the colours of the vis, or **+** (plus) or **–** (minus) on the number pad to change the screen resolution.

➤ Press **Esc** to return to the large display mode.

Clicking the down-arrow button in the upper-right corner of the large display replaces it with the medium display, shown below. This is a curvy little number that looks more like a futuristic handheld player.

The medium Sonique display has a nifty graphic depiction of the sound and a knob to raise or lower the sound's pitch.

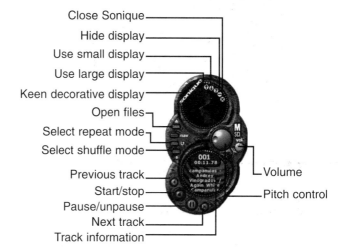

Close Sonique

Hide display

Use small display

Use large display

Keen decorative display

Open files

Select repeat mode

Select shuffle mode

Previous track

Start/stop

Pause/unpause

Next track

Track information

Volume

Pitch control

This medium display has most of the controls that are around the edges of the larger version. It also has a control knob that allows you to raise the pitch of the music, letting you turn even the most deep-toned singer into one of the Chipmunks. There's also an area for vis display. Point to this area and arrows appear that let you cycle through the various vis styles.

Where Are The Normal Players?

All the tricky buttons and fancy fonts are fun to look at but when I'm using a music player, I want to enjoy the music. There should be some full-featured player/encoder out there that just looks like a normal computer program. What would be so hard about having a play button that's actually marked Play, or a playlist that displays in the standard system font, or that uses the standard system colours? These features would make the player easier to work with and easier to understand. I don't want all the players to be straightforward and bland; I just need one that I can easily teach anyone to use.

Click the down-arrow button here and the display shrinks down to the smallest size possible, shown below. All this display shows is the track number currently playing and the time within that track. Point to this display, however and you see a minimal set of control buttons.

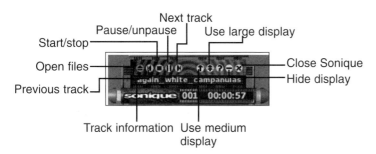

Sonique's small display has the minimum you need and it only shows that when you point directly at it.

Playlists In Sonique

To work on your playlist, you need to be using the large display. Click **Playlist Editor**. (If you don't see that option, right-click the display area and it will appear.) The interior of the display switches to display the playlist and playlist-related controls (see the next figure).

You can't drag and drop songs to add them to your playlist (if you try, it replaces the whole playlist with that one song). To add songs to the playlist, click **Add**. A file navigator appears. Use this navigator to select the song to add to the playlist. (When you're navigating a directory, you can add all the songs by clicking one song, pressing **Ctrl+A** and then clicking **Open**.)

Sonique's playlist editor appears in the large display's central area.

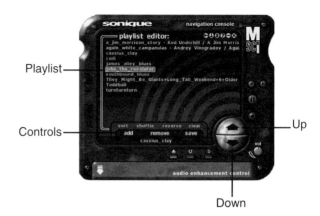

Playlist

Controls

Up

Down

To delete a song from the playlist, click the song name and then click **Remove**. You can rearrange the list randomly by clicking **Shuffle**, put it in alphabetical order by clicking **Sort**, or reverse the current order by clicking **Reverse**. To move any one song through the playlist, click the song and then use the up and down buttons to move it to the new location.

You can save the playlist by clicking **Save**. You can open a playlist in any display mood by clicking the **Open File** button and selecting the list from the file navigator or by dragging and dropping the playlist file icon on to the display.

To leave the playlist editing mode and return to the main large display mode, just right-click the central display area.

Soniqualizer

Sonique has an equalizer function, with a handful of preset arrangements designed to bring out the best in certain sorts of music. To use it, click **Audio Controls** on the large display's main screen. To use one of the preset equalizer layouts, put a tick in the **equalizer enabled** check box and then click the left or right buttons to cycle through the choices (Classical, Dance, Pop, Rock and Jazz).

If you want to design your own settings, click the down-arrow along the bottom of the large display. A 'drawer' opens, displaying 20 equalizer sliders, ranging from the deepest tones (at left) to the highest (at right). Push a slider up the screen to increase the mix of that tone, or down the screen to decrease it. Remember that this only works if the **equalizer enabled** check box is ticked. If you put a tick in the **spline tension** check box, then dragging one slider also repositions the ones beside it, keeping a smooth distribution of the sound. You can return all the sliders to the centre by clicking **Reset**.

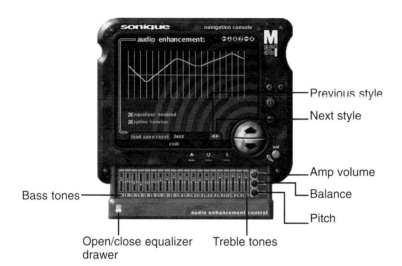

Sonique's equalizer allows you to save your bass boosting set ups.

Previous style

Next style

Amp volume

Balance

Pitch

Bass tones

Open/close equalizer drawer

Treble tones

When you have an equalizer arrangement that you like, you can save it to reuse at any time. Click **Save** and a list of 10 preset locations appears. Click any one of those 10 and your settings are stored. To return to that setting, click **Load** and the list of presets appears again. Click the setting you want.

To the right of the equalizer sliders are three knobs. The top one adjusts the amplifier volume, the second one the side-to-side balance and the third the pitch of the sound. To use one of these knobs, point to it, hold down the mouse button and move the mouse forward or back. On the Amp knob, pushing forward makes the music louder. On the Pitch knob, pushing forward raises the pitch. And on the Balance knob, pushing forward moves the sound to the right. You and I would probably design it so that dragging the mouse *right* shifts the sound to the right but that's why we aren't making millions in the software design business.

To close the equalizer drawer, click the down-arrow on its lower edge. To return the large display area to the main window, right-click it.

Expansionique

Various plug-in expansions are available for Sonique. Some provide support for additional audio file formats, while others add different vis styles. Both can be found at `http://www.sonique.com/plugs.html`. Don't try installing them before you've installed Sonique, used Sonique and then exited the program.

Sonique also supports *skins*, which can make your player look like anything from a portable CD player to a British flag. Skip on over to `http://skins.sonique.com` to find the latest and greatest skins to download.

45

Changing Your Default MP3 Player

Most of the MP3 players automatically configure themselves as Windows' default MP3 player when you install them. That way, when you double-click a song file icon, that program automatically starts playing the song. But what if you install the latest version of MegamaxiPlayer3 and decide that you don't like it that much and you would rather go back to using that version of Jane's Music Thingy you downloaded? Assuming that you haven't uninstalled Jane's Music Thingy, it's pretty easy.

First, find a song file icon, using either My Computer or Windows Explorer. While holding down the **Shift** key, click once on the icon to select it and then right-click the icon. Release the Shift key and choose **Open With** from the pop-up menu. A dialogue box appears, listing programs on your system. Click the MP3 player you want to use. (If it isn't on the list, click the **Other** button and use the file navigator to find the program file.) Put a check in the **Always Use This Program to Open This Type of File** check box, then click **OK**. *Voilà!* That's easier than memorising the lyrics to the Batman TV theme!

Players For Non-Windows Machines

There aren't nearly as many players available for the Macintosh as you might expect, considering how much of an artsy/college machine it is. If you want a player, check out the one available for download at http://www.macamp.com.

If your machine runs some other operating system, the best place for you to check is mp3.com's software section. They have a growing number of players for operating systems like Linux and BeOS and I suspect innovative programs will soon be offering an MP3 player that will run on your abacus.

Web Browser Power!

You can set up your Web browser to automatically start your MP3 player to play any MP3 song when you click its Web link. This arrangement can work out well if you have a high-speed connection to the Web (or to an intranet where MP3s are stored). It's really not that useful if you have a standard modem connection because you'll end up slowly redownloading the song every time you want to hear it.

Internet Explorer For Windows

For Internet Explorer 4 or higher for Windows, you first have to set the player to be your default system player, as described earlier. Next, click the **Start** button and choose **Programs**, **Windows Explorer**. When Windows Explorer opens, choose **View**, **Folder Options**. In the Folder Options dialogue box, click the **File Types** tab.

Now comes the tricky part: on an alphabetic list of file types, you have to find MP3. That sounds pretty easy, if you have most of the alphabet memorised. However, some programs change the name of file type to something like MusicMonster Audio File, putting the name of their player into the file type. So if you don't find it listed as MP3, look for the name of your browser on the alphabetic list. After you find the right file type, click it. In the File Type Details area below the list, it should say Extension: MP3. If it doesn't, you haven't found the right file type yet.

Next, click the **Edit** button and the Edit File Type dialogue box appears. In the **Content Type (MIME)** field, type audio/mpeg and then click **OK**.

Netscape And Other Browsers

For other browsers (including earlier versions of Internet Explorer), you have to set up the player within the browser's options. The browsers associate different programs with different file types. You want to tell it to associate your player with files with the extension .MP3 and the MIME type audio/mpeg. To do this, use your browser's **Options** or **Preferences** command.

Techno Talk

Musical Mimes?

The term *MIME* in computer jargon stands for *Multipurpose Internet Mail Extensions*. Basically, it's a standard description of a file type that your computer can use to recognise the type of file that it is receiving via email or the Web.

The Least You Need To Know

➤ Current versions of the Windows Media Player will play MP3s.

➤ Winamp is a popular music player that supports a range of interesting and useful plug-ins. Winamp is shareware and must be registered if you want to continue using it.

➤ MusicMatch Jukebox is a full-featured music player/encoder. The version on the CD-ROM is fully usable, except for some limitations on encoding.

➤ Sonique is a graphically impressive player-only program. The version on the CD-ROM is free for your use.

➤ Macintosh users don't have as many options when it comes to players. The most popular one is probably MacAMP, available at http://www.macamp.com.

Chapter 4

Finding And Downloading MP3 Files

In This Chapter

➤ How do you find MP3 sites?

➤ How do you find the tunes you want?

➤ How do you store the tunes on your hard disk?

So far, you've heard *about* MP3 files. Now you want to just *hear* MP3 files. And the first step is to get some MP3 files.

The CD-ROM that comes with this book has hours of MP3 files on it. That sounds like an awful lot but it's nowhere near enough to satisfy most music lovers. Luckily, there's plenty more music out there. How much? You could listen to MP3 music from dusk to dawn every day and never hear it all, because all the time you're listening, more new songs are being uploaded than you have time to listen to.

So now let's hunt down some of the most music-filled sites and see what they have to offer. (We're assuming that you know how to use the World Wide Web; if you don't, maybe you should head on over to the shop where you bought this book and see if they have a copy of *The Complete Idiot's Guide to the Internet.*)

mp3.com: Digitally Compressed Music's Central Core

The Web site mp3.com is the best known and the most active of the free and legal music sites. It boasts thousands of artists offering tens of thousands of tracks, leading to hundreds of thousands of downloads every day. It's popular because it has a lot of music and people keep putting more music there because it's popular.

Finding A Track On mp3.com

There are many different ways you can select music on mp3.com. For example, from the opening page you can:

➤ Click the **Song of the Day** link to get one new song selected each day by this book's American author, Rod Underhill. This should be a good song, although it may not be in your favourite style of music.

➤ Click one of the songs featured in the Hot New MP3s list. Each one is listed with its genre. This is a good place to find quality new tracks and tracks by big-name recording artists. (If you see an interesting track by a big name, grab it quickly! Sometimes the artist's label gets mad that the artist has uploaded it and moves quickly to get the song removed.)

➤ Click the **Music** link at the very top of the page to go to another page with links for many new artists and new tracks. It also has the Top 40 list, with links for the most popular songs currently on mp3.com. Some are popular because they are very good; others are popular merely because they have a cool title or have been well promoted. There's also a search field, in which you can enter a word to search for and then click **Search** to see a listing of all songs and artists with that word in the name.

➤ Click a musical genre on the **Songs by Genre** list to go to a list of sub-genres, see a listing of the top 40 MP3s in that genre and view a list of popular artists in that genre.

The only one of these techniques that immediately starts a download is clicking the title of the Song of the Day. Click any other song link and you'll be taken to a page on mp3.com focusing on that artist. It lists all the artist's available MP3 tracks. It also has a lot of information about the performer or group, such as a list of CDs available (many of which are available directly from mp3.com), the artist history, description and comments.

Buy A DAM CD – Pardon?

A lot of artists on mp3.com offer Digital Automatic Music (DAM) CDs on their page. These CDs are usually made up of a mixture of tracks available for download and tracks that can only be heard on the CD. What makes them different from standard CDs is that they also have all tracks on them in MP3 format, so you can put the disk in your CD-ROM drive and quickly copy the compressed tracks on to your computer.

Downloading Or Playing A Track

For each song on the artist's page, there are three links. The Play link is designed for people with high-speed Internet connections, such as a cable modem, a permanent network connection, or a direct line link at a university. Clicking this link launches your MP3 player and plays the song as it downloads, if you have your Web browser set up so that it knows where your MP3 player is (as described toward the end of Chapter 3, 'Installing and Using MP3 Software'). This process won't work if you're using a phone modem, because these modems are too slow. The player would have to keep stopping and waiting for the rest of the song to download before it can play.

Clicking the Save link is supposed to just save the file to your hard disk. Note that we said 'supposed to'. Depending on how people have used your PC and Web browser in the past, clicking this link may just save the file somewhere on your disk. Or it may open a dialogue box that asks if you want to save the file or open it (start playing it with your MP3 player when the download is done), or it may just open it without asking. Opening sounds good, right?

Well, it really isn't. When your Web browser thinks you want to open a file, it assumes you want to treat it like a typical Web page: look at it now and when you're done, you don't care what happens to it. So either after you close your MP3 player or after you've surfed the Web for a while longer, the song file is automatically deleted from your hard disk. If you want to hear that song again, you'll have to download it again and with a long, slow download that's a pain in the neck.

Unless you're using an old or strange Web browser, the browser has a command to save the file a link goes to. For example, Windows users should right-click the **Save** link. On the resulting pop-up menu, there is a command named something like **Save Target As** or **Save Link Document As** (the exact wording depends on your Web

51

browser). Choose this command and a file navigator appears letting you choose where to put the file.

Instant Play

The song's Instant Play link provides a way to start listening to a song almost immediately, even if you're just using a phone modem. However, it doesn't use MP3 technology. Instead, it uses a format called RealAudio. To be able to use the Instant Play feature, you'll either need to have the current version of the Windows Media Player or you'll need to install a piece of software called the RealPlayer, available for free from `http://www.real.com`. After you have RealPlayer installed, all you have to do is click the **Instant Play** link, wait a few seconds and you'll start hearing the song a few seconds later.

The quality of the sound is not as good as with MP3. Instant Play is best for trying out a song quickly before you decide whether it's worth downloading. Instead of tying up your modem for 15 minutes getting a song that's pretty weak, you can listen to the song's first 30 seconds and save yourself the time.

Techno Talk

Streaming Versus Downloading

You may wonder why MP3 addicts like the folks at mp3.com are using RealAudio instead of MP3 for their instant play features. Have they gone mad? Well, yes, some of them have, but that's not why. The RealAudio format and the RealPlayer were designed for streaming audio, listening to audio at the same time as it is coming across the Internet, without storing it on your hard disk. The MP3 file format was really designed around downloading, getting the entire file on to your hard disk and then listening to it.

The dividing line between the two types of audio format is blurring. As the Play link on mp3.com shows, MP3 files can be used in a streaming manner on high-speed lines (or with low bit-rate MP3s). And some of the MP3 encoders and players can also create and play back RealAudio tracks.

Other mp3.com Features

At the top of each mp3.com Web page is a series of links leading to different sections of the site:

> ➤ The News link takes you to probably the best-maintained site for news and opinions about MP3 and other compressed digital music formats. You'll find all sorts of information here on who's announcing what, who's suing whom and so on.

> ➤ The Software link takes you to pages where you can download a wide array of MP3 players, encoders and other MP3-related software.

> ➤ The Hardware link takes you to a page where you can find listings of various hardware-based MP3 players. Some of the listings are a bit too indiscriminate; you can't always tell quickly whether the item listed is something you can buy today at your local electronics shop, or whether it's just something that some students somewhere bet that they and some hired experts could come up with if they just had the money.

You can also find something called *radio stations* at mp3.com. These use the RealAudio streaming format to play music continuously. This is a nice way to listen to a lot of new music while you work, although it uses up some of your Internet bandwidth and thus slows down anything else you're doing on the Internet at the same time. Plus, the radio station often pauses while you do other things on the Net.

Most mp3.com artists have their own radio stations, which will loop through all the artist's available-for-download songs. There are also radio stations available for each genre of music on that genre's main page.

Non-Musical News, Non-Musical MP3s

Also on the front page of mp3.com is a Listen to the New York Times link. It can be a little hard to find, so if you can't find it easily, just go right to `http://www.mp3.com/audible/` to find the *New York Times* entry. That's right, headlines and articles from the *New York Times*, fresh every weekday, read out loud and stored in the MP3 format. Maybe they should change their advertising slogan to 'All the news that fits your RAM!'

Why All The Legal Sites?

You may wonder why the sites listed in this section are all ones that carry only legal MP3s, distributed with the permission of the creators. Aren't there sites out there that have all the latest CDs, ripped and compressed and ready for download? Of course there are but they come and go so fast it would be useless to list them all. The reason illegal sites disappear as fast as they appear is that they are, of course, illegal and their ISPs close them down rather than face the wrath of the record companies.

Record companies may seem like a legitimate target for piracy and pirating music may seem like a blow against big corporations. But it's not just the record companies who lose out with pirated music. The musicians and the people they work with lose out. Recording artists make most of their money off royalties – their cut of that £15 you shell out for a CD. It isn't a big cut but it's how they make their money, how they pay for the recording and all the people that helped them.

There are some standard arguments in favour of music piracy. Let's take a look at them:

'Well, I wouldn't buy the album anyway, so they're not really losing anything.' Except all that music you're stealing is filling your need for music and thus may be leading you to buy less legal music in general, hurting everyone in the business. And the recording artist is losing something: control over his or her music. Besides, if the recording isn't worth buying, is it really worth stealing?

'They should really be giving out samples for free anyway, to convince me to buy the CD.' But because it's their music, isn't that their choice? If you believe in free samples, you should be supporting the artists who give out free samples, which is what all those songs on the free and legal sites are.

'But I could listen to this song for free on the radio and there's no difference between that and listening on my computer.' Actually, there is a difference: the radio station is paying for playing the music.

'Information wants to be free!' Funny how the recording studio time doesn't want to be free, the cups of coffee don't want to be free, the braces for the mixing engineer's daughter's teeth don't want to be free...

peoplesound.com

peoplesound.com is the newest and brightest of the sites offering exposure to budding artists. The Web site was launched in the UK in October 1999 with a huge record industry party and they've continued to spend loads of money promoting the site in national magazines and on advertising hoardings since.

The site features the peoplesound.com Navigator, a unique tool for finding the type of music you like from amongst the wealth of talent available. The Navigator counters a common fault of sites as rich in content as mp3.com and peoplesound.com: information overload. Finding the type of music you like is not always easy.

Using The Navigator On peoplesound.com

peoplesound.com's Navigator works by asking you to tell it the type of music you like, naming three of your favourite tracks for accompanying everything from driving your car to having a bath! It then matches music by the artists in its data base with your preferences and finds tracks by peoplesound.com artists that match your tastes.

To use the Navigator, click on **Use Navigator** on the home page of peoplesound.com at `http://www.peoplesound.com`. This will bring up a new page with nine option squares asking your opinion on the following question. What do you listen to when you are... **Relaxing with Friends?**, **In the Bath?**, **Working Out?**, **Getting ready for the big night out?**, having a **Candlelit dinner?**, **Pissed off?**, **Out driving?**, **Doing the ironing?** or when you've simply **Got the blues?**

Choose a square, any square, by clicking on it. Another smaller page will pop up asking you to list three bands that you listen to while performing the activity you've chosen. Fill in your three favourite artists for listening to while you're having a bath or whatever you've chosen and click on the button marked **Results**. You'll be taken back to the page with all those option squares but this time the square on the option you've chosen will have some different text in it.

There'll be the name of a peoplesound.com artist and one of their tracks. This has been chosen by the peoplesound.com editors as being suitable for you to listen to while bathing or whatever, according to the preferences you've just expressed. You can choose to download the whole track to your hard drive as an mp3 file and play it with your mp3 player software by clicking on **Download**.

Alternatively, if you have RealPlayer software installed, you can listen to the track immediately by clicking on **Instant Play**. This will open up RealPlayer and start streaming the song. If you really like it you can choose to download it to disk. Below these two options are a tick and a cross either side of the text **Vote**. If you like the track click on the tick and if you don't click on the cross.

If you do like the song and you've chosen the Instant Play option it's wise to download it before voting as voting will refresh the page with a new song chosen for you according to how you voted for the previous number. You could find the song again on peoplesound.com but that might take some time and effort so why put yourself through all that aggravation?

You can repeat this process as long as you like. With thousands of tracks for it to choose from, the Navigator has got as long as you can afford to spend online to keep presenting you with more options. It's a good idea to go through as many listening-to mood activities as you can, voting on the music offered each time, as each successive option and vote helps the Navigator to find the music you *really* like.

Other Ways Of Finding Music You Like On peoplesound.com

As well as the Navigator, peoplesound.com lets you choose your music by genre. Select the link marked **Choose Genre** from the home page at http://www.peoplesound.com to be taken to another page where you can peruse the content on peoplesound.com by musical genre, from electronica to jazz. Selecting one of the genres or sub-genres, from ambient to vocal, will present you with a randomly chosen selection of tracks in the style you have chosen.

Alternatively you can let peoplesound.com choose a selection of tracks for you according to your mood. Follow the link marked **Choose Mood** on the home page at http://www.peoplesound.com and answer the question, How Do You Feel Right Now? by selecting from the range on offer, from 'seriously up for it' to 'laid back'. Once you've decided how you feel, which isn't always easy, you are presented with another randomly chosen selection of tracks that peoplesound.com's editors have decided suit that particular mood.

Download Or Instant Play?

Tracks on peoplesound.com are marked with two options, **Download MP3** or **Instant Play**, except in the Navigator where Download MP3 is shortened to simply **Download**. Select **Download** or **Download MP3** to, er..., download the MP3 file. Although clicking the Download MP3 link should save the file to your hard disk, depending on how your PC is configured, clicking this link may just save the file somewhere on your disk. Then again, it may open a dialogue box that asks if you want to save the file or open it. Remember that opening an mp3 file from within your browser means it will be deleted from your hard drive once you close your browser. If you want to listen to that track again you'll have to log on and download the track all over again.

To make sure this doesn't happen right-click the **Download MP3** link. On the resulting pop-up menu, choose the command named something like **Save Target As** or **Save Link Document As** (the exact wording depends on your Web browser). A file navigator appears letting you choose where to put the file. Chose a directory to download the file to your hard disk where you can play it using your MP3 software.

If you decide you must hear the song *now,* select **Instant Play** to hear the song while you're online. Remember you must have RealPlayer installed before you can use this link. You can download a free version of RealPlayer from `http://www.real.com`.

There's More!

Once you've decided you really like the track you're listening to and would like to find out more about an artist and perhaps buy their CD, click on their name to take a closer look. Alternatively you can click on the link marked **More Info**. Either will take you to a new page with another free track for you to download along with some information about the artist and a review of their album.

Once you've downloaded the second free track and digested their biographical details you may be really sold on this band and decide you want to buy a CD. Typically, peoplesound.com will show a tracklist of the album and a short review of it in the middle of the page. Below the track listing you'll see a link marked **Buy Now!**.

Click on **Buy Now!** and a new, smaller screen pops up showing the album you have just selected in your virtual shopping basket. Beside the details of the album you've just ordered is a section called **Change Quantities**, showing **+1** and **–1**. If you want to buy a copy for your friends, click on the **+1** link and the page will refresh with the new quantitiy now showing. If you change your mind and decide you really don't want the album or you have fallen out with the friend you were buying the album for, click on the **–1** link. The page will be reloaded showing the new quantity. If you had only ordered one copy the new page will show that your shopping basket is empty.

Once you've decided you really do want to buy the album, enter your details in the boxes provided. You must fill in a contact phone number, your home address (if that's where you want the albums delivered to) and the country you're residing in. If you leave out any of this information a dialogue box pops up, prompting you to fill in the information you've omitted.

Once you've completed this section, click on the button marked **Save Details**, at the bottom of the page. You'll be taken through to another page showing your order and the delivery address you've just entered. This page looks very similar to the page you've just left and has the same button marked **Save Your Details**. This is so you can change the delivery address if you decide you'd really rather recieve the CD at work or if you've made a mistake entering the address.

Assuming you've got your address details right, you can now click on the words, **Go to checkout**. This will take you to a new page where you will be asked for your credit card details. peoplesound.com uses Secure Server Technology to ensure your details are encrypted before they leave your browser and so cannot be read by anyone else on the Internet. Once you've filled in your credit card number and card expiry date, click on the button marked **Submit Order**. You'll receive a confirmation message telling you your order has been accepted and that the CD will be delivered to your doorstep within a week.

Finding An Artist Again

Once you've decided you like an artist on peoplesound.com you might want to return to see if they've put any new tracks online or released another CD. Some artists already have more than one CD available for sale and you may want to return and buy their second album if you've received the first and have fallen in love with it or the lead singer.

On the front page of peoplesound.com is a drop-down menu marked **Who's your favourite artist?**. This is a quick link to the Navigator and entering a favourite artist in here and clicking on **go** will present you with a selection of tracks that peoplesound.com's editors have decided are similar in style to that artist.

If you want to find out more about a favourite peoplesound.com artist, click on the arrow next to the pop-up link. From the menu that is displayed choose **Find a peoplesound artist**. Now type the name of your chosen peoplesound.com artist in the text box and click on **go**. You'll be taken to a new page listing peoplesound.com artists whose name matches the name you've just typed in. click on the link marked **Go To This Artists Page** to proceed to the page featuring that artist's biographical details and details of available albums and free tracks for download.

EMusic: Music Worth Paying For

EMusic, located at `http://www.EMusic.com`, is the leading commercial MP3 download site. That's right, you have to pay for most of the songs on EMusic. But for the price (generally, 99 cents per song, charged to your credit card), you're not getting the same would-be up-and-comers that make up most of the tracks on the free sites.

Instead, you get commercial recordings from some medium-to-big name folks. Some of the biggest names are actually big-but-dead names, ranging from Leadbelly to Frank Zappa. And these folks aren't offering entire albums but a song or two from one CD and a song or two from another, so you're really buying more of a sampler than a full album. If you're really into these artists, you probably won't be satisfied with what you get here.

But they do have other, living, breathing recording artists. Many are folks who are seemingly past the peak of their career, generally people who have left their major label and are moving on. This doesn't mean that their music isn't better than ever, it's just not what the kids are buying these days. If you're into what The Pixies were doing, you can check out front man Frank Black's new recordings with his band The Catholics. If you like Gene Loves Jezebel, their new music is here as well. And with these folks, you aren't just getting individual tracks; you are getting entire albums.

You can buy an entire album for $8.99, or you can buy any individual track off most albums for 99 cents. There's even one free track on many albums, something you can download and listen to and then decide if you want the whole thing.

Look for EMusic to grow into carrying not only a larger selection but also more impressive work as time goes on. They've announced a new album by respected off-beat pop charmers They Might Be Giants, an album that will not be released on CD but will be available only in MP3 format.

Getting MP3s From EMusic

On the EMusic front page, click the **Artist Index** link and you are taken to a list of the performers they currently carry, which number in the hundreds rather than the thousands you'll find at a good CD store. Click the name of an artist to be shown a list of the albums and non-album tracks he or she has available (see the figure below). Click on an album name to see a list of tracks on that album.

For each listed track, you can download a sample clip. Just right-click the icon in the MP3 column and select **Save Link As** or **Save Target As** or some similar command (depending on your browser), then use the file navigator that appears to navigate the file list. The same instructions go for the **Free** link on the free tracks. (Some tracks also have a RealAudio symbol that you can click to hear the track more quickly but at lower quality, if you have a RealAudio player installed.)

An example of an EMusic page for an artist who offers just individual songs, not an entire album.

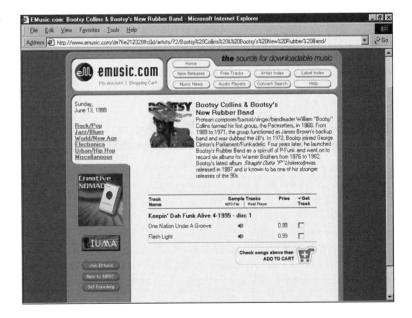

Is Buying An Album Online Worth It?

Whether shelling out the money to download an album is worth it depends on how you're listening to your music. Let's consider, for example, Gene Loves Jezebel's album *VII*. If you want to buy the album in a store, the list price is $16.97. Of course, most stores discount some from the list price but you may have a tough time finding this album in a store because it's not by a currently hot band. If you order the album from online discounter CD-NOW (`http://www.cdnow.com`), it'll cost you $11.88, plus shipping and then you have to wait days for it to arrive. But then, you actually have a physical CD. If you're not totally converted to MP3, you can still play it in your car CD player, on your Discman and so on. And when you're tired of it, you can probably sell it for a couple of pounds to your local secondhand music shop.

Still, if you've built your previous musical life around CDs, you probably already have enough CDs to serve your car and Discman needs... and you can store up the money you save towards buying that portable MP3 player that will let you take it on the road.

Ordering Individual Tracks

Each track you can purchase has a check box next to it. Click on the box for each track you want to buy. After you've ticked off all the tracks you want for the page, click the **Add to Cart** button. Doing so adds these tracks to your online shopping cart, a list of the things you plan to buy. When you add items to your cart, you will be shown a list of everything in your cart. This list also has controls that allow you to remove items from your cart. One of the nice things about a virtual shopping cart is that, unlike a real shopping cart, when you remove something from it, you don't have to look both ways to make sure that nobody notices you sticking the item back on the wrong shelf.

Ordering An Album

When you've found an album on the artist's page that you want to order, click the **Download Album** link under the album's cover image (shown in the next figure). If you don't have an account, you are taken to the Log In screen; go through the steps described in the following section, 'Getting an EMusic Account', to create your account. If you do have an account but have told the system not to remember you, you must enter your account name and password now. After you do so, the album is added to your shopping cart.

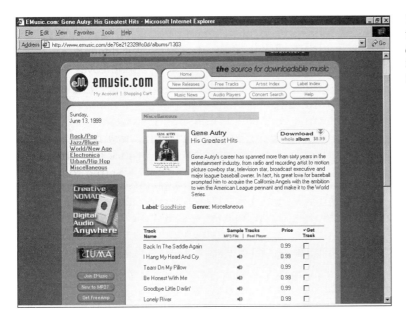

You can select any individual song from this album. The link to buy the whole album is at the top of the page.

Getting An EMusic Account

Before you can pay for and download all those tracks you've put in your shopping cart, you need to have an EMusic account. Otherwise, they won't deal with you.

To set up your EMusic account, click the **My Account** link toward the upper-left of any EMusic page. You are taken to a Log In screen, where the system wants to know your name and password. You don't have a password? No surprise, because this is your first time here!

Click the **Create New Account** link to set yourself up. A form appears asking for your name, email address and your choice for a password. Fill out this form and then click **Update Our Records**. Now you have an account! You also have a screen listing various mailing lists you can join. If you join a mailing list, you will get occasional emails about EMusic, their partners, or specific musicians, depending on the topic of the list.

Getting The Music You've Ordered

"They'll Sell My Details To The Devil!"

If you're worried about what EMusic will do with your name and email address, check http://www.emusic.com/help/privacy for their privacy policy.

After you've got all the songs you want in your shopping cart, it's time to check out. Click **Shopping Cart** at the top of any page to view the contents of your shopping cart. You'll see a list of the items you've put in the cart, as well as the price of each. If you've changed your mind about an item, click its **Remove** check box and then click **Update Cart**.

When you're happy with the list, click **Check Out**. If you haven't logged in this session, you'll need to enter your email address and password, so EMusic knows that it's you. The log-in form also has an option that instructs the system to always remember you, so when it's time to log in, you can just click the **Log In** button and skip entering your name and password. This option is a good idea for your computer at home because it saves you time each time you use EMusic. It's a bad idea for your computer at work because EMusic will think that anyone who uses your computer is you, even if they have a really bad haircut.

An invoice of what you've ordered appears. At this point, they're going to want a lot more information so that they can charge your purchases to your credit card. Click **Add a New Credit Card** to get a form of credit card information. Fill out the form and then click **Add Credit Card**. On the next screen, click the **Continue** button. (You'll only have to go through this rigmarole the first time; after that, EMusic remembers your credit card information as part of your account info and you can charge automatically to that card.)

After you've entered your credit card information, EMusic puts the purchase order through, so your credit card is charged. A list of songs you've ordered appears. Each of these songs has a download link. Use these links to download the songs, as described earlier.

Yes, it does take quite a while to download entire albums. Don't worry about something going wrong in the midst of a download; after you've purchased a song, you're allowed to download it up to three times.

Remember that you don't have to wait for one file to finish downloading before you start the next. Your Web browser can usually handle several files at a time. That way, you can start the various files downloading just before going to bed, or before heading off on a trip to the Himalayas. Those of you with high-speed links shouldn't have much problem getting the music you bought but those of us still using the same phone modems our grandparents used when they were kids will find getting that album a bit more trying.

Combatting Credit Card Crime

If you're worried about someone stealing your credit card number when you send it over the Internet to a site like EMusic, you're causing yourself unneeded stress. Modern major browsers all support *secured* mode; a communications mode where everything you send via a Web form is encoded so that people using Internet snooping tools can't read it.

You can tell when your browser is in secured mode by looking at the bottom bar of the browser window; if you see an unbroken key or a closed padlock, the security is in force.

Other EMusic Features

EMusic doesn't just support music by selling MP3s; it offers a number of useful informational links. Other features of the EMusic site include:

➤ A page of downloadable MP3 players (not nearly so many as mp3.com but with more description).

➤ A concert search (you can find out the next time that The Wascally Weasels are coming to your town).

➤ A general music news page (so you can find out that The Wascally Weasels have broken up because the lead Weasel got elected to Congress).

Amp3: Music And Just A Little More

Amp3 seems to have taken a cue from commercial radio. At Amp3.com, you can download free music from hundreds of bands. And that's not all! In addition to the free music, there's something else you get for free: advertising.

That's right, attached to each song is a short little advertclip, just a few seconds long. Every time you play the MP3, you'll hear a little jingle for some sponsor.

So why would you download from here when you can be downloading advert-free music from other places? After all, if you're a fan of music, you don't really want to have to sit through even a few seconds of adverts and if you're a fan of adverts, you really don't want to have to sit through several minutes of music to hear each one.

The answer is that Amp3.com hopes to provide you with better music because of the adverts. Every time someone downloads a song with an advert in it, the advertiser pays Amp3.com money. When that happens, Amp3.com passes half of the money to the performer. By doing this, they hope to attract musicians whose music is worth paying for. The deal for the musicians is actually quite attractive because the amount they get paid per download (ranging from 5 to 25 cents) is around the same rate they would get paid for the song if it were on a CD. In the long run, you may see people building careers from this sort of distribution, rather than getting some attention with a few free tracks and then hopping off the MP3 bandwagon on to the CD bandwagon.

Getting this arrangement fully working and profitable is a long-term goal for Amp3; at the moment they don't have everything going quite as well as they probably hope to since the ad jingles they run are jingles for the one advertiser they can most easily land: Amp3.com. And they give themselves a discount on the ads, only paying the performer 2 cents.

Finding Music On Amp3.com

The front page of the site has a list of their recent Pick Hit Of The Day picks. This is a spot that their artists really desire; not only does it mean a lot of visibility and more downloads but they get a $50 bonus for being the Pick Hit. Better still, if the same song is a Pick Hit for two days, they get $1000 and for three days, $10 000.

Running down the left edge of the page is a list of musical genres, ranging from alternative to zydeco. Click any of these links and you'll see the most popular downloads in each category. When I visited, their genre list was a bit overzealous, as I found at least one genre for which they had no music. That's another sign that their goals are set well beyond what they've achieved.

Every Web Site Aims To Grow

In our coverage of Amp3.com, you'll see a few comments noting that they clearly aren't yet at the level of success that they are aiming for. Does this mean they're failures? Absolutely not! Few of even the most popular Web sites have achieved their goals. Even those sites whose stocks are skyrocketing are losing money by the bucketful and aren't that worried about it. They know that if they can get their Web site established now, there will be plenty of opportunities to make money when the Web has even more users and a much larger bandwidth.

For each song listed, you can use the link for the name of the song to download it, or click the performer's name to see an information sheet on that performer and a list of all their songs available to download, each with a download link.

Other Amp3.com Features

At the time of this writing, there isn't much more there. They have an introductory MP3 guide, some hardware reviews and some links to a handful of MP3 software providers. Again, expect this site to grow.

RioPORT

RioPORT is a site run by Diamond, manufacturers of the Rio portable MP3 players and other multimedia gadgets. As such, there is a visible emphasis on providing music for people with Rios and convincing people who come looking for music that they should get a Rio to play it on.

Head on over to `http://www.rioport.com` and you'll see what I mean: some large adverts for the Rio and Rio-related stuff, plus an alphabetically ordered list of links to various musical genres. Click one of those links and you'll get a handful of tracks in that genre displayed, each with an illustration. The download link for the track is the track's title. There's another link for each track with the name of a Web site that includes the artist; click that link to see the Web site.

When you select a genre, you also get a list at the left of the screen of Web sites that provide authorised MP3s of that sort of music. You can click any one of these links to visit that site.

All in all, there aren't that many songs on the RioPORT site (although they are hand-picked ones and thus tend to be good quality). What the site does best is help you find other MP3 sites that have music in a given genre.

Other RioPORT Features

In addition to musical genres, RioPORT has a list of spoken word genres (news, comedy and so on). These categories all link to the Audible.com site, which we'll discuss in a little bit. The news is the same *New York Times* news that mp3.com carries. (Oddly enough, although clicking the link on RioPORT pulls up the Audible.com page with the *Times* news, a similar link on one of Audible's pages pulls up the mp3.com page!)

The RioPORT opening page provides music and news links.

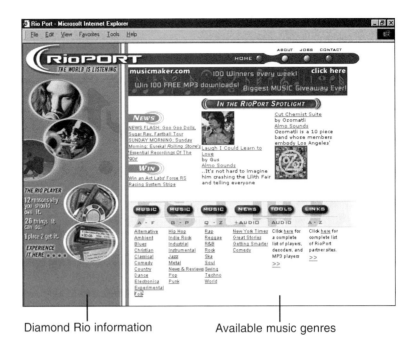

Diamond Rio information   Available music genres

RioPORT has every kind of musical genre, even folk music.

Sources for other tracks in this genre ➤

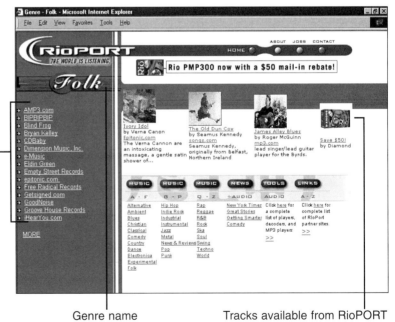

Genre name   Tracks available from RioPORT

Audible: Words, Not Music

New Jersey-based Audible, Inc., is an interesting company. Years before the first portable MP3 players were available, Audible had their own portable electronic compressed audio player, the Audible MobilePlayer. This little handheld device doesn't have as much memory as the MP3 players (even the newer MobilePlayer-Plus has only half as much memory as the earliest Rio) but they've been able to get hours of playtime out of the memory by using higher compression rates. The sound wasn't as high quality as a good MP3 but that didn't matter so much for its intended use. Audible wasn't trying to replace CD players with their device; their target was the books-on-tape market.

Books on cassette tape are a huge market in the United States. I know that when I was driving from Minnesota to Alaska, my spirits were kept up by listening to such things as Richard Feynman's lectures on physics. Of course, that subject isn't to everyone's taste. (Some people I know would drive from Minnesota to Alaska just to avoid six hours of physics lectures.) But the good news is that all sorts of books, from the utterly vapid to the completely inscrutable, are available on tape.

One of the problems with books on cassette tape, however, is that they aren't cheap. Even an abridged edition will often take up four or six cassettes. Get a nice thick book like Stephen King's *Four Past Midnight* and you'll find that the cassette edition is four volumes totalling 20 cassettes. That version will cost you about $100 more than buying the printed book in paperback, which runs to about $8. The people at Audible realised that if you didn't actually have to manufacture the cassettes, the costs came down a lot. If all they had to do was to have you download the electronic files, they could offer a lower price and still make a good profit. For example, King's *Bag Of Bones* – clocking in at more than 21 hours – costs about $60 on cassette and $80 on CD but if you download it for your MobilePlayer, it costs just $18. That's less than the hardback ($20), although still more than the $8 paperback.

Granted, the MobilePlayer costs something (starting at about $80) but it doesn't take a lot of Stephen King audio recordings to save you money. Plus, the ability to make a recording available quickly online means that they can offer things that would be impractical to offer on a cassette, such as fresh National Public Radio news and interviews.

What's This Got To Do With MP3?

Audible realised that the Diamond Rio was a hot seller. Suddenly, loads of people were getting this player that worked a lot like their own. If they could just sell the files in the MP3 format as well, they could open up a large market of people who might not cough up $80 for a non-music player. And so they began converting the books that they offer to the MP3 format and snuggled up with Diamond so that they could help each other. (They may be delayed by the people who license them the rights to the recordings. After all, an MP3 of a book faces the same copying concern as an MP3 of a song.)

Despite being close to Diamond, Audible will tell you that their own player is actually better for books than the Rio. After all, if you pause the Rio in the middle of a chapter and don't start playing again soon, Rio resets to the beginning of the chapter and when you want to listen again, you'll have to fast-forward to find your place. The Audible player doesn't lose its place. Because they're friendly with Diamond, however, they don't tell you that some of the *other* MP3 players (such as the MPMan) also don't lose their place.

Because of the higher level of compression (using a non-MP3 format) they use, the MobilePlayer-Plus can actually store more audio than the standard Rio.

So Where Do I Get These MP3 Books?

Surf on over to `http://www.audible.com/mp3/` to get to their MP3-oriented site. After you get there, you'll see that they really want you to sign up with them. They'll want your name, phone number and email address.

At Audible.com's MP3 site, you'll find links for a number of types of spoken information and entertainment. They have news, literature, humour and more. They even have some alternative rock and jazz. Click one of these links and you'll see a list of available items for download. Click one to get a fuller description, with a download link.

At the time of writing this, most of the downloads are shorter items (20 to 80 minutes), which are available for free, as samples. Soon (perhaps by the time you buy this book), you can expect to see more material available for sale.

They Want Your Number

Beware when someone wants more personal information than they legitimately need before you can access their site. The Audible MP3 site asking for your phone number is a clear example of that. How do you know they won't give your number to the fine folks at Evil Jack's Phone Company, who will call you at 3 am to offer you their new phone plan ('Buy 10 minutes of long distance for £30 and your next 10 seconds are free!')? Some sites at least offer you a privacy policy letting you know what they might do with your information before you give it to them; no such luck at Audible. And some sites don't mind if you leave out some information; again, no such luck here. So consider these facts before you decide to give any site your information.

Mac Maniacs, Beware

To make longer works easier to handle, some of them are broken down into separate MP3 files for each chapter. In some cases, you can download a book chapter by chapter, which is fine. In other cases, however, they have combined the book's files into a single file that has a built-in program to split its component files apart again. This program is for Windows; it won't run on the Mac. If you see that the file you're downloading from Audible ends in .exe instead of .mp3, it isn't Mac-friendly.

MP3now: An MP3-Less MP3 Site

The site at http://www.MP3now.com is supposed to be a central site for the MP3 fan. You might think they would have a lot of MP3s, some MP3 software, all the latest MP3 news articles, perhaps a search engine that lets you find the MP3s you want (legal or, alas, otherwise) and so on.

Actually, they don't have any of that stuff.

Links, Links, Links

What they *do* have is *links* to all that stuff. You can click a link on the site to pull up mp3.com's top 100 list from their site, another link to pull up the list of downloadable music from an online rap label and so on. They have reviews of software and they have a download link but that link starts the download from someone else's server, not their own. Click one of the MP3-related news headlines and it'll pull up the page from someone else's site, not from MP3now.com itself.

And whenever you do link to a page on another site, MP3now.com opens that page either in a new window or in a frame on the existing window, making sure that you still have their site open.

The site does offer some music and a top 100 list that it *says* is part of MP3now.com but if you look at the URL in your browser window, you'll discover that it really comes from another Web site, http://www.nordicdms.com. If you surf on over to that site, you'll see that they offer all those songs themselves.

Do They Have Anything Of Their Own?

They do have some original content, material that talks *about* MP3 in some way. They have information on how to make and play MP3s, reviews of MP3 software, things like that.

They also own Findsongs.com, a site designed to help you search for MP3s. But in the MP3now.com tradition, this site doesn't actually have a search engine of its own. Instead, it lets you enter the information you're searching for, selecting the engine to search with from a long list of search sites. The results get displayed in a frame, so you're always kept at the Findsongs site.

A Disposable Web Site

So if MP3now doesn't have original material, does that mean that it's useless? Not really. It's useful like a disposable tissue is useful: use it once.

MP3now.com can be a good place to find out about other MP3 Web sites. Go there once, see if any of the sites that they link to are interesting and add them to your Web browser's bookmarks. You don't need to keep going back to MP3now.com every time you want to get back to a site that they link to because doing so will just slow you down.

The Least You Need To Know

➤ Go to `http://www.mp3.com` for tens of thousands of free, legal recordings to download.

➤ Go to `http://www.peoplesound.com` for even more legal recordings to download.

➤ `http://www.EMusic.com` offers downloadable tracks by known musicians for sale.

➤ `http://www.Amp3.com` offers free downloadable songs with a short advertising jingle attached to the beginning of each one.

➤ Diamond has a Web site at `http://www.RioPORT.com` that offers free music as well as information on the Rio portable players.

➤ The company Audible, set up at `http://www.audible.com/mp3/`, sells mostly spoken word recordings but it now offers plenty of free samples, including complete stories.

➤ At `http://www.MP3now.com` you'll find links to content on other MP3-related sites.

Chapter 5

MP3 Hardware

In This Chapter

➤ Portable MP3 players

➤ MP3 for your stereo system

➤ MP3 for your car

➤ MP3 for your PDA

MP3 music on your computer is great but it's only useful as long as you're sitting in front of your computer. Now, if you spend all day in front of your computer, that should be good enough. But if you do spend all day in front of the computer, you should get out more. There are a lot of exciting things happening out there, a whole life to lead.

And we're not the only ones. A whole industry has popped up to create other types of MP3 players, so don't feel you have to stay stuck in front of your PC in order to hear your favourite tunes.

Diamond Rio PMP300/PMP500: Little Gems

The best known MP3 player is the portable Rio PMP300, manufactured by Diamond Multimedia, previously best known for their high-quality PC video cards. The Rio is about the same size as a deck of playing cards.

The Rio stores music in *flash memory*, a type of computer memory. Flash memory is different from the standard memory in your PC, because flash memory retains data even when the power is turned off. The basic PMP300 (priced at £149.99) comes with 32 megabytes of flash memory, about enough to store half an hour of songs in CD-quality compression, or more if you use a lower grade of compression. (You can keep a fairly sharp sound and get a full hour of music in it.) The PMP500, priced at £229.99, comes with twice as much memory.

There is also an expansion slot, so you can add another 16 or 32 megabytes using a standard SmartMedia flash memory card. These cards cost from about £50 to £100 apiece, depending on whether you're buying 16 or 32 megabytes' worth.

Don't Forget These Facts About Flash Memory

More and more folks are using SmartMedia flash memory cards in their digital cameras and other digital appliances. If you've got some of these and want to use them in your Rio, be careful! First, flash memory cards come with different voltage ratings; some of the flash memory cards out there are 5 V and the Rio needs 3.3 V.

More importantly, once you use a flash memory card in the Rio, you can't use it again in your camera or in other products! The Rio changes the internal formatting of the memory, so that other devices can't understand it. (This is Diamond's way of addressing a US law that requires that the Rio not be able to transfer files to other devices.)

Installing The Rio's Battery

The Rio takes a single AA battery but it's a little tricky to install. The plastic battery door is on a metal hinge on the bottom of the Rio but in addition to pivoting on that hinge, the door can slide along the hinge.

To open the battery door, use your thumb to push it toward the side of the Rio, sliding it along the hinge beneath. Once you have it pushed out the hinge will flip open easily. The battery goes in positive end first. (That's the end with the little bump sticking out of it.) Closing the battery door is the tricky part – you have to make sure that the door is slid all the way out along the hinge, then close the hinge and then push the door in along the hinge. It's easy to make the mistake of first trying to slide the door in and then trying to force the door inward. At best you'll be frustrated. At worst, you'll damage the little door and you'll have to hold together this nifty cutting-edge electronic device using a piece of sticky tape and that isn't cool! (Then again, if you own a pager, you're probably used to this awkward little battery dance.)

If you're not going to use your Rio for days at a time, take the battery out. Even when you're not using it, the Rio will slowly drain the battery. If the battery isn't in it, it can't get run down. Perhaps more importantly, you eliminate the chance that an ageing battery will start leaking battery acid all over the inside of your player, turning the electronic marvel into a low-quality paperweight. The good news is that because the Rio uses *flash memory* you don't lose the music when the battery is removed.

Save Money *And* The Planet

If you find yourself going through a fair number of AA batteries in your player (and in other uses), consider switching to rechargeable batteries. They cost more initially (particularly since you have to buy a battery charger), but can save you money in the long run. Plus, it's more ecologically sound.

Hooking The Little Box To Your PC

In order to make use of the Rio PMP300 you're going to need a PC that runs Windows. (The Macintosh only works with the PMP500.) But don't worry, you don't have to carry the PC with you everywhere you go. You'll need the PC when you want to add or change the songs in your Rio.

The Rio comes with two sets of software on CD-ROM. It comes with a copy of MusicMatch Jukebox software, as seen in Chapter 3, 'Installing and Using MP3 Player Software'. This is not a fully registered copy of MusicMatch; it can handle all your encoding needs for a while but it will stop encoding after you've encoded 50 songs, while the rest of the functions will continue working. You can use MusicMatch to turn tracks from your favourite CD-ROM into MP3s, so you can put them on the Rio.

The other set of software is special Rio software. While it can be used to play MP3s, its main use is to send files to the Rio and to remove older files to make space. Before you can do any of this, however, you'll have to connect your Rio to your PC. To do this, follow these steps:

1. Shut down your PC.
2. Unplug your printer cable from the back of the PC.
3. Plug the Rio adapter into the printer port.
4. Plug your printer cable into the adapter.

5. Plug the Rio cable into the special slot in the adapter. The side of the cable marked UP goes away from the printer connector.

6. Plug the other end of the Rio cable into the Rio. The side of the cable marked UP goes toward the face of the Rio.

7. Turn on your PC.

Printer Confusion

These days, there are a lot of non-printer devices that use the printer port. For example, you may have a scanner that plugs into the printer port and then a printer plugged into a port on the scanner. The problem is that devices like that or like the Rio adapter assume that they're the only device using the port besides the printer. With the adapter plugged into the PC, the scanner plugged into the adapter and the printer plugged into the scanner, some printers start acting crazy the moment you turn on your PC. If you plug the scanner into the PC and the adapter into the scanner, the PC can't communicate with the Rio.

How can you get around this problem? Well, you can get rid of any non-printer items connected to your printer port but that's probably not practical. Some PCs have multiple printer ports, in which case you can just plug the Rio connector into a different one than your other non-printer devices. Or you could unplug your other devices when you want to use the Rio.

If you're going to be using the Rio and the other devices fairly regularly, however, you'll probably want to avoid the difficulty and wear and tear on the parts of constantly unplugging and re-plugging. What you'll need to do is purchase an A/B switch, which is a box that plugs into your printer port. It will have two different out ports, one that you can connect the Rio to, the other for your other device. Then you just turn a knob or push a button on the A/B switch whenever you want to change which device is connected. When you buy your A/B switch, make sure that the package says that it *passes through* (connects) all 25 leads from the printer port; cheaper A/B switches only pass through the few leads that printers use and won't attach the leads that other devices use.

Installing Rio Software

To install the Rio management software, stick the Rio's software CD-ROM into your CD-ROM drive. On most people's PCs, the installation program will start automatically after a few seconds. If it doesn't start for you, double-click **My Computer**, right-click the icon for your CD-ROM drive, choose **Explore** to see the contents and then double-click the icon marked **Setup.exe** or just **Setup**.

The installation program suggests a folder to store the program in. Click **Next** to accept this folder. Then a list of suggested installation options appears, with the most appropriate choices already checked off. (If you already have a current, registered version of MusicMatch running on your system, you'll probably want to clear the check box next to the option to install the new one.) Click **Next** again. On the next screen, click **Next** again. The installation takes place and you'll be informed when it's done. Click **Finish** to acknowledge that it's done.

But wait! It may not be all over! If you chose to install MusicMatch, the MusicMatch installation program will automatically start. Just follow the instructions to complete that installation.

Sending Music To Rio

To copy MP3 songs from your PC to the Rio, first start the Rio software by clicking the **Start** button and choosing **Programs**, **Rio**, **Rio Manager**.

The window that opens up is a basic Windows MP3 player as shown in the figure below. As a player, it's rather basic. If you just want to play MP3s on your PC, you'd be better off using the MusicMatch software. About the only reason you'd really want to start this player is so that you can click the **Mem** button.

——The Mem button

When you start the Rio manager, you get a basic MP3 player with a vital button marked Mem.

When you click that button, a Rio Internal Memory window opens up (see the next figure). The program communicates with your Rio and displays a list of all the songs stored in the Rio's *internal memory* (the memory that's built in to the Rio, as opposed to any add-in memory card you have installed, which would be considered *external memory*). The first time you run it, there won't be any music there, of course.

The easiest way to add a song to the list is to drag and drop the song's icon on to the song list. You can also add a song by clicking **Open** and finding the song using the file navigator that appears.

The Rio memory manager manages Rio memory in a reasonably memorable manner.

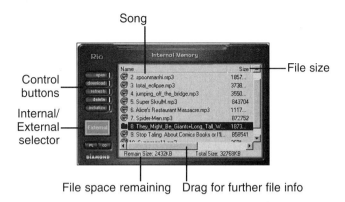

Song

Control buttons

Internal/ External selector

File size

File space remaining   Drag for further file info

If the song file is bigger than the remaining space in your Rio, you'll get a dialogue box telling you so in nice, non-insulting terms. You can make room for the song by deleting other tracks. To delete a track, just click on it and then click **Delete**.

Once you have the right set of songs on the list, click **Download** and any new files you added to the list will be downloaded to the Rio. This may take a few minutes. (A standard, unexpanded Rio without any files on it takes about six minutes to fill up.)

If you do have a memory card inserted into the Rio, you have to set up a separate list of music that will be stored on it. Click **External** and the manager switches to managing the memory on the card. To return to managing the internal song list, click **Internal**.

Once you've finished downloading, unplug the connector cable from the Rio. You can leave the other end plugged into the adapter, so that you don't have to reconnect it every time you want to download to the Rio.

Using The Rio

Plug a set of headphones into the Rio and you're ready to start high-quality digital listening. You can use the headphones the Rio came with or any other headphones with a standard Walkman-style jack.

To start playing the downloaded songs, just press the **Play/Pause** button. The Rio will automatically turn on and quickly display the amount of memory the system has and then a second later, you'll be hearing pure digital sound, assuming you remembered to stick the headphones in your ears.

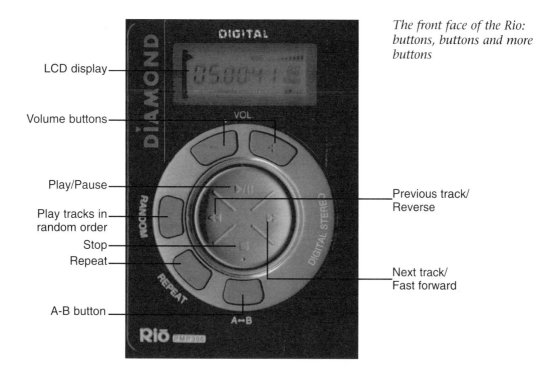

The front face of the Rio: buttons, buttons and more buttons

LCD display

Volume buttons

Play/Pause

Play tracks in random order

Stop

Repeat

A-B button

Previous track/ Reverse

Next track/ Fast forward

The main controls are on the front face of the Rio, as shown in the figure above:

➤ Press the **Play/Pause** button to start playing music. Press it again to pause the playing and then again to restart it. (After you've paused a track for about half a minute, the Rio will lose its place in the track; press **Play** after that and you're back at the start of the song.)

➤ Quickly press and release the **Next track/Fast forward** button to skip to the next song. If you hold down the button, you'll fast-forward through the current song.

➤ Quickly press and release the **Previous track/Reverse** button to skip back to the previous song. If you hold down the button, you'll zoom backwards through the current song. (You won't actually hear the music while fast-forwarding or reversing. You can only tell where you are in the song by looking at the display.)

➤ Press **Stop** once to stop the music playing. Pressing it a second time turns off the Rio. (The Rio will turn off automatically after about 15 seconds if there isn't any music playing and you're not doing anything, unless you're in Pause mode.)

➤ Use the **+** and **–** volume buttons to increase and decrease the volume. The Rio has 20 different volume levels, which should be enough to enable you to find a level that is audible but comfortable in most situations.

➤ Press **Random** to hear the songs play in random order. (Even in this mode, you will hear songs stored on the internal memory first and only once you've heard all of those will you hear songs from the external memory card.)

➤ Pressing **Repeat** cycles between repeating one song, repeating all the songs (automatically restarting the first track when the last song is done) and just playing through the songs once and then stopping. If you're in one of the repeat modes, the display will show an arrow turned back on itself in the lower-right corner, followed by either 1 or All, depending on the repeat mode.

➤ The **A-B** button is used to repeat a short segment of a song. For example, if the singer is singing, 'You're a simple pleasure like hot dogs, like discovering new songs,' you can press the button once after the word 'hot' to set the start of the repeating segment. Press the button again in the middle of the word 'discovering' to set the end of the repeating portion. Suddenly, your Rio will start repeating the phrase 'dogs like disco' time and time again. Press the button for a third time to resume normal play.

The Rio also has three buttons across the top:

➤ The **Menu** button is one you won't be using often. It only works when the music is stopped. Press it once to go into menu mode. The letters tI will be displayed, followed by the number of total internal memory megabytes. Press the **Next track/Fast forward** button repeatedly to see the total external memory (tE), the amount of unused internal memory (RI), the amount of unused external memory (RE) and the version number of the software built into the unit (V). Press **Menu** again to return to music playing mode.

➤ Press the **EQ** button to cycle between the four different sets of equaliser settings, optimised for different types of music. There are settings for normal, classic (misspelled clasic), jazz and rock.

➤ Press **Intro** to hear the first 10 seconds of each song. This makes it easy to find an individual song when you don't remember what order the songs were stored in. When you find the song you like, press **Intro** again to return to normal playing mode.

The final control is on the side of the unit. It's a small, unmarked switch. Slide this switch up and none of the buttons will work anymore. Why would you want this? Well, if you're going to stick the Rio in your pocket, or somewhere else where it's going to get banged against things, having this **Hold** button on will keep your music from starting, stopping, or being otherwise abused by accidental button pushes. Just slide it back down when you're ready to take control again.

Rio's Display: Information In Formation

The Rio has a convenient display on the front, shown in the next figure. Convenient, that is, unless you're using the belt clip on the back of the unit to hold it to your trousers. Then you have to bend yourself in half to see the display and even then it will appear upside-down. Either that or you can just briefly unclip it and lift it to your eyes.

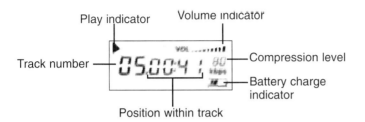

The Rio display is actually clear to read, just hard to photograph.

The Play indicator in the upper-right corner displays an arrow when playing or two parallel lines when the song is paused.

The Volume display indicates the sound level as an idea of line segments of increasing size. The more segments displayed, the louder the play is. It's not a precise display (it only shows 10 different volume levels, when there are actually 20) but it's close enough.

The battery charge indicator gives you an idea of how much energy is left in your battery. The more black showing in the image of the battery, the more power remains. When you get down to just a small segment of black remaining, carry a spare battery with you.

Techno Talk

Maybe The Writer Was On LSD?

The Rio manual repeatedly refers to the display as an *LED* display. Problem is, it's not true. *LED* stands for *Light Emitting Diode*. LED displays are ones with glowing figures, as found on the front of most VCRs. The Rio display is neither light emitting nor made of diodes. It's properly called an *LCD* display, the same sort of display that most digital watches have. *LCD* stands for *Liquid Crystal Display* (which means that *LCD display* stands for *Liquid Crystal Display display* but that's just normal technical silliness).

Thanks For The Memory Card

To add additional memory to the Rio, insert the memory card into the slot at the bottom of the unit. (A diagram on the back of the unit shows you how to orient the card for proper connection.) When you push the card in, the large slider on the back of the Rio will slide up. Once the card is in place, push the smaller slider to the left to lock it into place.

To remove the card, push the small slider to the right and then push the large slider down.

Down To Rio

The Rio is a rather nifty gadget. The sound quality coming from songs compressed at 128 Kbps is amazing. The unit is rugged, making it great for use while you're jogging (or sitting in the park laughing at the joggers). Its small size means that it can be carried in a large pocket so you have it when you want it... just try that with a portable cassette player or a CD player.

However, the 32 megabytes of memory that the basic unit has stores only half an hour of that high-quality compression. If you're going for a longer jog, you'll have to settle either for repeating the same music, or using higher-compression, lower-quality audio. Even if you throw in money for additional memory, you top out at a couple of hours of music.

And just as headphones can point up the strengths of high-quality audio, they also accent the weaknesses of lesser quality. If you use files compressed down to 80 Kbps or even 64 Kbps, you'll hear a metallic echo to the music, as if your favourite band was playing in a ditch. The higher the compression rate, the deeper into the ditch they get.

This Rio is clearly a member of the first generation of MP3 players. Assuming that memory prices continue to fall, you'll soon be able to carry several hours of high-quality audio with you at all times. With that much, you'd be able to keep a lot of music with you, rather than redownloading a half-hour or hour of music each time you plan to go out. But then, with technology changing so fast, you can count on something better coming out in a few months no matter when you buy.

Best Got Better: The Rio PMP500

The Rio PMP500 improves on what is already a great player by upping the internal memory to 64 MB. This gives you an hour of listening straight out of the box and, with the addition of a 32-MB memory card, takes your uninterrupted listening pleasure up to a train ride to work's worth of 90 minutes. At £229 it's a little more expensive but well worth the extra money.

To compensate for you having to fork out a bit more money the PMP500 comes in currently stylish see-through coloured plastic, which doesn't make it sound any better but makes it look really cool. Rio have also thoughtfully added a back light to the LCD display, which is very handy in dark and moody locations. Because it works through a USB port the Rio provides faster downloads than any of the other machines can achieve through the slower printer port. Typically, you can download an hour of music to the PMP500 in just a couple of minutes. The use of the USB port also means that Mac and iMac users can plug the Rio into their computer and so enter the portable MP3 revolution.

Rio have also introduced a new piece of software, at least on the PC, called the RioPort Audio Manager, which lets you encode CDs into MP3s, keep a library of your MP3s *and* copy files on to the player. Mac users get the excellent SoundJam software, which does the same thing. You get the same outstanding sound quality as the original Rio, a choice of see-through blueberry or grape and an hour's worth of listening without any additional memory card. The best just got better and the rest will have to catch up.

Rio have taken the MP3 revolution to heart with their website, `http://www.rioport.com`, which offers lots of information about MP3 and links to files for you to download.

Thomson Lyra: Memory Free

The Lyra, from Thomson Multimedia, has no flash memory built in. If you want to listen to any tunes you must plug in the 64-megabyte card that's included with this £199.99 unit.

There is no memory built in to this device because you won't be connecting the Lyra to your PC to download. Instead, you have a separate memory writer connected to your PC, a spaghetti-like concoction of leads that plug into your printer port *and* your keyboard socket. Insert your memory card into this device, download your songs into the memory and then insert the memory card into the Lyra.

With the PC connector and the memory writing capability built in to a separate device, there's that much less hardware that needs to be built in to the portable device, although that doesn't seem to have made the Lyra that much smaller or lighter. In fact, because the Lyra carries two AA batteries, it weighs a bit more than some of the other machines. On the plus side the use of two batteries, instead of one as on most of the other players, means that the Lyra will run for up to 20 hours without a battery change.

Although the leads offer a through port for your printer and, naturally, a through socket for your keyboard, as with most of the portable players it didn't like having a printer attached at the same time when we tested it. The enclosed software for connection of the memory device actually managed to disable the use of the printer on one machine, forcing the printer software to be re-installed before everything would work normally again.

Sound As A Pound

The Lyra is one of the most solidly built players we've had the opportunity to review and certainly impresses with its build quality and excellent sound reproduction. It is one of the few players on offer to design into its LCD the ability to display song information (title, artist's name, track playing time, etc.) while the track is playing. This is a strange omission in the other players as this facility is one thing that MP3 can do that CD players don't and it's nice to see it make an appearance. Only Lyra and the Elex JazPiper, of all the review models made available to us, let you see what you're listening to.

The Lyra uses RealJukebox to download tunes to the memory card and encrypts the files as you download them which is why Virgin Music has endorsed the player. As well as selling it in their stores, the Lyra comes with six tunes from Virgin music on the accompanying CD-ROM. The encryption means that once you've downloaded a track to the Lyra you have no way of copying it on to any other device or back on to your hard drive. You and I might see that as a disadvantage but the music lawyers probably think it's a good idea!

With the ability to play Windows Media files as well as encrypted MP3s, the Lyra is the darling of the SDMI (Secure Digital Music Initiative) and this will certainly ensure it is supported by other music companies as the MP3 revolution gathers pace. You can find out more about the Lyra, as well as downloading MP3 files, at `http://www.thomson-lyra.com`.

LG Electronics MF–PD330 MP3 Player And AHA–FD770 MP3/Cassette Player: What's In A Name?

The LG Electronics range of MP3 Players have the least inspiring names of all the machines but are actually both very impressive. The two players on offer provide a very solid build quality alongside reliable software that does an excellent job of transferring files back and forth between the player and your PC. In fact this was the only software that didn't seem to mind if you had a printer attached to the parallel port at the same time. That's not to say you can print *and* send files to the LG at the same time mind. PC parallel ports aren't up to that!

The MF-PD330 is the basic model, an MP3 player with bass boost (called X-Live sound) and two memory card slots. As with the Thomson Lyra there is no onboard memory on the LG players and they only come with two 16-MB cards as standard, meaning you'll have to fork out for two 32-MB cards if you want to enjoy more than 30 minutes of music. Allowing for that, the MF-PD330 retails at a very affordable £129.99 and is very good value for money.

Turn On, Tune In, Play MP3s

The sister model to the MF-PD330, the AHA-FD770 is unique amongst MP3 players in embracing old technology alongside new. Thus it features a cassette player and is quite happy playing this early music-copying medium that once had music lawyers in as much of a tizzy as MP3 does now. It also features an FM tuner, allowing you to listen to your favourite radio station once you've exhausted the rather meagre 30 minutes of listening that the supplied 2 × 16-MB memory cards allow you. At £199.99 you're obviously paying for the FM tuner and cassette playing functions at the expense of that extra 32 MB of memory. As the man said, you pays your money and you takes your choice.

Find out more about the LG MP3 players and download software updates at `http://www.lge.co.kr/english/main.html`.

Philex MPress3: Dressed To Impress

The Philex MPress3 is a fashion self-conscious piece of hardware that comes on like something Austin Powers would carry if MP3 had been around in the sixties. With its decidedly psychedelic decoration and packaging the MPress3 is proof that MP3 players are aiming to become as much of a fashion item as mobile phones are.

The MPress3 plays MP3 files of course and does this rather well, with excellent sound quality, assisted by a mega bass switch for those dance and hip hop aficionados amongst us. There are also the obligatory EQ presets, classical, jazz and rock, plus a user mode, which lets you set your own levels of bass and treble. The MPress3 comes with the familiar 32 MB of onboard memory and is expandable with a smart memory card, in similar fashion to the Rio.

Dictaphone Functions

You can record speech on the MPress3 through its built in microphone, thus using it as a memo machine. Speech is recorded at a low quality facilitating the storage of several hours of *aides memoire*. With additional software installed on your PC you can also record voice files on your PC and download them to the MPress3 for later listening. There is even a socket for external input allowing you to plug in the output from your cassette player and record music that way, although it's hard to see why you would want to. Unlike the Rio you can also use the MPress3 as a storage device for other files, text documents, spreadsheets, etc. and transport them from one PC to another in this way.

Although the MPress3 and its Web site come tricked out in the latest retro-psychedelic fashion the software used to download files to the MPress3 is more prosaic in its appearance and decidedly functional in its approach. The MPress3 File Manager lets you download files to the unit as well as upload them back to your hard drive and also permits you to upload voice files from the unit to your PC. In addition it will play MP3 files on your PC's hard drive but doesn't provide any facility for encoding MP3 files, whether from a CD drive or from WAV files. At £149.99 the MPress3 is an affordable and useful player which may well suit your style.

For a taste of Philex's decidedly groovy approach to MP3 players and to download the latest updates to its software check the MPress3's very own website at `http://www.mpress3.com`.

Elex JazPiper: Who Calls The Tune?

Where the MPress 3 has a retro-groovy approach to fashion, the Elex JazPiper adopts a decidedly modern cool approach to fashion. With an oval window on its LCD display and matching oval button for play functions, the JazPiper's style is more rooted in the seventies than the sixties. Like the MPress3 it allows you to record voice files via a built-in microphone and upload them to your PC. It also lets you store your friends' contact names and telephone number details, making a bid to become an indispensable part of your everyday life.

The JazPiper is impressive in operation, with a clear sound quality, ably assisted by its equaliser function, rather grandly called DSP (Digital Signal Processing) mode. Despite the grandiose title the JazPiper still offers the familiar presets of normal, pop, rock and classic, with no jazz or dance on offer. There is also no sign of a bass boost, although for the price of £129.99 perhaps that is asking too much.

Jaz, Jet And Zlurp!

The JazPiper comes bundled with a confusing set of software. First off is the JazDesk. This is how you transfer files to and from the JazPiper. It will allow you to upload voice files you have recorded previously to your PC but will not, however, let you upload MP3 files back on to your PC's hard drive. When you attempt this a copyright warning notice appears, advising you that 'Uploading of MP3 files is an infringement against international copyright laws'. At least it will keep the lawyers happy.

Before you download files to the JazPiper you will want to convert them from your CD. The other bundled software, Jet-Audio, is a wonderful piece of software that plays audio CDs, MP3 files and MIDI files, with excellent EQ features and effects too, so you can add loads of echo, flanging or reverb to your favourite MP3 files. Sadly, it only encodes CD tracks randomly and one at a time, which isn't really much use. To encode CD tracks to MP3 JazPiper supply you with a trial copy of Zlurp!. As Zlurp! is a trial copy it will expire after three weeks and then you will have to buy a copy.

Check out the JazPiper and download updates to its software at `http://www.jazpiper.nl`.

The MPMan F30: First Out Of The Box

The Saehan MPMan F10 was the first MP3 player on the market, beating the Rio by a narrow whisker to the US shops, but it was never released in the UK. It's finally hit the streets here in its third incarnation, as the MPMan F30. As you would expect, they have improved on the original and added new features, some of which have since appeared on other devices. The MPMan F30 is shown in the figure below.

The MPMan F30 – definitely a distinctive design.

There is now a voice recorder built in to the MPMan allowing you to record voice memos and an electronic memo feature so you can store and browse telephone numbers and memos. This is a feature that is appearing on more MP3 players as they prepare to compete with their latest rivals in the market, PDAs (personal digital assistants) and mobile phones.

Whereas the F10 used a docking device, in similar fashion to the Thomson Lyra, the F30 now connects to your PC through a 25-to-15 pin parallel cable. You can use this link to transfer non-MP3 files from one PC to another. Just download the file to the F30 and then carry the F30, cable and software disk to another PC, install them there and upload the files. This may seem a little awkward but if you're trying to move a 20-MB file and don't have a compatible large-size disk drive, it's a method that will work.

MP3 Goes Everywhere!

Several mobile phone manufacturers are planning to include MP3 players in their latest models and there is already a PDA featuring the ability to play MP3 files, the Cassiopeia E105 (see later on in this chapter). In addition there is now software available to upgrade older PDAs to play MP3s. Try `http://www.xaudio.com/wince/` for a demo version of software enabling most Windows CE devices to play MP3s.

As with most players, the F30 will take 3.3-volt SmartMedia flash memory cards and reformat them, rendering them unusable for any other purpose. However, the reformatted card can be moved from F30 to F30, data intact. That way, you can load your latest recording on to a memory card and pass it on to a friend, who can put it into their F30 and listen to it. At the time of writing the Saehan MPMan F30 had a RRP of £199, making it £50 dearer than the MPress3, which is the most comparable in terms of functions (the MPress3 and the LG players are the only other units that feature a bass-boost). For that you get a slightly better build quality than the MPress3 and the ability to store phone numbers and memo information which neither the MPress3 or LG players offer.

Samsung YP-E32: Just Say 'Yepp'

Samsung must have realised that YP-E32 was hardly an inspiring or memorable moniker and thus they decided to christen their player 'Yepp', which is at least memorable, if not elegant. The Yepp comes in a configuration which should be familiar to you by now: 32 MB of onboard memory, which can be expanded by the addition of a SmartMedia flash memory card; voice recording; and data storage. It is shown in the next figure.

Yepp, It's Easy

Where the Yepp scores is in ease of use. Its front-panel rocker switch is easy to use and there is a nine-character LCD screen, which displays track name and number, playback time, battery health, volume level, and the setting of a four-band graphic equaliser. Yes, that's a four-band equaliser, the most bands on offer yet although it's a case of swings and roundabouts as there is no bass-boost. It can also record your voice via its built-in microphone and can be used to transport non-MP3 data as it will be recognised as a hard drive when attached to your PC. With a faster MP3 data link than most, the YP-E32 can fill up its 32-MB memory in just one minute.

The Yepp looks smarter than its name.

Samsung's multilingual Yepp Explorer software makes it easy to assemble compilations and categorise recordings under groups, singers, genres, etc. Another feature that is becoming more prevalent is that the Yepp implements a security feature to prevent you copying MP3 files from one machine to another. At £149.99 it certainly packs a lot of features into a good-quality case and the £79.99 cost of Samsung's flash memory cards is an added bonus.

Cassiopeia E105: This Time It's Personal

At £499.99 the Cassiopeia 105 must rank as the most expensive MP3 player yet, but there is more to this than meets the eye, or ear. You see, the Cassiopeia is a PDA, or personal digital assistant. What this means is that the Cassiopeia will let you keep a record of all your addresses, phone numbers and email addresses, appointments *and* let you send emails and surf the net, as well as playing MP3 files. The Cassiopeia is a precursor of the wired future where your mobile phone is a PDA and an MP3 player (shown in the next figure) as well as an appointments diary and contacts database.

Picture this, you're on the train, on your way to work, when your friend calls you on your mobile phone. 'You must hear the new track on Radio Internet', he enthuses. So you log on to their Web site, download the track to your PDA and listen to it for the rest of your journey. If this sounds far-fetched then consider this: with the Cassiopeia you can do just that – right now. OK you might need a flash modem card (plus a special lead to connect the Cassiopeia to your mobile phone) but you *can* do it. New mobile phones due out soon will enable you to do all that from the phone itself, as well as enabling you to keep a track of your appointments, contacts and tasks.

The MP3 Audio Player supplied with the E105 looks pretty cool but lacks any equaliser functions.

More Flash Memory Please

As with most of the machines featured here, the Cassiopeia's 32 MB of onboard memory is expandable with SmartMedia flash memory cards. In the Cassiopeia's case this is essential if you want to listen to more than a couple of songs as the onboard memory also has to store the programs and information that make it so useful as a notepad, appointments diary, task scheduler and email client.

The sound quality on the Cassiopeia is pretty good, let down only by the lack of a graphic equaliser to beef up the bass (or whatever frequency you want boosting). The sound is loud and clear and the Cassiopeia can even play videos (once they've been converted to its own format with the enclosed software), making it a pretty impressive machine for technophiles and early adopters. The rest of you may want to wait until Casio introduce a lower-priced model.

Portable MP3 CD Players

As attractive as the all-electronic players are, the limited memory size really means that they can't hold much. OK, you can buy external flash memory cards for most of them and carry multiple cards with you to switch songs in and out, but the flash memory to hold half the music from a CD will cost several times the price of the CD.

As an alternative, manufacturers like Pine (http://www.pine-dmusic.com) are developing portable CD players that can read CD-ROMs filled with MP3s. These are aimed mainly at people who have CD-R or CD-RW drives on their computers, so they can make their own CD-ROMs filled with MP3s. You can store about 12 hours of music at typical compression rates on one CD-ROM, or about 50 hours of reasonably good voice-grade recording. The players, a little larger than a typical portable CD player, can read the MP3 files and playlists from the CD-ROM. They can also play standard audio CDs.

The drawback to these players (in addition to requiring the user to have a CD-R or CD-RW drive, which start at around £150) is that they still have a lot of moving parts. As such, they don't replace the all-electronic player. However, they do a fine job of replacing the standard portable CD player. You can carry an assortment of discs with you and quickly change what you're playing. After you've spent a while with a portable MP3 player planning and downloading the day's music in advance, this becomes a very desirable feature.

AudioReQuest: Music Is For Stereos, Not PCs

Let's face it, your PC is not the ideal place for playing music. Even the high-grade PC speakers are designed for playing to someone seated at the PC, not the crowd at your party. If you want to hear a song now, waiting several minutes for your PC to start up is a pain in the neck. You've got a nice hifi system in the living room and you'd really rather hear your music through that.

A new breed of MP3 players is arising, designed to be part of your stereo system. These fall into the category of *non-tethered* systems, because they are designed to be connected (tethered) not to your PC, but to be their own devices. The AudioReQuest by ReQuest, Inc. (www.audiorequest.com), available in the later half of 1999, is at the forefront of these devices. For about US$600, you can bring MP3s to your stereo system.

Two Drives, No Waiting

The AudioReQuest looks a lot like a standard component CD player and it connects to your amplifier in the same way. However, in addition to having a CD drive, it also has a hard drive built in and a parallel port that can connect to your PC's printer port. Using these features, the AudioReQuest can:

➤ Play standard audio CDs.

➤ Take an inserted audio CD, encode the tracks and store them on the hard drive, for playing at any time.

➤ Copy MP3s from your PC to the system's hard disk, for playing at any time.

➤ Play MP3s encoded on CD-ROMs.

➤ Copy MP3s from CD-ROMs to the hard disk, for playing at any time.

➤ Connect other audio devices (record players, cassette players and so on) to the AudioReQuest's line in port, so you can digitise, encode and store music from other sources.

The main goal is to get your favourite music on to the hard drive, which holds about 300 hours of music. (That's about 5000 songs or one really overindulgent drum solo. ReQuest does plan to offer units with larger hard disks, if two solid weeks' worth of music just isn't enough for you.) Once the music is there, you have a high-quality, high-capacity jukebox. You can set up playlists to have your favourite music for different moods.

Look At All The Pretty Music

AudioReQuest includes a video-out connector, which you can use to connect it to your TV. If you do so, you can watch all sorts of hypnotic displays to accompany your music. Bouncy coloured blobs that mesmerise and create an inexplicable fascination… now go and turn the TV on. Switch it over to watch the patterns generated by AudioReQuest and you get pretty, captivating colours that move in time to the music without wrecking your cerebral cortex.

You can even create your own visuals. AudioReQuest lets you transfer scanned photos and other images for display while playing your music.

That's not all the TV connection is for, however. It also allows you to control your AudioReQuest through on-screen menus. This isn't needed for simple things like playing an individual song, but it comes in handy when you're doing more complex things, like building a playlist. (AudioReQuest can read song ID information that's encoded into the MP3s. If you're digitising your music by putting your CDs into AudioReQuest, however, you should consider throwing down the extra money for the optional wireless keyboard, which makes entering data a lot easier.)

FutuReQuest

With all of the competition in the compressed audio field, it's clear that MP3 won't be the only popular format in the long run. AudioReQuest also supports Microsoft's Windows Media Audio (WMA). AudioReQuest is designed so that you can upgrade its software to play whatever new standard takes hold.

ReQuest, Inc. is looking at a number of other functions for future upgrades and new versions. Most notable among these is some form of Internet connection (possibly through your PC), which would let the AudioReQuest look up the album name, performer and track titles for any CD you insert, thus saving you the effort of entering all that information yourself. They are also considering adding support for some sort of removable recordable drive (such as a Jaz drive or a Zip drive), to allow you to effectively expand the unit's capacity.

MP3 On The Motorway: A Player For Your Car

We all love listening to music in our cars. Not only does it make those long commutes cheerier but it also helps us deal with that annoying little grinding noise that would cost about £2000 to repair properly but can be drowned out with a twist of the volume control.

Getting MP3s into your car is many people's dream. In fact, if you surf on over to `http://www.mp3.com/hardware/` you will find a healthy list of sites describing various devices for playing MP3s in your car. Follow most of these links, however and you'll discover that it's some hobbyist who decided to build an entire PC into their car boot and then connect that up to their car's stereo with a remote control. These homebrew projects sound like a wild idea but they aren't what we'd recommend to, well, sane people. (There are even commercial versions of these but they still seem like bodges rather than proper long-term solutions.)

However, there are now emerging some genuine MP3 players for your car which let you have at your fingertips far more music than any car CD changer will ever give you. At the forefront of this is Empeg.

Empeg: A Hard Drive To Make Your Drive Easier

The Empeg player, manufactured by Empeg Limited (http://www.empeg.com), fits into a standard European dashboard slot (or, with a common adapter, a US dashboard slot). Behind a fancy glowing display is a hard drive that holds your MP3s and playlists. The base model, which will cost you about £1000, has a 4-GB drive, which stores about 35 hours of music. Expanded models are available with up to a 28-GB drive, storing over 400 hours of music.

The Empeg is removable. This not only makes it easy for thieves to steal it (alerted to the unit's presence by the bumper sticker and window decal that come with each unit, letting everyone know you have this expensive unit in your car) but it also makes it easy for you to take it with you so that thieves can't get at it. Even if crime weren't an issue, the removability is important because it lets you take the Empeg inside and hook it up to your PC, so you can transfer all your MP3s on to it. Otherwise, you've just paid a thousand quid for a fancy blue digital display. It supports both serial connections (mostly used to connect to older PCs) and USB connections (which transfer data much more quickly and are supported by most modern PCs).

In order to use the Empeg you'll need to have an amplifier of some sort already in your car. It does have standard audio-out connectors, which you can connect to the audio-in jacks on many car stereos, or to a dedicated amp. There simply wasn't enough room in the Empeg to build an amp in. (In fact, to fit everything into the unit, they had to use the smaller hard drives made for laptop computers... which is just as well, because those drives are made for the sort of shaking and battering that driving along bumpy roads will provide.)

The unit also has a radio tuner built in. Alas, it's FM only, since the unit's internal circuitry would wreak havoc with an AM signal.

A small remote control gives you access to the full range of the player's functions. The included home power supply can be used to run the unit as part of your home stereo system.

All in all, it's one powerful box.

MP3 For Your Car – Quick, Easy And Cheap!

Most of the designs for car-based MP3 players assume that your goal is to store dozens of hours of audio in your car, for playing any time. A laudable goal, that. However, if your goal is simply to listen to a given MP3 while you're on the road (for example, if you've downloaded an audio book and want to listen to it on your way to work), you can do it a lot more cheaply. In fact, you may already have everything you need!

You will need a portable MP3 player – a Rio, an MPMan, a Yepp, or anything like that will do fine. (Obviously, if you don't have one of these anyway, this is a major expense.) You'll also need a CD-to-car cassette adapter; this looks like a cassette tape with a cable coming out of it. If you don't have one lying around (they come with many portable CD players), you can buy one for about £15 at most stores that sell portable CD players. And you'll need a cassette player fitted in your car.

➤ First, turn the volume on your MP3 player all the way down. (This is important; if you set the volume too loud, there's a slight chance you will do damage to your car stereo.)

➤ Unplug the headphones from the player and plug the cable from the cassette adapter into the headphone jack.

➤ Turn on your car radio and set the radio's volume to a level you like. Push the cassette adapter into your car's cassette player.

➤ Press the Play button on your MP3 player and then slowly turn the volume on the MP3 player up.

➤ You will start hearing the sound from the MP3 player coming out of your car stereo. Keep turning the MP3 player volume up until it matches the volume you heard coming from the radio before.

Whatever you do, don't just wear your MP3 player headphones and listen to your MP3 player as you drive! Driving with headphones on is dangerous (it can block out vital road sounds) and may cause you to run into trouble with the police.

Rejig Your Empeg

The Empeg runs on the Linux operating system, an operating system popular with hardcore computer users. The dazzling user interface is written in Python, a computer language popular with Web designers because of its relative ease. If you're a computer programming nut, you can redesign the user interface to meet your needs.

The Least You Need To Know

➤ All-electronic portable MP3 players like the Rio let you download music from your PC and carry it with you anywhere.

➤ Portable MP3 CD players will read MP3s off CDs you make yourself, enabling you to carry around 12 hours of music on each CD.

➤ Tethered systems are stereo system components that connect to your computer, letting you build a library of MP3s to play on your stereo.

➤ You can connect your all-electronic MP3 player to your car stereo.

➤ The Empeg is the first commercially available MP3 player designed for a car. It's removable, so you can take the player to your PC and download your MP3s from the PC to the car player.

Part 3
Making MP3s

Making your own MP3s is easy. Soon you'll be taking every CD, LP and cassette that you own and transferring it to MP3 format. The uses of MP3 don't stop there though. If you make your own music, you can make it an MP3. If you want to send an audio letter to your mother, you can record it, 'MP3 it', and ship it to her via email. In the following chapters we'll show you how to do all of this and more.

Chapter 6

Ripping CD Tracks

In This Chapter

➤ Copying audio CD tracks on to your hard disk

➤ Ripping with MusicMatch Jukebox

Ripping CDs isn't what a shoplifter does in your local music megastore and it isn't what music pirates do when they bootleg CDs. The term means to copy the digital audio recording from a CD to an uncompressed file on your hard disk. Thus you are ripping the music from the CD and placing a copy of it on your hard drive.

Why People Used To Rip Songs

In the old days (and by old days, we mean 1998; things move pretty fast in the MP3 world), if you wanted to encode an MP3 track from a CD, it took two steps. First, you would use a *ripper* program to *rip* the song, copying the digital-format audio from the CD to an uncompressed WAV-format file. Then you would run your *encoder* to turn the WAV file into an MP3 file.

However, modern all-in-one MP3 programs can skip the middleman, reading the song from the CD and encoding it directly, without ever writing a WAV file. So if you're using MusicMatch and want to start turning your CDs into MP3s, head on down to Chapter 8, 'Compressing Music', to see how it's done.

Why People Still Rip Songs

Ripping has not disappeared, for a number of reasons. Many people aren't using all-in-one products; they are still ripping and encoding. But even if you're using the all-in-one products, there are times when you might want to just rip.

For example, let's say that you have a recording of Evil Nasty Demons' medley of Abba tunes. You don't like the whole medley; you just like their cover of 'Dancing Queen'. If you convert the medley into a WAV file, you can load it up into any standard audio editor (such as the Sound Recorder program that comes with Windows) and remove the rest of the medley, leaving only the part you like.

Or if you're a DJ and really enjoy playing records at the wrong speed, you can use better sound editing software to speed up 'When Doves Cry' (by The Artist Formerly Known As Prince) by about a third. (It turns into a wicked dance track at that speed.) Take an old Chipmunks tune and slow it down and you'll hear what the guys singing really sound like!

Getting Ready To Rip

In order to rip, you're going to need a computer with a CD-ROM drive. That doesn't sound very tricky but there is one problem: it won't work with all CD-ROM drives.

You see, when they started making CD-ROM drives, they decided that you'd be using them for one of two purposes. Either you'd be using them to read data off a CD-ROM, or you'd be playing audio from an audio CD and sending it to your sound card. They didn't realise that people might want to read data off an audio CD, so they didn't set up the CD-ROM drives to do so.

As time went on, they figured out that we crazy folks were wanting to do things with their CD-ROM drives that they had never intended, so they started making drives that support Digital Audio Extraction (DAE). However, there are still drives made today that do not support this feature.

How Do You Tell If A CD-ROM Drive Can Rip?

Most of us don't have the high grade of X-ray vision needed to stare into our CD-ROM drives, look over the internal schematics and see if it supports DAE. If you happen to know your drive manufacturer and model number, you can surf on over to `http://www.mp3.com/cdrom.html` where you will find a well-maintained list of CD-ROM drives and whether they support ripping.

You can also just try to use ripping software and see what results you'll get. Not every piece of software supports every DAE-enabled CD-ROM drive but the Windows version of Digital Audio Copy, available from `http://www.windac.de` on the Web, supports the vast majority of them and the programs covered in this chapter support most you are likely to have.

Not All CD-ROM Drives Are Created Equal

While CD-ROM drives are extremely careful in making sure they've read programs correctly, they are not so careful in checking data from CD audio tracks. If they misread something, they may not go back and double-check it. Because of this, the ripped file may not be an exact copy of the original audio track, even on the best of CD-ROM drives. Generally speaking, drives connected using the SCSI standard will read more cleanly than drives using the ATAPI or IDE standard. Setting up a PC for SCSI does cost more, though. I know people who absolutely swear by the quality of Plextor CD-ROM drives for this purpose; again, they generally cost more than the bargain brands.

If your CD-ROM drive doesn't support DAE, that doesn't mean that you can't convert your CDs to MP3s. What it does mean, however, is that you'll have to convert them by having your CD-ROM drive play the audio (converting the digital encoding into an analogue audio signal). The audio will be picked up by your sound card, which will re-digitise it, converting the analogue signal into a digital format. This sounds like more complex an effort than it really is; programs like MusicMatch will do it automatically. However, when you do this, you will lose some sound quality.

Ripping With MusicMatch Jukebox

In order to start ripping with MusicMatch Jukebox, you're going to need to install the program, as described in Chapter 3. You're also going to need to have an audio CD in each of the CD drives on your system the first time you run the program. (You probably have only one but some people who have CD-R or CD-RW drives also have a standard CD-ROM drive.) This is because the first time you run MusicMatch it tests all your CD drives to see which ones are capable of Digital Audio Extraction.

Start MusicMatch by double-clicking the MusicMatch icon on the Desktop. To get into the recording process, click the **Record** button (the one with the round dot) on the main MusicMatch display. A Recorder window opens up (as shown in the next figure) and MusicMatch will test the CD-ROM drives. The test will only take a few seconds.

When the testing is done, right-click the top bar of the Recorder window and select **Recorder**, **Quality**, **WAV Format** from the pop-up menu. Right-click again and select **Recorder**, **Source** and then choose the CD drive with the CD you want to record from on the submenu.

Selecting And Recording

To select individual tracks, just tick the box next to the track name. You can select all the tracks by clicking **All**, or clear the selections by clicking **None**. (If the track names aren't listed, either MusicMatch hasn't connected to the CDDB via the Internet, or the CDDB doesn't recognise your CD. There might be an Internet Connection dialogue box in which you need to click **Connect** to complete your connection. Otherwise, just select each track name and type in the real name.)

You May Already Have A Ripper!

If you have a CD recorder (either a CD-R or CD-RW) that came with software to help you make an audio CD, that software probably has the ability to rip. (It may describe it as *pre-recording*.)

Got Clicks In Your Music?

If you hear a clicking noise or gaps in your music when played from the WAV file, there were probably problems with the ripping. To minimise the chance of repeating the problem, eject the disk, reinsert it, select the track you want to rip and rip it again. Don't play the track before you rip it and eject the disk between each track you rip. Doing so will clear the buffer and minimise the chances of the sort of reading error that causes this clicking.

Select all tracks   Select no tracks

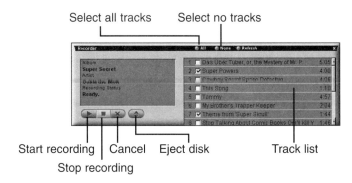

*MusicMatch's Recorder
window might look a bit
different, depending on
the theme you have
selected*

Start recording | Cancel | Eject disk   Track list

Stop recording

To start ripping, click **Record**. MusicMatch will rip one track at a time, with a completion meter on the track listing showing you what percentage of the track is ripped at any one time. If you need to stop the ripping, click **Cancel**. (If you just click **Stop**, MusicMatch abandons that track immediately and starts ripping the next selected track.)

Catch A WAV

To find out where your WAV file ended up, right-click the top bar recorder window and choose **Recorder**, **Settings** from the pop-up menu to get the Options dialogue box. On the **Recorder** tab, click the button marked **Songs Directory**. The dialogue box that appears will list the directory where the files are stored. It also lists a variety of other options in the creations of subdirectories for individual albums, as well as in how the files are named. You're more likely to be using these options when you're encoding MP3s, so we've covered them in Chapter 8.

Stop AutoPlay

Windows is usually set up to automatically start playing an inserted audio CD. To get around this, press **Shift** while inserting the CD and hold it down for several seconds.

Mac The Ripper

As noted elsewhere, there is a shortage of good Mac software for MP3 users. If you're encoding MP3s on your Mac, you're probably using Xing's AudioCatalyst (see http://www.xingtech.com for ordering). This program does have ripper capabilities built in.

The Least You Need To Know

➤ Ripping means copying recordings digitally from an audio CD on to your system into an uncompressed format.

➤ These days, most MP3 programs read the digital audio recording and encode it as a single step, eliminating the separate ripping step.

➤ Ripping without encoding is still used for getting tracks you want to edit.

➤ Some CD-ROM drives cannot be used for ripping.

➤ One of the programs included with this book's CD-ROM, MusicMatch Jukebox, has ripping capabilities.

Chapter 7

Digitising Music

In This Chapter

➤ Transfer cassettes and records on to your PC

➤ Record your voice with your PC

➤ Get your original music ready to be compressed

Not all music comes on CDs. Odds are good that you have a few cassettes in your music collection. If you're a DJ you've probably got all your favourite tunes on vinyl.

Just because you can't stick a record into your CD-ROM drive don't think that you can't get the music from these non-digital sources on to your PC. All you really need to do is play the music from these sources into your PC and use your PC to re-record it in digital mode. This is called digitising the music. If you want to create MP3s of music that is not already digitised (including your own performances), you'll have to learn to digitise it yourself.

Digitising Equipment

In order to digitise music, you're going to need whatever device plays the music you have to digitise. If you have a big pile of records but no turntable, then you're just plain out of luck. It's time to go shopping for a player, or perhaps marry someone who has one.

You're also going to need a computer with a sound card, which you probably already have. (The bad news is that many computers come with the cheapest possible sound card and they won't do as nice a job of digitising as a better sound card will. If your digitised recordings sound a lot worse than when you listen to the recording directly on the player it may be time to buy a better sound card.)

Finally, you'll need cables to connect the two items. That's so tricky that we'll give it its own heading.

Digital Duplication

If you're copying from a digital medium, such as *Minidisc or Digital Audio Tape* (DAT), you'll get the best quality results if you don't try to re-digitise the music. Instead, you want to copy the digital information from the player to your computer. To do this, you'll need a sound card that supports digital input and output (digital I/O). For example, Creative Labs' SoundBlaster Live sound card (but not the SoundBlaster Live Value Edition) has the ability to connect to some types of digital I/O. (But to connect to optical digital I/O, as many minidisc and DAT systems use, you will need to buy an add-on card.) The software needed to copy tracks digitally will come with the card.

Concocting Cable Combinations

Standard sound cards are expecting to get sound in from a miniplug (also known as a 3.5-mm plug), the same sort of plug that you use when plugging headphones into a portable cassette or CD player. However, the device you're recording from may use one of three different sorts of jacks that you need to connect to.

➤ If you're recording from a portable player of some sort, you'll be connecting to the line out connector (if it has one – most cassette players don't but many CD players do) or the headphone jack, which is the same sort of miniplug jack as the sound card has. You'll need a cable with miniplugs on both ends.

➤ If you're recording from a typical stereo component, it will have a pair of RCA jacks. These are generally marked line out or audio out, with one for the right channel and one for the left. You'll need a cable linking two RCA plugs to a single miniplug; these cables are often included with portable CD players. The red RCA plug goes into the jack for the right output and the other RCA plug (either white or black) goes into the jack for the left output.

➤ If you have a cheap all-in-one system, it may not have RCA jacks. Instead, you'll have to connect to the headphone jack. You'll need an adapter for connecting miniplug headphones to full-size headphone jacks (these often come with the stereo, or with mini headphones) and a cable with miniplugs on both ends.

If you're connecting to a record turntable, there is an additional concern. The basic turntable setup doesn't put out a strong enough signal for your sound card to make much out of it. You're either going to need a turntable that has a built-in amplifier or get an external preamplifier to connect it through (that'll cost you £30 to £50), or simply plug your turntable into the turntable inputs of your stereo amp and connect the computer to the amp's line out or headphone jacks.

A good audio electronics shop should be able to supply you with any of these cables, pre-amps, or adapters.

Quality Cabling

To get high-quality digital music, you want to make sure that the music doesn't get degraded on the way into your PC. To that end, the length of the cable can be very important. Instead of buying a long cable to run all the way from your cassette deck in the living room to your PC in the den, take your cassette deck and move it close to your PC and use a shorter cable.

When you do run the cable, try to avoid running it against electrical cables. The electrical current causes a field that will interfere with the audio signal. (This is, by the way, good advice for all your audio and video equipment.) You should also try to avoid running it by electrical appliances, particularly phones, speakers and computers. Of course, you can't avoid bringing it to the computer entirely but try not to have the length of the cord wrapping around the computer.

Techno Talk

Socket To Me

A *socket* (a connector with a hole for something to be inserted into it) may also be called a *jack* or a *female connector*. A *plug* (a connector which is designed to stick into a socket) may also be called a *male connector*.

Double-check to make sure that you are connecting to the right socket on your sound card! You want the line in socket, not the microphone in socket or the speaker socket, both of which also use miniplug sockets. Many sound cards have the sockets marked, although some of them are indicated with little pictures. If you're not sure which sockets are which check the manual. Don't just guess; there is a potential for damaging some of your equipment (and a likelihood of making some ugly loud noises) if you connect up the wrong things.

105

Using Your Computer As A Stereo Base

You can check to make sure that your hook-up between your audio player and your computer is working before you try to digitise anything. That way, when something goes wrong (and it will), you'll find it a lot easier to isolate the problem.

Before trying to use your PC as an amp for an external audio device, play an MP3. Doing so will let you know that your PC sound system is working and is set to a reasonable volume.

Mark It!

Once you figure out which port is which on your ill-marked sound card, use small pieces of masking tape next to the sound card to mark which socket is which. It'll save you time in the future!

Volume Controls

Next, start up your volume control program. Click the **Start** button and you'll find the program in either: **Programs**, **Accessories**, **Entertainment**, **Volume Control** or **Programs**, **Accessories**, **Multimedia**, **Volume Control**. The program will display volume controls for several different sound sources (see the figure below). For example, take a look at the one marked Wave. That one sets the sound level for the MP3 you just played (and, for that matter, any WAV, MP3, or other digitised sound file you play). It's got a slider at the top to adjust the balance between the left and right speakers and a vertical slider for setting the total volume for audio from that source. It also has a Mute check box, which you would check if you didn't want to hear any audio coming from that source.

Your volume control window may look different, depending on the options you have selected.

Wave volume controls   Auxiliary volume controls

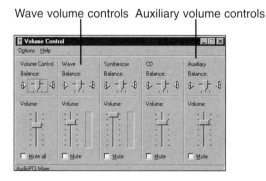

The volume control that you really want to use may not be visible, however. There are so many possible audio sources these days that you can't display them all. If you don't see a volume control marked Auxiliary (which is the one we want), here's what you do:

➤ Choose **Options**, **Properties**.

➤ In the dialogue box that appears, click the **Playback** option button.

➤ On the scrollable list below that, put a check in the **Auxiliary** check box.

➤ Click **OK**.

Setting The Volume Levels

The volume controls for the sound you'll be playing into the computer will be marked Auxiliary. Set the volume level for this control to the same level that the Wave control is set for. Click on the **Mute** check box for each of the other input volume controls, to turn them off for now. Don't click on the **Mute All** check box, or you won't be able to hear anything!

If you connected your cables to the line out connectors on your audio player, you can start the audio player playing and the sound will come out through your computer. If you connected it to a headphone output jack, however, you'll need to turn the player's volume all the way down first. Then, after the player has started playing, slowly turn the player's volume control up. You should start hearing the sound come out of your computer's speakers. When the sound is about as loud as the MP3 file you played earlier, you've got the player's volume at the right setting. (This step is important; playing too loud an audio signal into your computer may possibly damage some components.)

When you're done with this test and finished doing all your digitising, clear all those Mute check boxes on the volume control. Otherwise, you won't be able to hear all your system sounds.

Other Volume Controls

Your PC may have an additional volume control program already installed. Many sound cards come with their own mixer programs, which do pretty much the same things as the Volume Control program but may have added features. You can search your Programs directory for these, or just try double-clicking the Volume Control or Mixer icon on the right end of your taskbar to see what appears!

WAV Goodbye!

Now that you know you can successfully play sound from your record or cassette player through your computer, it's time to try using the computer to catch some of that sound. In order to do this you're going to need a sound recorder program.

The good news is that Windows comes with a sound recorder program built in, cryptically named Sound Recorder. The bad news is that Sound Recorder isn't very good. It doesn't have a lot of features (although it has the basic ones that you need). The real problem, though, is that it tries to record all the sound into your RAM and high-quality sound will fill up your RAM right quickly. On most systems, Sound Recorder usually quits recording after about one minute. The only song you can fit in that space is Cliff Richard's version of 'Of All The Girls I've Loved Before'.

You may already have a good sound recording and editing program. Many sound cards come with a bundle of programs, including those. Also, some advanced CD creation programs include recording programs for people who are trying to convert their LPs to CDs. Easy CD-Creator Deluxe Edition, for example, includes recording software that will help you get rid of the noise from old records.

Depopping Pop Music

If you're turning old records into WAV files, you may be picking up a lot of popping noises. If you don't want to shell out the money for Easy CD Creator Deluxe Edition, you can try using the shareware program Popfix. This is free to try, or $25 to register. Download it from `http://www.newave.net.au/~voskulen/popfix/popfix.html`.

Recording WAVs With MusicMatch Jukebox

If you have a proper WAV file recording/editing program, you are probably better off using that to record your WAV files. Those programs generally offer a lot of handy recording features, as well as the ability to trim excess material from the beginning or end of a recording. However, if you don't have such a program, MusicMatch Jukebox can handle basic recording needs, although it doesn't handle editing.

To record using MusicMatch, click on the **Record** button. The Recorder window opens up. Right-click on an unused part of the Recorder window and choose **Recorder**, **Settings** from the pop-up menu. On the Options dialogue box that appears (why can't software manufacturers ever decide if these are *settings*, *options*, or *preferences*?), click the **WAV Format** option button to choose to record to a WAV file rather than directly recording an MP3.

Why Not Record Directly To MP3?

Because programs like MusicMatch can record directly to MP3 format, you may be tempted to use that ability. When you try recording directly to MP3, the program has to compress very quickly in order to keep from falling behind and it may not make the best choices in compressing. If you record to a WAV file and then com-press the WAV file, the program can compress at its leisure and you are likely to end up with better sound quality. Also, having the WAV file first lets you do things like trimming the file in a standard sound editor. If you're encoding your own per-formances, you'll want to keep the WAV file for your own permanent records. The WAV file doesn't have the data loss that your MP3 file has and you can back it up to avoid the decay concerns that will hit your audiotape original.

This isn't to say that you should never record directly to MP3. However, if you want to do that, make sure that you have a fairly powerful computer and test it out on a couple of tracks before making it your usual way of recording. And again, if you're recording your own original performances, you should always make and keep a WAV file of it.

While you have this tab open, there are a couple other things you should take a look at. You should make sure there isn't a check in the **Mute While Recording** check box. Otherwise, you won't be able to hear the song you're recording to know when it ends. Click **Song Directory** to get a dialogue box that lets you select which directory the WAV file ends up in. This dialogue box has a lot of options, which are described in Chapter 8, 'Compressing Sound'. Click **OK** to get rid of the New Songs Directory Options dialogue box and then click **OK** to get rid of the Options dialogue box.

Right-click on the Recorder window again and select **Recorder**, **Source**, **Line In**. This lets the recorder know that you will be recording from the auxiliary audio input. When you select this, the Recorder display changes somewhat from the way it looks when you're recording material from CD.

You probably won't use MusicMatch to record the album Nat Gertler's Greatest Hits *but he did!*

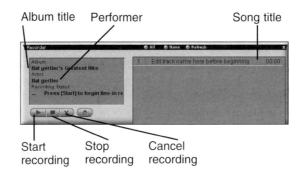

Album title   Performer   Song title

Start recording   Stop recording   Cancel recording

Before you start recording your first track, MusicMatch wants you to name three things (see the figure above). Click the album name area on the left side and type a title for the album the track comes from. Click the artist name area below it and type a name for the musician. Finally, on the right side of the window, click **Edit Track Name Here Before Beginning** and type a name for the individual track. MusicMatch will use these three pieces of information in naming and placing the file. (Recorded WAV files do not get added to the music library.)

Microphone Master

Most of the instructions in this chapter will also serve if you are recording live from a microphone that's plugged into your sound card's mic in port. Just substitute the terms microphone or mic in for the terms auxiliary or line in. Also, put a tick in the Mute While Recording check box on the Recorder tab of the options dialogue box.

Recording

Click the Record button and start your audio player. When the song has finished playing, click Stop and then stop your audio player. MusicMatch will finish writing the track to the hard disk. Then it's time for the next track.

For each additional track, click **Edit Track Name Here Before Beginning** and type a name for the individual track. Click **Record**, restart the music and click **Stop** when the song is done.

Now, I know what you're thinking: you can just play the album all the way through, rapidly clicking Stop and Record between tracks. After all, you've got a quick mouse button finger. Unfortunately, that's not going to work; every time you click Stop, the system needs a few seconds to take care of the file. If you click Record before it's finished stopping the previous track, it'll put up a dialogue box telling you that it is recording already. By this time, the next song has started and you're out of luck.

But what you can do, if you have enough disk space, is record the entire album side as one track. Then you can use a good WAV editor to select portions of that long recording and save them as separate WAV files.

How Much Space Is Enough?

A WAV file in CD-quality resolution takes up about 10 megabytes per minute of recording. Thus an hour's worth of stereo recording will take up about 600 megabytes of your hard drive. Try and keep at least a gigabyte free if you want to record this much music.

Tips For Top Taping

To make sure that your taping goes smoothly, you should avoid running any other programs while recording. Make sure you have plenty of space on your hard disk and defragment your hard disk at least once a month.

If you've been running your computer for a while without rebooting it, you may want to reboot it. The more you do with your system without rebooting it, the more it slows down.

Digitising For The Macintosh

There are a number of good audio recorders and editors for the Macintosh. The AudioCatalyst all-in-one MP3 program from Xing (`http://www.xingtech.com`) can also handle recording.

The Least You Need To Know

➤ Digitising means converting analogue audio into a digital format.

➤ You can digitise music from cassettes, LPs and other media by connecting the player to the line in or auxiliary socket on the sound card.

➤ A special sound recorder/editor program is the best thing to use to digitise songs. One may have come with your sound card.

➤ To tell MusicMatch that you want to record the input from the sound card's line in connector, right-click a blank area on the Recorder window and choose **Recorder**, **Source**, **Line In**.

➤ You can tell MusicMatch that you want to store files in WAV format using the Recorder tab on the Option dialogue box.

➤ To record in MusicMatch, enter the album name, artist name and song title and then click **Record**. When the song has finished playing, click **Stop**.

Chapter 8

Making MP3 Files

In This Chapter

➤ Turn a CD track into an MP3

➤ Turn a WAV file into an MP3

➤ Turn an MP3 into a WAV file

Finally, it's time to actually make MP3s. To make an MP3 file, all you need is digitised music (a CD or a WAV file), an MP3 encoding program (such as MusicMatch Jukebox or RealJukebox) and a computer to run it on.

How Much To Compress?

Before you compress your music, you're going to have to decide how much to compress it. Compression is measured in how many *kilobits per second* (Kbps) the compressed sound takes up. A *bit* is the smallest unit of computer data, able to hold either a 0 or a 1. A *kilobit* is 1024 bits, about enough space to store the following sentence: 'The word "problematic" always seemed to me to be a very good name for a machine that the world really doesn't need at this time'.

Most of the MP3s you'll find on the Internet are compressed to 128 Kbps, which means it takes roughly a megabyte to store a minute of music. This rate provides fairly high quality, which some people refer to as *near CD-quality* and other people will claim to be *CD-quality*. It's certainly good enough to be giving people a sample of your music over the Net. Some hardcore audiophiles insist that to really get CD quality, you have to compress your files less, giving larger files (up to 256 Kbps, which takes about two megabytes of disk space per minute). And there are always some purists who will tell you that any compressed sound can't be as good as the original and that even CDs aren't as good as the high-quality non-digitised audio you get from a good record played on an expensive record player. Sometimes, people get so smug about it that you want to tell them to take an analogue walk off an uncompressed pier.

You'll have to judge for yourself how much compression is acceptable for you and your favourite music. Part of the decision will probably rest on how much disk space you have available and on the quality of the sound system you'll be playing the music through. A high-quality sound system will let you hear the difference between 112 Kbps and 128 Kbps but you may not hear the difference in the same files when heard through cheap computer speakers.

Variable Bit Rate

Some encoders now support *variable bit rate* (VBR) encoding. This term means that the whole song is not compressed at the same rate. Most of the song is compressed at a standard rate but detailed sections of the music that would lose quality from such compression are compressed less. This process leads to larger files but better sound. However, not all players will play VBR MP3s.

To help you work it out for yourself, we've thrown something special on the CD-ROM. The fine folks with Wacky Lemon Hello have let us take their song 'Trust' and compress it at several different rates. In the directory Rates, you will find the following files:

➤ TRUST.WAV (the source file)

➤ TRUST256.MP3 (compressed to 256 Kbps)

➤ TRUST160.MP3 (compressed to 160 Kbps)

➤ TRUST128.MP3 (compressed to 128 Kbps)

➤ TRUST112.MP3 (compressed to 112 Kbps)

➤ TRUST096.MP3 (compressed to 96 Kbps)

➤ TRUST080.MP3 (compressed to 80 Kbps)

➤ TRUST064.MP3 (compressed to 64 Kbps)

➤ TRUST032.MP3 (compressed to 32 Kbps)

➤ TRUST016.MP3 (compressed to 16 Kbps)

➤ TRUSTV75.MP3 (variable bit rate compression set at 75%)

➤ TRUSTV25.MP3 (variable bit rate compression set at 25%)

This song was selected not because it tests the limits of compression but to be a pretty typical example. It's really going to sound lousy at the smaller bit rates; anything below 48 Kbps you will probably use only for spoken word recording, since it takes away all the magic that gives music its power. You can still hear the song at 16 Kbps but it sounds like it's playing in the car next to you, with the volume turned up but all the windows closed. Notice also that the sound difference is more apparent in the louder sections of the song with more instruments and complexity than it is during the song's quieter moments.

Compressing With MusicMatch

The unregistered version of MusicMatch included on the CD-ROM can encode any CD track or WAV file. It does, however, have one strong limitation: it will not encode at any bit rate greater than 96 Kbps, nor will it encode using variable bit rate. You can use it to learn to encode, or to encode music for cases where you want to fit a lot on to a disk. If you want the higher sound quality that comes with larger bit rates, you will need to register your copy. If you surf over to http://www.musicmatch.com and register (it costs $29.99), they'll transmit to your PC a secret key that will unlock MusicMatch's ability to encode at bit rates as high as 320 Kbps.

For instructions on installing and starting MusicMatch, see Chapter 3, 'Installing and Using MP3 Player Software'.

Optimum Options

To set the MP3 recording options click **Option** and choose **Recorder**, **Settings**. The Option dialogue box opens up showing the Recorder tab. It's full of MP3 recording settings and options (see the next figure).

The most important option to set is your recording rate. You can use an option button to choose 64, 96, 128 or 160 Kbps MP3s. Select the **CBR** option and you can use the adjacent slider to select from 15 different bit rates ranging from the hard-to-hear 16 Kbps to the huge 320 Kbps. If you have registered your copy of MusicMatch, choose **VBR** if you want to use variable bit rate encoding, choosing a variation rate from 1% (worst quality) to 100% (best).

MusicMatch recording options give you a lot of control over your recording.

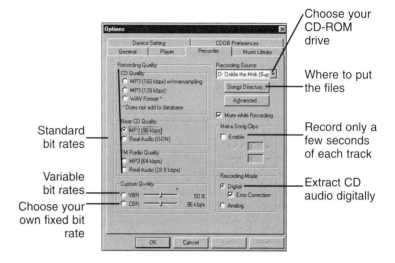

Choose your CD-ROM drive

Where to put the files

Record only a few seconds of each track

Extract CD audio digitally

Standard bit rates

Variable bit rates

Choose your own fixed bit rate

If you're going to encode from CDs, use the **Recording Source** drop list to select the CD-ROM drive you'll be using for your CDs. Next, head down to the Recording Mode area and click **Digital**, to choose to read the digital audio data directly from the CD. Putting a tick in the **Error Correction** check box will slow down the process somewhat but will avoid some noises that might be added to your music if the CD isn't read properly.

Where To Put The Music

Click the **Songs Directory** button to get a separate dialogue box that controls where on your computer the MP3s you encode will be stored and what the files will be named (see the figure below).

You can spend more time deciding where to put your files than you do encoding them!

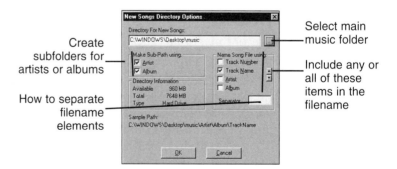

Select main music folder

Create subfolders for artists or albums

Include any or all of these items in the filename

How to separate filename elements

To pick the main directory, click the enigmatically marked **...** button to the right of the text entry field. (It might help if you know that ... is Morse code for the letter S, which perhaps is short for Select-a-directory.) A dialogue box opens up listing devices and folders on your system. Double-click any device or folder to see the subdirectories it contains. When you find the folder you want to use as your main music folder, click it and then click **OK**.

The **Make Sub-Path Using** options are used to create individual subfolders for each artist or each album, making it easier to find songs so they aren't all in one huge folder. If, for example, you are MP3ing the song 'A Hole in the Head' from the album *This Is Not a Drill* by the Savage Dentists and you didn't have either of these options selected, the song would end up in your main music folder. If you had just the **Artist** option selected, MusicMatch would create a subfolder called Savage Dentists and the song would reside in there. If you had just the **Album** options selected, the main folder would have a subfolder called This Is Not a Drill, which would hold the song. If both options were selected, the main folder would be called Savage Dentists and in that folder would be a folder called This Is Not a Drill and that's the folder where MusicMatch would place the song.

Automatic Song Naming

MusicMatch can automatically name MP3 tracks using any combination you want of the album name, the artist name, the track number and the track name. To design your own name order, first clear all the check boxes in the **Name Song File Using** area. Next, click on the check box for the element you want to be first in the filename and then click the up-arrow button. The element you want will move up in the list of elements. Keep clicking the up-arrow button until it has moved up to the top spot.

If you want a second element in the filename, click on the check box for that element and then use the up-arrow to move it into second place on the list. If you want a third element, click on the check box and then move it up to the third place on the list. If you want all four elements included, put a tick in the last remaining check box.

If you're using more than one element, you can also use the **Separator** field to choose how to mark the end of one element and the start of the next. Usually, you'll just put one character in here, such as a dash, an underline, or an exclamation point. However, you can put more characters in there. For example, if you were using album name, artist name and track name (in that order) as the elements of your filename and you typed QUACK into your separator, you would end up with files like this:

    SurrenderQUACKThe Chemical BrothersQUACKHey Boy Hey Girl.MP3

As you work on setting up the folder and filename, the dialogue box shows an example filename and path.

When you're finished with this dialogue box, click **OK**. When you're finished with the Options dialogue box, click **OK**.

117

Option Overload

Click the **Advanced** button on the Recorder tab and you'll have access to a handful of other options. If you're getting clicks and noises in your recording, go here and turn the **Multipass** option on; this will slow the recording but eliminate the errors.

Recording From CD

Before you open up MusicMatch's recorder window for the first time, put an audio CD in each of your PC's CD-ROM drives. The program will test out your CD-ROM drives to see if it can read the digital audio data directly, or if it will have to play the CD into your sound card and have the sound card re-digitise the music. The former method is both faster and gives better quality sound.

Be aware that MusicMatch is about to try to use the Internet, so if your modem is using your main phone line, make sure that no-one is using the telephone. When you start the recorder, MusicMatch reads an identification number off your CD and sends it to an online source called CDDB. The CDDB site responds with the name of the album, the artist and song names... if it knows them. Their database will have most of the CDs in your collection, as they have an awful lot of the commercially released CDs. However they won't have that homemade CD of your Uncle Chester yodelling the theme from *Mission: Impossible*, sadly.

To open the recorder window, click the **Record** button on the player window. (That's the button with the red circle on it.) The first time you open the recorder window, MusicMatch will run the CD-ROM test we mentioned earlier.

The next figure shows the recorder window. The left side of the window displays the name of the album and the artist. The right side of the window lists the name of each track, with a check box for each. If you don't see actual track names, click **Refresh** to force MusicMatch to check the CDDB for the information. If CDDB doesn't have the CD on record, you can click on the artist name, album

CD Not Found?

Do everyone a favour and enter the information about that CD into the CDDB database! Surf on over to `http://www.cddb.com/user-faq. html` to find out how.

name and each track area and type in the appropriate name. (If you don't see the check boxes, MusicMatch was probably last used to record from some other source than the CD-ROM drive. Choose **Options**, **Recorder**, **Source** and select your CD-ROM drive from the list.)

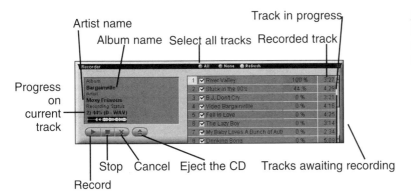

Artist name

Album name Select all tracks Recorded track

Track in progress

Progress on current track

MusicMatch's Recorder: better than those plastic recorders they taught you to play in music class!

Stop Cancel Eject the CD Tracks awaiting recording

Record

Put a tick in the check boxes of each track you want to record. If you want to record all the tracks, just click **All**. If you don't want to record any of the tracks, you can click **None** but then if you don't want to record any of the tracks, what are you doing here in the first place?

Start the recording by pushing the **Start** button. The speed at which MusicMatch will record depends on what record options you chose and the speed of your CD-ROM drive. In most cases, it will record in a fraction of the time it takes to play the CD. If you need to interrupt the recording process, click **Cancel**.

Making A Little Splash With Compressed WAVs

As you saw in Chapter 6, 'Ripping Music', and Chapter 7, 'Digitising Music', there are a number of ways that you can end up with uncompressed audio in the form of WAV files. To convert these, choose **Options**, **File**, **Convert**. A File Format Conversion dialogue box opens up, as shown in the next figure.

First, select **WAV** on the **Source Data Type** drop list. Then find the folder with the WAV files in the Source Directory list. You can see the subfolders in any folder or device by clicking on the + next to it. Once you've found the right folder and clicked on it, a list of the WAV files in that directory will appear on the list below.

Converting MP3s to WAV files is a very efficient way to fill up your hard disk.

What folder has the WAVs?

Put the MP3s in what folder?

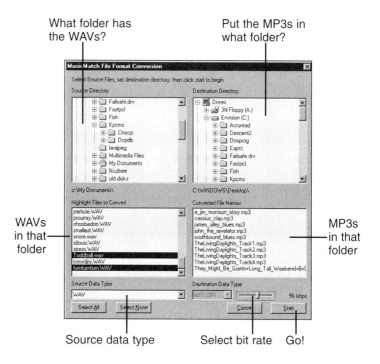

WAVs in that folder

MP3s in that folder

Source data type   Select bit rate   Go!

Click the name of each file on the list that you want to convert. When you click it it becomes highlighted. If you change your mind about converting a file, click it again and it becomes unhighlighted. If you change your mind again, you are too indecisive and should resort to flipping a coin.

Next, choose a folder to put the files into, using the Destination Directory section. (Don't be worried when a list of files appears below that, they're just whatever MP3 files were already in the folder.) Use the slider near the bottom of the window to choose the bit rate of the MP3s you're making. Finally, click **Start** and let your PC do its work!

Some Things Need Editing

Remember, you want to sample a song as a WAV (despite its size) if you plan to edit the resulting file.

Mono: The Space-Saving Option

If you're doing a recording that isn't going to rely on sound quality (such as recording an audio letter that you're going to email to someone, or perhaps a book read aloud), you can choose to forego the stereo signal. Choose **Options**, **Recording**, **Settings**. On the Options dialogue box that appears, click **Advanced**.

120

On the Advanced Recording Options dialogue that appears, choose **Mono** from the Channels drop menu. With this option selected, MP3 file space will not be used up storing the information that normally separates what the left ear hears from that the right ear hears, leaving it more room to properly track a single signal.

For an example of high-compression mono recording of spoken words, check the directory *book* on the CD-ROM. The files natstar.mp3, monkey.mp3 and angel.mp3 are recordings of Nat Gertler, one of the American authors of this book, telling the tales of his work as an acting extra on the films Primary Colours and Mighty Joe Young and the TV show Teen Angel. Because these recordings were made with a typical cheap PC microphone, they aren't going to sound great even in high resolution but they are certainly clear enough to hear compressed to 32 Kbps.

Making WAVs

To convert MP3s into WAV files, start a new playlist with only those MP3s on it. Next, choose **Options**, **Playlist**, **Convert Playlist to WAV**. A dialogue box appears where you can select a directory to put the WAVs and enter names for the WAVs. Take care of that and then click **Start** and you'll be making WAVs.

Tagging MP3s

MusicMatch lets you edit tags, little pieces of information about the song that get embedded into your MP3 file. These can be useful when you're creating your playlists. They can be extremely useful when you're going to be distributing your own original music, since you can put lyrics, your biography, your Web address and even a picture of your album cover where the listeners will be able to find them. Many MP3 players automatically display tag information while the song is playing.

To add tags, first open up the Music Library window by choosing **Options**, **View**, **Music Library**. The window appears and among the songs it lists are all the songs you compressed from CD. MusicMatch automatically added them to the database when you compressed them. (If you compressed a file from a WAV, drag the icon for the compressed version on to the Music Library window to add it to the library.) Find the song you want to add tags to, right-click it and choose **Edit Track Tag** from the pop-up menu. A Tag Songs dialogue box appears, filled with spaces for you to add tag information (see the next figure).

You may end up with more words in your tags than there are words in the song!

Track and album information

Musical style

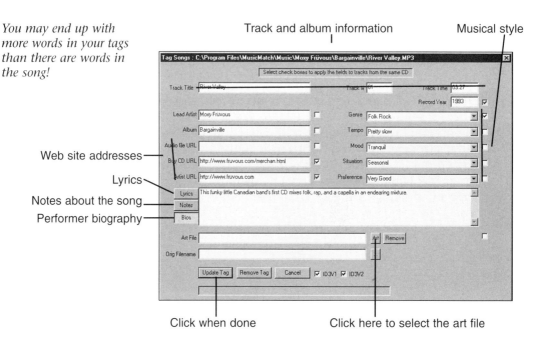

Web site addresses

Lyrics

Notes about the song

Performer biography

Click when done

Click here to select the art file

The form has many different tag entries that you can edit to give more information about the song. These fall into five basic categories:

➤ Basic track information – this includes the song name, which track it was on the CD, the year it was recorded, the artist name and the album title. If you encoded this track from a CD, MusicMatch will probably have already added most of this information (except the year) using the information it downloaded from the CDDB.

➤ Style information – the drop-down lists running down the left side lets you describe the song in terms of genre, tempo, mood, quality and the situation where you'd want to listen to the music. For all the categories except genre, you can type in your own description instead of selecting one from the list. These selections can be very useful for building playlists, as described in Chapter 3.

➤ Web addresses – you can enter three Web addresses (URLs): one where the song file is available on the Web, another for a Web site that sells the CD and one for the performer's home page.

➤ Detailed information – click **Lyrics** and you can enter the words to the song into the big text field. Click **Notes** and the field becomes a place for the story behind the song, or the names of the musicians, or any other information you want. Click **Bio** and you can use the field for the performer's history.

122

➤ Song art – you can scan the CD cover into your computer, or design your own art to accompany the individual song. The only limitation is that the art must be stored in the Windows Bitmap format (files ending with .bmp) or the JPEG format (files ending with .jpg) and should be exactly 100 pixels wide by 100 pixels high. Click **Art** and a file browser appears. Select the file with the art in it and then click **Open** to add this tag.

Most of the fields have a check box next to them. Put a tick in one of those fields and MusicMatch will add that tag info to all the songs compressed from the same CD. That way, you can quickly mark all the songs from TLC's latest album as being ballads or apply a photo of your pet puppy to all the tunes from the stage version of Cats.

When you're done, click Update Tag and all the information you entered will be added to the MP3 file.

Fee Versus Free

You may have heard that there are free unrestricted MP3 encoders out there and wonder why we haven't included these on the CD-ROM. The folks who came up with the MP3 audio format have patents on it and they make their money licensing the right to make encoders out to software companies. These free encoders are generally made without getting a license, meaning that they are violating patents. Just as musicians deserve to be paid for their labour, so do inventors, and giving out these encoders would work against that. (It also would open us up for whopping-great lawsuits.) Give your support to the software makers who support the inventors... and who, by the way, are more likely to offer you support and timely upgrades.

Mac Compression

AudioCatalyst from Xing (http://www.xingtech.com) can compress from CD and from WAV files. As this book is being written, MusicMatch is working on a Macintosh version of their Windows product; it may be available for download by the time you read this. Surf on over to http://www.musicmatch.com to see if it's available.

Decompression Without A Compressor

Winamp and Sonique can't be used to encode MP3s. That's how they can get away with being cheap shareware and freeware, respectively; they don't have to pay the encoding licence. They can, however, do quite a nice job of decoding MP3s and saving them as WAV files. Decoding, like butterflies, is free.

Windowsamplifier: Winamp Decompression

To turn an MP3 file into a WAV file, first click on the upper-left corner of Winamp's player window. On the menu that appears, choose **Options**, **Preferences**. A Preferences dialogue box appears.

Click **Output** in the left pane of the window. A list of output plug-ins (different programs for handling Winamp's output) appears in the right pane. Normally, when you want Winamp's output to go to your speakers, Nullsoft WaveOut Plug-In will be highlighted. Click on **Nullsoft Disk Writer Plug-In** to choose to output to your disk instead of to the speakers.

To choose where on your disk the files end up, click **Configure**. A dialogue box appears listing folders on your hard disk. Click the **+** next to any folder to see the subfolders in that folder. When you find the folder you want to store your WAV files in click it and then click **OK**. Click **Close** on the Preferences dialogue box.

Now you're set up to decompress! Just drag any MP3 file's icon onto the player portion (the upper left) of the Winamp window. Winamp will run the conversion, which it can do quite quickly. When you want to go back to using Winamp as a player rather than a decompressor, bring up the Preferences dialogue box again, click Output and reselect **Nullsoft WaveOut Plug-In**.

Decompressionique

The version of Sonique included in the CD-ROM has a feature to convert MP3s into WAVs – sort of. I say 'sort of' because it has all the commands for the feature but they don't work. However, the programmers know the problem and by the time you read this, a newer, fixed version of Sonique will be available for download at the http://www.sonique.com Web site. The feature will work like this:

To turn Sonique into an impressive decompression contraption, click **Setup Options** on the main menu in large display mode. (If you don't see that, right-click the main display area and it will appear.) On the Setup Options display, click **Audio**. Click the up-arrow at the end of the Setup Options field, until **WAV Disk Writer** is displayed.

Next, click the **WAV Disk Writer Path** field. A dialogue box appears listing storage drives on your system. Click the + next to any drive to see the folders on that drive, or the + next to any folder to see the subfolders in that folder. When you find the folder you want to store your WAV files in click it and then click **OK**. Right-click the display window to return to the main menu. Then just use Sonique's standard commands to play any song and instead of coming out of your speakers, it will end up in a file in the directory you selected.

The Least You Need To Know

➤ Compression quality is measured in kilobits per second (Kbps). High Kbps rates mean big files but high quality sound reproduction. Low rates mean small files but poor reproduction.

➤ A registered copy of MusicMatch Jukebox can convert CD files and WAV files into MP3s, ranging from 16 to 320 Kbps. It can also convert MP3s into WAVs.

➤ An unregistered copy of MusicMatch is limited to creating MP3s at 96 Kbps or less.

➤ Winamp can convert MP3 files into uncompressed WAV files.

➤ The version of Sonique on the CD–ROM cannot properly convert MP3 files into WAV files, but the new version on the Sonique Web site at `http:/www.sonique.com` can.

Chapter 9

Distributing Your MP3s

In This Chapter

➤ Where is the best place on the Internet to put your MP3 files?

➤ How do you set up a free band page on the Internet?

➤ How do you upload MP3 files to your band page?

World, Hear My Song

All artists want people to enjoy their artistic creations and musicians are no different. Well, some of them still wear baggy clothing and say 'Wicked', but for the most part they are just like you and me. Isn't that wicked? (Oops, I just spilled fruit juice on my baggy trousers.)

Let's learn how to arrange for a whole lot of people to have a chance to listen to your music. Yes friends, step right up and meet your potential audience: the world. That part of the world that is hooked up to the Internet, that is, which is certainly a large number of people. Just try fitting that many people into a concert hall. You could perform in a standing-room-only sports arena every night for a month and not begin to reach the number of potential fans waiting for you on the Internet. Distributing your MP3s on the World Wide Web allows your music to reach a staggering number of people from nearly every nation on planet Earth.

Before you will be able to entrance fans from France, or sing your heart away to some person from Mandalay, you'll need to find a home for your MP3s on the Internet.

Space On Your Home Page

If you have a home page of your own with enough space to house your MP3s, you could set them up there. You would simply place a link to your MP3 file and your new fans in Sweden (and everywhere else) could download your song and groove to your musical genius.

Before you post your MP3s, however, be sure to check the arrangement with your Internet service provider (ISP). Some ISPs offer free Web space but limit either the amount of storage space or the amount of information you can transmit to the Web per month. A popular MP3 site could rapidly exceed both of those restrictions, which in turn could cause your ISP to charge extra.

Newsgroup No-Nos

You could also find an MP3-related Internet newsgroup where you could post your MP3s. Before you do, however, take one important fact into consideration: never place an MP3 or other digital file into a newsgroup unless you are absolutely certain that binary files are accepted. The newsgroup will usually include the word binaries someplace in the title. If you are not certain that MP3 files are welcome in the newsgroup that you are interested in, don't upload them. If you do, you'll make a very large number of people very upset. That much concentrated ill will could – broadcast your way from across the globe, even – cause you to have a nasty headache.

That doesn't mean you can't take advantage of the non-binary newsgroups. Post your latest rap, 'Hard 2B a Gangsta in Berkshire', on `alt.binaries.sounds.mp3.1990s`, which has the word binaries; then go to `alt.music.gangsta.rap` and post a message telling everyone to head over to the binary group to check out your new track. You can also post a message containing a link to your MP3 file on a Web page.

Newsgroups

Want to learn more about news-groups? Go check out `http://www.dejanews.com` for more info. Learn how to find discussions on just about any topic imaginable.

Songs In The Key Of Email

Emailing your MP3s as an attachment to your friends is also a lot of fun. If you email them, make sure you alert your friends that you are sending an MP3. Better yet, send them a short email first asking if it's okay to send them an MP3.

Why? Because as emails go, MP3s are pretty big. Your friend may be sitting there, tapping his or her fingers, waiting for this all-important contract via email, or perhaps a love letter from a partner. When the mail program finds your letter first, the modem line could be tied up for 15 minutes downloading your latest masterpiece.

Binary Newsgroups

The binary newsgroups that exist to carry MP3s include:

➤ alt.binaries.sounds.mp3.1950s

➤ alt.binaries.sounds.mp3.1960s

➤ alt.binaries.sounds.mp3.1970s

➤ alt.binaries.sounds.mp3.1980s

➤ alt.binaries.sounds.mp3.1990s

➤ alt.binaries.sounds.country.mp3

Go to http://www.dejanews.com *to learn about newsgroups.*

American Online (AOL) and CompuServe have music forums with file libraries, which may very well be places for you to place your MP3s. (Check the forum rules to make sure that what you want to upload is acceptable.) While this might be a wonderful place for you to put your MP3s, you'll find that the World Wide Web is the most popular location for MP3s. Why? Because of the 'world' part of World Wide Web. Only members of AOL or CompuServe can access those libraries but the Web is open to everyone.

The Internet allows you to reach a very large number of people. A whole world's worth of people. There are many sites out there offering to put your music online. We'll look at the oldest site offering to put your music online, mp3.com, and the newest, peoplesound.com.

mp3.com: The Site Of Sites Of MP3

The largest and most wel-known Internet location for MP3s is mp3.com. More than six million people come to mp3.com each month looking for music to listen to. Here your songs will mingle with both new artists and some of the most famous musical artists in history. Billy Idol, The Band, The Beach Boys, Dionne Warwick, Willie Nelson, Ice-T and Tom Petty have all placed MP3s on mp3.com for the world to enjoy.

Hundreds of musical areas, genres, are available on mp3.com which helps you find the best possible spot for your music. For example, instead of offering simply an electronic area, mp3.com offers acid, ambient, break beat/breaks, dance, drum and bass, house, techno, industrial, detroit, goa, rave, trance and many more. They'll have a home for whatever type of music you make.

Best of all, their service is completely free to all artists. You'll be able to obtain a Web page, have your music available for download, hear your music play on one of their genre-specific Internet radio stations and enjoy lots of other cool features – all for free. Isn't that great? mp3.com is located at `http://www.mp3.com`. Regardless of how many Internet sites you select to house your MP3s, your first stop should be mp3.com.

mp3.com And You

You can find mp3.com at – where else? – `http://www.mp3.com`. Once your friendly computer takes you to its home page (shown in the next figure), scroll down and you'll find a portion of the front page that says Artists/Labels. The sign-up process begins when you click **New Artist Signup**. You'll see the first of a series of helpful pages that will walk you through the artist sign-up procedure. Before you go any further, look for a link to Artist FAQs. This link refers to Frequently Asked Questions (also known as FAQs) that relate to artists.

The mp3.com homepage lets you post your own recordings.

You might not be an artist to your friends but you are in the eyes of mp3.com. When they mention 'artists', they are talking about you. Make sure you follow that link and read all the FAQs so that you can learn about any recently added features.

The services of mp3.com are completely free to artists. All they ask is that you place one complete song on their site. Many cool things can happen once your music is on mp3.com. Some mp3.com artists have ended up being on MTV, as well as other national television and radio programs.

Successful artists on mp3.com can find doors opening that might have otherwise been closed. If you are a talented performer, your new fans will surely find you and mp3.com is always coming up with new ways to promote their resident musicians.

No doubt your eyes are open wide at this point as you think about all the exciting possibilities for your own music. Are you wondering what happens if mp3.com doesn't like your music?

Fear not! You will never face rejection from mp3.com as long as you own the music that you want to upload. mp3.com is happy to let the world judge your music. They accept every artist who wants to place an MP3 on their site. Aren't they wonderful?

No Strings, No Obligations

Here are two magic words that apply to mp3.com: no obligation. mp3.com doesn't require an exclusive relationship with its artists. You are free to put your files on mp3.com and any other MP3 Internet site that you want. You can also terminate your relationship with mp3.com at any time and remove your music.

The Free mp3.com Band Page

You are offered a free band page on mp3.com and the basic design work has already been done for you. They know how busy a talented musician can be. All you have to do is sign up for their service and give them some information – away you go to set up your page.

How long does it take – from start to finish – to set up your page? Once you have a CD of your song in your hands, you could encode your song into an MP3, set up your band page and have the world listening to your song within 48 hours after you've uploaded the MP3. That's fast.

Basic mp3.com Artist Requirements

The basic artist requirements are quite simple: you need a band name and an email address. Try to pick a unique band name – you already did, didn't you? – because mp3.com does not allow duplicate band names on their site. After all, the world doesn't need two bands named Pro-Life Cannibals.

Of course, if you're a solo performer, you probably already have a name. Thank your parents for that.

Your Own Secret Code

When you sign up as an artist with mp3.com, you are given a password and a username. This amounts to a secret code so that you and only you can log into your band page's admin area. You select the username; mp3.com selects the password. You must enter both the password and the username when you return to your mp3.com band page to make changes or additions.

Want to change the band photo? Add a new song? Exchange an updated version of one song for another? Your secret code (password and username) allows you to do so. Your password and your confirmed username are emailed to you automatically after you sign up with mp3.com.

What If I Lose My Secret Code?

If you lose your password or forget your username, don't panic. When you log into your mp3.com band page, you'll see a link that says **Lost Your User Name Or Password**? Click here. If you click that link, you will find your password and username automatically sent to the email address that you gave mp3.com. No mucking about with questions about your mother's maiden name. The helpful little email will show up almost instantly, too.

And This Is A Photo Of My Band...

While a one-of-a-kind band name and your email address are the minimum requirements for enrolling with mp3.com, there are several optional features that will help make your band page colourful and exciting. Do you have a cool photo of your band handy? You can scan that great work of art and load it to your band page if you want. Most CD covers aren't blank, right? Art helps sell CDs. You don't have to use this spot on your page for a band photo. You can also scan any original art that you happen to have on hand, or put up a photo of something that is meaningful to your band.

The image that you upload to mp3.com has to be in JPEG or GIF format and should be exactly 270 pixels wide by 180 pixels high.

My Musical Influences Are...

You are also encouraged by mp3.com to provide your fans with a description of your band, a statement about your musical influences, popular artists you sound similar to, a history of your band and more. You can even list your band members, the instruments you play, albums you have recorded, upcoming concert dates, press releases and other types of information designed to create excitement about your band.

It's best to organise all this information before you set up your page so that you don't find yourself making it up while you are filling out the online mp3.com forms. Take a look at some of the other band pages on mp3.com to get some ideas and then write your own material. This will make setting your band page up that much easier and will also help give your band page a more professional appearance.

Basic Requirements To Place An MP3 On mp3.com

As a new artist, you need to prepare before you sign up. You will, of course, need at least one MP3 file. You also need to know the title of your song and prepare a one-line description of your song. If your song is on a CD that you've already made, be prepared to list the name of that CD. If you have a record label, mp3.com will want you to tell the world about that, too. Some artists use this spot to say 'I have no record label as of yet but would like to be signed by one', or language to that effect. If you would like to be signed by a record label, you might as well go ahead and say as much.

A place to list the credits for the song is also provided. That area is most often used by artists to list who wrote the song and whether the songwriter is a member of ASCAP or the BMI, the performing rights societies in the US. You will also find that they provide a spot to place the entire song's lyrics.

Album Cover Art: Smaller But More Plentiful

You can also place a small JPEG or GIF version of your album cover. This image is different to the band photo. It's a lot smaller, for one thing – 70 pixels by 70 pixels, or about a centimetre square. Plus, you are only given one spot for your band photo; the album cover art can be placed next to each and every song on your page. You can have a different image for each song, if you want.

Some people use this spot to put small animated GIFs if they don't have an album cover to show off. You can put any image there that you want. Again, you're bound to get some cool ideas when you look at several other band pages.

The only thing mp3.com actually requires is the MP3 file itself and the title of the song. The lyrics, cover art, credits, record label and song description are all optional; mp3.com will give you a special password so that you can return to the site as often as you want and change things. You can put up cover art, change your song title, add lyrics and so on, whenever you feel so inclined. If all you do at first is upload your MP3 file and name your song, that's perfectly okay, you can do the rest later.

Play Musical Genres

You'll also have the ability to select a genre for your individual songs. Hundreds of musical categories are available on mp3.com that you can select from. Try to select the most appropriate genre for your song. Doing so helps people find your music. If you perform gospel music, you'll want gospel music fans to find you, right?

Don't purposely place your song in a genre that you know is inappropriate. For example, don't place your heavy metal song into the polka genre just because you think that would be funny or because you've decided that it is time for those silly polka lovers to learn about the pleasures of heavy metal. This advice isn't limited to MP3s that you might put on mp3.com but is for all the MP3-related sites that you find on the Internet.

Your Own Custom Band Name 'URL'

A custom mp3.com Internet address is also provided: `http://www.mp3.com/your bandname`. This unique address will make it easy for you to tell your friends how to find your band page on mp3.com. When you sign up as an artist, you'll find an easy form to complete regarding this feature.

Why Isn't My MP3 On My Page Yet? I Uploaded It Hours Ago

After you've uploaded your MP3 file, the song will become available to the public to listen to in a day or so. The encoding of your song must first be verified and your song is actually listened to by a real living person (or at least an mp3.com staff member, which is almost the same thing) before it is released to the public.

Trouble Tickets: Reporting Problems

If at any point you have trouble creating your band page or uploading your art or songs, you can fill out a *trouble ticket*. If you click the corresponding link, you can report to mp3.com any problems you are having during sign up. A helpful mp3.com person will respond to you within a day or so. You can also use the Trouble Ticket link to report problems with your page at any time during your relationship with mp3.com.

Overview Of The Sign-up Process

Here's a quick sketch of what you do to sign up as an artist on mp3.com. Remember that the New Artist Signup link is on the front page of mp3.com, underneath the Artists/Labels heading. Click that. Now you are in the Artist Area-New Artist Sign Up section. Remember to follow the link to Artist FAQs if you haven't already.

Now click **Go Straight to Step One**.

mp3.com Music Submission Agreement

Step 1: This is an online contract that you must read and sign before you can go any further in the sign-up process (see the next figure). Read this contract carefully (don't worry, there isn't too much small print); if you agree to the terms of the agreement, complete the blanks and move on to the next step. You must be at least 18 to sign this contract. If you are under 18, you need your parent or guardian to do it for you. If your parents won't sign the contract, you can hold band practice in the front room until they see reason.

You don't exactly sign the contract. Instead, you type in your name and click a few boxes that mp3.com ends up accepting as a signature.

Step 2: Here you supply mp3.com with a mailing address. Not an email address but a street address. This step is very important because mp3.com sometimes mails out freebies such as t-shirts and the like to their artists. If you make up an address, somebody that you don't know might get some great stuff meant for you.

Supplying your mailing address is vitally important if you plan to use mp3.com to make and distribute CDs. This is something covered in detail in the next chapter. No reading ahead! I don't want you to spoil any surprises. You can supply mp3.com with a post office box address if you like. In any event, your address is not for viewing by the general public and does not show up on your page.

You click a few boxes to accept the mp3.com Artist Agreement.

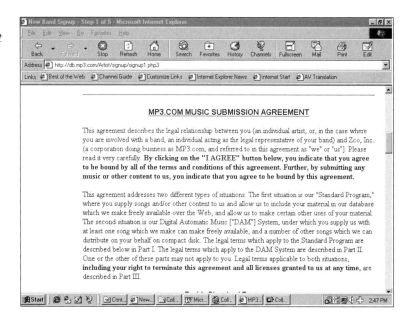

Step 3: This page asks you to review and confirm the artist information that you've entered. After you've double-checked your entries and made any corrections that are warranted, go on to the next step.

Step 4: Upload your band picture (see the next figure). Remember that it should be exactly 270 pixels wide and 180 pixels high. If your image doesn't appear on your page for some reason, try increasing the size of your image by one or two pixels more than 270 × 180. Research has shown that more people download songs from bands that have their photo on their band page, so don't be shy.

The ability to have full-colour cover art for the CDs that they can make for you has been recently added by mp3.com. We'll cover that in more detail in an upcoming chapter.

As you build your band page, you will see a preview of what the page will look like, including the art. Remember that this is simply a preview. The art won't show up on your page until mp3.com has approved your band.

Step 5: You are now finished with the Artist Management menu. You have to upload a song. Click the **Add New Song** link and move on to the next step.

Adding Your Music: The Fun Starts Here

Step 1: Enter your song information, which consists of the song title, a brief description and your credits. Here is an example:

Song Title: 'My Pet Charlie'

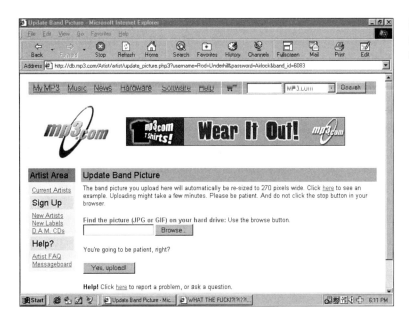

Uploading your band art on mp3.com doesn't take much time.

Song Description: 'I love my pet Charlie so much that I made up a song about him. Sadly, he blew away yesterday before I finished this tune and he never had a chance to hear it.'

Credits: 'I wrote this myself.'

Step 2: Find the MP3 file on your hard drive and upload the file. You'll notice a line on this particular page of the mp3.com sign-up process screen that reads like this: Find the MP3 file on your hard drive: use the Browse button. You will also notice an empty rectangle next to this statement. Empty rectangles are boring, so fill it with something appropriate. A window will open when you select the Browse button, showing you various files on your hard drive.

Simply follow the path to the file where your encoding software has stored your MP3 file and click the actual file when you locate it. You will see the file (and its path) automatically appear in the once-empty window. Windows users will see something like C:\Program Files\Encoderdelux\Music\Songs\music.mp3.

Now click the **Upload MP3** button. Your song will automatically be sent to mp3.com. Depending on your Internet connection speed, this process might take up to 45 minutes for every song you upload. If you have a slow modem connection, this might be a good time for you to write another song. After the song is uploaded, proceed to the next page in the sign-up process.

Step 3: Upload the album cover image. Remember that this picture must be 70×70 pixels. The art will appear next to your song on your page. You can provide a different one for every song that you upload. If you have several songs on your page, having matching cover art for each song looks really great. The uploading of your art will be quite brief compared to the time it takes to upload your MP3. You'll only have enough time to write a title for a song at this point.

Step 4: mp3.com provides a special button for pushing if your song should have a parental advisory warning. If your lyrics are a little on the adult side, please put a parental advisory on the page next to your song. The warning is set up by you but someone at mp3.com might request that you do this if you forget.

Here's a good rule of thumb: songs that contain profanity or explicit lyrics should bear a parental warning. Also, please keep your band names and song titles relatively clean as well, or you might find your band sequestered in an adults-only area on mp3.com. This would limit the exposure that your music would get because these areas aren't as well travelled by music fans.

Now decide where you want the song to be available. Remember, at least one complete song has to be available to the public as a free MP3. You can also allow MP3 to play the song on its Internet radio network and to place your song on one of its great promotional CDs – all at no charge to you. Three check boxes are selected automatically for you; the selections allow your songs to be on MP3, on radio stations and on possible compilation CDs. Simply deselect those you are not interested in for a particular song.

You're finished! Repeat the uploading process for each song that you want to place on mp3.com. You can return to mp3.com and to your band page as often as you want to add new songs, update current songs by giving them a new version (which retires the older version automatically), delete songs and change where the songs are available.

The Artist Currently Known As 'You'

After you've joined mp3.com as an artist member and successfully set up your band page (complete with at least one MP3 version of a song), you no longer have to go through the artist sign-up procedure. Instead, you'll return to mp3.com's front page and once again go to the area marked Artists/Labels; this time, however, you click **Artist Login**.

You then see a page, as shown in the next figure, where you type in your username and password. Remember that the usernames and passwords are case sensitive. In other words, if your username is John Smith, type John Smith, not john smith.

After you log in, you see a friendly greeting from mp3.com welcoming you back to the site. You also see a list of fun activities. Want to change your band info? Upload a new MP3? Change the art? Each function is clearly marked for you to follow with ease.

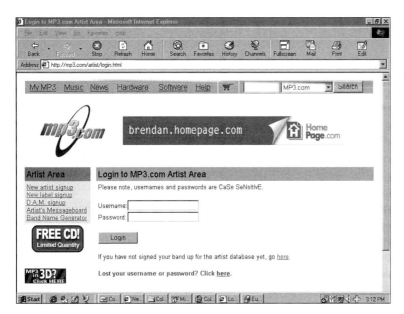

Here's where you log in to add songs and make other changes on your artist page.

mp3.com Internet Radio

Your MP3 file will be converted by mp3.com into a RealAudio file to allow them to play it on one of their Internet radio stations. All you have to do is give permission to do it. They have a Top 40 program, plus a station for every one of their many genres. Since mp3.com also breaks the larger genres down into smaller ones, you could also find your electric blues music playing on their electric blues station and your acoustic blues songs playing on their acoustic blues station. They will also provide you with an Internet radio station of your very own – that plays only your music. Your very own private radio station! Besides being yet another free service for artists, mp3.com does all the work for you. All you have to do is upload your MP3s and let them know that you want your music to be played on their various Internet radio programs. You could find your song being played on several different Internet radio stations at the same time. A great way to get new listeners!

mp3.com's 'We'll Do It For You' Program

If you don't want to bother encoding your song into a MP3 file and uploading it to mp3.com, you're in luck. mp3.com has a special program you should love. It's called the 'We'll Do It For You' program. Perhaps they should have called it the 'I Got Better Things to Do with My Time Than Wait 45 Minutes to Upload an MP3' program but they didn't.

mp3.com will encode your songs for you. However, while they will encode your MP3s, you still have to complete all the steps required to sign up as an artist, as well as those for setting up your band page and list of songs. That means doing those steps online at the mp3.com site.

However, you will simply skip over the one step that requires you to upload your MP3s to mp3.com. Instead, you'll mail your CD to mp3.com with a cheque for $20 and they will do the encoding for you. The fee covers all the songs on your CD that you want encoded, from one song to a full CD's worth. Remember that they won't set up your band page or scan your art. This program only includes the encoding of your CD and they can't work from any medium other than an audio CD.

Because it can take up to 40 minutes to send a song to mp3.com over a standard 56 K modem, this service is quite a bargain if you are planning to upload several MP3s. Look how much time you save if you are going to upload an entire CD's worth of MP3s. You'll find a set of FAQs regarding this program in the Artist area of mp3.com. Check it out to see if there are any recent updates to the 'We'll Do It For You' program.

Remember the basic facts of this program: you must set up your band page with the band photo, cover images, band information and song information just as you normally would but here you skip over the upload MP3 part of the process. You then complete the online 'We'll Do It For You' program forms. The forms tell mp3.com what songs to encode. Finally, you mail your CD to mp3.com, who do the encoding for you.

Your CD will not be returned by mp3.com but kept in their library in case they have to re-encode the songs.

What peoplesound.com Does For You

One of the newest and brightest sites available for getting your music online is peoplesound.com at: `http://www.peoplesound.com`. The Web site, shown in the next figure, was launched in October 1999 with a huge record industry party and they've continued to spend loads of money promoting the site in national magazines and on billboards since. All of which is good news if you're a budding artist who wants to get your music *out there*. Even better peoplesound.com offers a £100 cash advance to everyone who is successful in getting their music online. They also offer another £50 advance for every new artist you introduce to them.

peoplesound.com, they'll pay you to put your music on their site!

The site features the peoplesound.com Navigator, shown in the next figure, a unique tool for finding the type of music you like from amongst the wealth of talent available. The Navigator counters a common fault of sites as rich in content as mp3.com and peoplesound.com: information overload. Finding the type of music you like is not always easy and the Navigator makes light work of that by asking people to enter their favourite artists then matching these up with peoplesound.com music that their editors have decided is similar in style. This is good news if you're trying to get your music heard by people who want to hear it, including those all-important A&R men from the record companies, many of whom now use peoplesound.com as a first stop in their search for new signings.

Getting Your Music On To peoplesound.com

Unlike mp3.com, peoplesound.com doesn't invite you to simply upload tracks and create your own Web site. Because they take a more editorial interest in your music, reviewing and categorising it before putting it online, the process is slightly different. There's no guarantee it will get online with peoplesound.com either – if they decide it's not good enough it won't go up there.

What peoplesound.com ask you to do is submit two tracks to them in Audio CD or MP3 format that you are happy to make available as a free download from their site. There is a simple form for you to fill in giving your details and an agreement outlining the terms under which peoplesound.com will put your music online. You can download a copy of this agreement from their website at `http://www.peoplesound.com/artists/new_artists_sign.doc`.

peoplesound.com's Navigator – find the music you like!

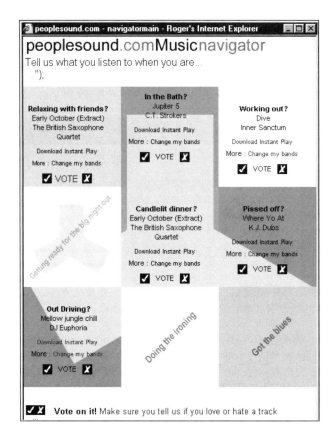

Alternatively, there's a copy of the form on the CD-ROM accompanying this book in the following directory: peoplesound\artistsagreement.rtf. Open the application form and fill it out. Classical artists have their own special form also available from the peoplesound.com website at `http://www.peoplesound.com/artists/classicalagreement.pdf`. You can also find a copy of the form on the CD-ROM accompanying this book in the following directory: peoplesound\classical agreement.pdf.

Send in your music by post to:

> peoplesound.com
> 20 Orange Street
> London
> WC2H 7ED.

Please note – they only accept music on CDs or in MP3 format, no cassette tapes please. Cassette tapes simply aren't good enough quality to be converted into MP3s or burnt on to a CD. The peoplesound.com A&R team will process your application as soon as possible. If you're successful you'll get a cheque for £100 in the post, your own Web site and 50% royalty on CD sales.

Setting Your Sites Higher

Of course, mp3.com and peoplesound.com aren't the only MP3 sites out there. They're the biggest and therefore probably the best ones to start with but you should take advantage of other sites as well. Take a quick look at Chapter 4, 'Finding and Downloading MP3 Files' for a list of some of the other major MP3 sites. Those that distribute tracks for free are generally glad to have you upload yours. Each site has a different procedure, so read through their guidelines carefully.

The Least You Need To Know

➤ The most popular place to put your MP3 on the Internet is mp3.com.

➤ peoplesound.com is one of the newest sites offering to post your MP3s and pays you a cash advance if you're accepted.

➤ Your band page can contain photos, art, lyrics and other promotional information along with your MP3s.

➤ Scan your photos, title your songs and prepare your band-related text before you begin setting up your page on mp3.com or any other MP3-related site.

Making Money From MP3s

MP3s On CD: A Lot Of Music On One Disc

Take a look at any one of your commercial audio CDs and count the number of songs on it. You'll discover around eight to 12 tunes. The average blank CD can actually hold up to about 74 minutes of music but few people take advantage of this capacity.

Now consider this: if you put music in the form of MP3s on a CD, it can hold nearly 10 times as much music as a standard audio CD. Of course, having an MP3-filled CD means that you have to upload the MP3s to your computer and play the songs on the computer's speakers, or perhaps download the MP3s to a Diamond Rio or some similar device. But wouldn't it be great if you could play a 100-plus song MP3 CD in your car, or on a home CD player?

Soon you will be able to. MP3s are a very new technology and hardware manufacturers are just beginning to catch up. CD players are now appearing on the market that can handle both formats: standard CD audio tracks and MP3s. That means you can pop in an MP3-based CD and dance for hours without having to put in a new CD. How come? Because the new players will instantly know if the CD is a standard audio CD or an MP3 CD and will play both types of recordings.

This is where you come in. Let's say you have an album's worth of material ready to go. Why stop there? You could place loads of material on the CD that fans would be interested in. Start of course by putting your basic collection of 10 (or so) songs on the CD. Then, why not add a few bonus tracks, such as some demos that you might have done? After that, why not add a half an hour of interviews with the band, broken into five-minute segments?

You could also add a few live tracks and a couple of versions of your songs with the vocals mixed out so that your fans could have some fun and sing along with your band. In short, jam that CD with as much audio material as you can possibly think of.

Then, sell the CD at your live shows. You could be the first band on your block to be ready with a lengthy and interesting MP3 CD when the new players start showing up in neighbourhood stores. You could also sell your CD on the Internet from various locations like http://www.cdbaby.com or from your own Web page. The point is that you should be ready to exploit the new MP3 technology by preparing in advance your MP3 CD and have it ready to sell when the MP3 home and auto players first come out. It will be a while before the major record companies come out with 10-hour long CDs at any affordable price. You will be able to be ahead of the game if you plan now.

Naturally, it might be difficult for you to come up with 10 hours of material for your CD, or even two hours of material. So, why not team up with other bands and get a great, massive CD together? You can easily meet bands that you like on mp3.com or other MP3-related communities.

mp3.com And 'DAM CDs'

mp3.com has an ingenious way of helping to sell your MP3s: the 'DAM CD' system, which stands for 'Digital Automatic Music'.

Once you have enrolled as an artist on mp3.com, you can elect to sell your music on CD. You set the price for the CD, which is offered for sale on mp3.com. Your fans can download samples of your album, since you have to give at least one free MP3 away to qualify for a band page. The rest of your music, including the free MP3, can be available on the CD that mp3.com will manufacture for you.

mp3.com prints the CD and full-colour cover art, places the CD in a jewel box and ships the CD for you. The fans pay for the CD with their credit cards. You are given a full 50% of the sale price of the CD, which you collect after a $100-worth of CDs are sold.

The DAM CD contains both MP3 versions of your songs and standard CD tracks that mp3.com automatically creates for you. That means your CD can be played both on a standard CD player, such as in your car, and on your computer!

The Future Of Getting Paid For Your MP3s On The Internet

It is important to remember that the concept of MP3s is still very new. Because of this, ideas for helping bands to make money with their MP3s are currently under development. As MP3 becomes more of a household term, the popularity of the format will surely grow. Now is the time to get your music into MP3 format and on the Internet. Better and more effective ways of making money with your MP3s will surely follow. Remember: the current main goal for you should be getting lots of listeners. After you achieve that goal, hopefully some money may follow.

Enrolling In The DAM CD Program

Once you've signed up as an artist on mp3.com and your MP3s have been approved for release, simply log in to your artist page on mp3.com. Remember how you do that? Go to the mp3.com home page and find the link that says **Artist Login**. Click on that and you'll be taken to a new page that has two boxes: one for your username and one for your password. Just fill in that information and you'll be taken to the Artist Admin Area (shown below), where you can make changes to your band page.

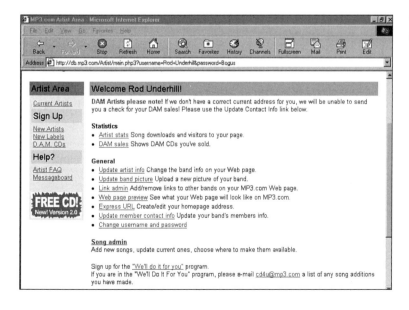

The Artist Admin Area on mp3.com.

Creating Your DAM CD On mp3.com

In the Artist Admin Area, scroll down the page until you find the link that says **DAM CD admin** (shown below). Click on that and then scroll down the next page until you see a link that says **CREATE NEW CD**. Click on that.

*Click on the link **DAM CD admin.***

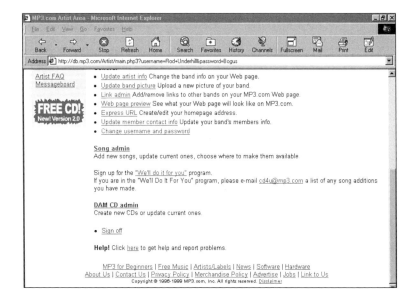

Now you will see a list of your approved songs. All you have to do here is click in the box next to every song that you want to appear on your album.

You will also give your CD a title by filling in that information in the CD Name box. You can use a maximum of 30 characters. You will also set your CD price on this page by going to the pull-down CD Price window and scrolling down the available prices ranging from $5.99 to $10.00. Pick the price that you want and then you are ready to move on to the next step.

After you are ready to go on to the next page, just click on the **Continue to Step 2** box.

Step 2 of the CD creation process is easy. Here you just list the order of the songs for your CD. See the boxes next to each song. Just pull down the little windows and scroll to the order number that you want to set for each song.

When you have finished, click on the box on the bottom of the page and move on to step 3.

148

Cover Art For Your DAM CD

Colour cover art for your CD is a relatively new feature on mp3.com. Step 3 is where you set up your album cover art. This is not to be confused with the 'cover' art that is mentioned elsewhere on mp3.com that refers to the small, 70 × 70 pixel images that go on your band page next to your songs. Those images are essentially small thumbnail pictures of any art that you want to use to jazz up your page. The 'cover art' that we are talking about here is specifically the cover art that will be printed for your CD.

This would probably be a good time for me to tell you the specifics that you should know so that you can do a good job of creating your cover art.

You will be sending the image to mp3.com through the Internet and that means that the picture will have to be turned into a certain type of graphics file. You've learned already that an MP3 is actually a compressed file format for music. There is also a type of compressed file for pictures called a JPEG.

The JPEG, or .jpg file as it is also called, can be created by any one of several computer art/photo programs. Perhaps you already have a program such as Painter or PhotoShop. If you do own such a graphics program, please refer to the instructions that came with it for more information about JPEGs.

If you don't own any art or photo software, don't get upset. You can obtain the shareware program Paint Shop Pro if you are using a Windows-based computer or the shareware program GraphicConverter if you are using a Mac. These programs will happily create JPEGs for you. GraphicConverter can be located at `http://www.lemkesoft.de` and Paint Shop Pro can be found at `http://www.jasc.com` on the Web.

Where should you get the art for your CD cover? You can paint your own picture, take a photo, or create your own original art in any way that you want. Digital cameras are great for this sort of thing. But one thing that you can't do is use art that you do not own. That means you can't simply scan in somebody's art that you find in a book, magazine or postcard.

Use your graphics program to create a file that is 1435 pixels wide and 1425 pixels high. Your resolution must be set at 300 dpi to make sure that the resulting CD cover appears nice and crisp.

If you don't want to create your own CD cover art, mp3.com will provide you with some nice default art.

Techno Talk

Who's PEG then?

JPEG stands for *Joint Photographic Experts Group*, a committee of the ISO, the same folks who brought you *MPEG*.

Additional Tips For Making Money

While you may experience various levels of success regarding selling your MP3s, you can make additional money by selling T-shirts and other promotional materials and by getting people to come to your shows. Make sure that you collect the email addresses for all the people you meet on and off the Internet and set up mailing lists so that you can tell your fans about your new songs, your shows and your products. Ask your fans to tell other people about your band! The future of music may not be in selling your music but giving it away freely and making money on shows and other product sales.

Additional Revenue Ideas

A few Internet MP3 sites are experimenting with paying bands for the downloads of their MP3s. One such company, Amp3.com, offers two cents per download. The downside to this is that the company adds a three to five second advertisement jingle to the beginning of your song. That means that if people download their songs from Amp3.com and add them to their playlist, they'll have to put up with an advertisement as an intro to each song that they listen to, which can be rather disconcerting.

Amp3.com may also be able to help you find a higher-paying sponsor for your music. Again, a brief ad would be added to your song but you would qualify for some sort of compensation. Check out `http://www.amp3.com` for the latest details on this and other revenue-sharing programs for their artists.

mp3.com regularly runs news stories regarding MP3s and the Internet. If you read these news stories on a steady basis, you will pick up information regarding MP3 sites from all over the Internet and learn of any new ways you can earn a buck with your MP3s.

The Least You Need To Know

➤ Get ready for the upcoming CD players that will handle both MP3 CDs and regular CDs by preparing your MP3 CDs now.

➤ Sell your MP3s on CD at mp3.com through their DAM CD program.

➤ Keep your eye on upcoming ways that you can make money with your MP3s by visiting mp3.com often.

Part 4

Music Police – MP3 And The Law

No, the Music Police won't come over to your house and confiscate your copy of 'Achey Breaky Heart'. There are, however, serious laws that you need to be aware of that affect MP3s.

In this part, you will learn about the legal history surrounding MP3s, pirated music and legitimate sources from which you can encode MP3 files. You will also learn how you can get permission to record your favourite song and release it as an MP3 on the Internet.

Chapter 11

Making Money From Other People's Music

In This Chapter

➤ What is bootlegging?

➤ What is a music review site?

➤ What are the different types of review sites?

➤ How do I make money with a review site?

Become A Music Tycoon!

Perhaps you love music a great deal but have absolutely no ability to play an instrument or sing. Maybe you can't even carry a tune. Don't worry! There's still a place for you in the world of MP3-related commerce.

There are at least two great ways to earn some money by using your newfound knowledge of MP3s. But before we walk down either of those golden paths, let's take a look at one way you can't make money with MP3s – at least legally.

Bootlegging: A Shortcut To Trouble

Some people might think that the rich bounty of CD-quality MP3 music on the Internet is a licence to steal. These unprincipled persons might consider downloading oodles of fantastic MP3s and then use them to burn their own custom CDs, which they would in turn sell to their friends. They might even come up with the idea of selling them in markets or car boot sales. Is this a good idea? No! It's a serious crime.

This activity is known as bootlegging and is illegal. Don't even consider doing it. After all, it got Al Capone in trouble and he probably had a better lawyer than you do. Besides, there are other, legal methods to earn a living within the exciting musical world of MP3s.

Music Review Sites: The Land Of Gold

The Internet is rich with tens of thousands of free MP3s. Many of them are recorded by artists with little talent. Although there are huge numbers of gems, searching through the chaff can be daunting and time-consuming. This is where you come in.

You can easily establish an Internet site where you review MP3s of high quality. Are you an expert in a particular type of music? Wonderful! If not, you can always partner up with someone who is an expert in a certain type of music. Or, you can list MP3s by artists who are playing live in your own city and let your users make their own decisions about the abilities of the acts in question.

Here's the best part of this whole idea: you don't have to keep the MP3s on your own server space but can merely link to the remote location where the MP3s are kept. This keeps your space requirement for your page down to a minimum. In fact, such a site can easily fit on the free Web space many ISPs offer with your email account. Low overhead means higher profits!

Make sure that you set up links to MP3s that are legitimate and authorised by the performers. Never link to pirated music because doing so can still get you in loads of trouble.

Lycos Falls Into Copyright Trouble

Lycos operates a very powerful and popular Internet search engine. The International Federation of the Phonographic Industry (IFPI) became upset when Lycos licensed an MP3 search engine and database that was owned and operated by a Norwegian business called FAST Search & Transfer ASA. Essentially, the FAST company provided links to hundreds of thousands of MP3s on the Internet. Evidently, the IFPI must have felt that a certain number of these MP3s were actually pirated from various record companies that the IFPI represents. The issue of whether FAST has in some way violated Norwegian copyright law remains unresolved at this point, as the case remains in litigation. It is important to remember that record companies are very serious about protecting their copyrights.

Thinking Of Linking

Before you set up your review page on the World Wide Web, make sure that the locations that you are linking to are happy for you to do so. Most MP3 sites encourage other Internet sites to link to them but you should always ask if you aren't certain. mp3.com, for example, encourages review sites to link to their site and even provides art that you can use on your page for just that purpose.

But some MP3 sites will become angry if you link to them. For sites other than mp3.com, you should ask first before you set up your links. You can usually find a link on the page to email the Webmaster, which is a fancy title for the person who runs the site. (And when you're finished, you'll be a Webmaster too!) Also, read the materials on any site carefully to see if it has posted its policy on this subject.

You should also check with each artist whose MP3 you intend to review (and link to) to make sure that it's okay with them. You should find that nearly every artist will absolutely love the idea! Why? Because you are helping to drive new fans to their Internet pages and they want all the new fans that they can possibly get. You'll be a hero! On mp3.com, each artist has a special email link on their page that makes contacting them easy to do. Tell them that you only review music that you like and they'll jump at giving you permission!

You can see the mp3.com listing of review sites at `http://www.mp3.com/artistspotlight/`, shown below. If you want to submit your own review site to mp3.com for listing on this page, you'll find a handy link right there just for that purpose. Click it; an email window opens up and you can send mp3.com details and the URL address of your review site. Good luck!

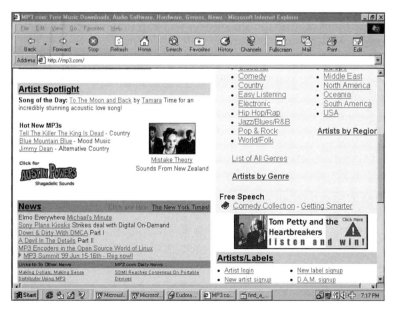

The Artist Spotlight page on mp3.com offers a listing of review sites.

MP3 Review Model One: Be Specific

The first example of a possible review page is one that concentrates on one type of music. For the purpose of having a good example, let's arbitrarily select 'soul' for our genre of music.

Your first step is to search out the best soul on the Web that's offered in free MP3 format. Start your search at peoplesound.com and mp3.com, the largest repositories of free, authorised MP3s.

You'll need to listen to all the soul that you can. If you have a slow modem, you'll find the going easier if you listen to the 'Instant Play' version of the song, which streams out in low-fi, mono RealAudio format. If you need to study the music in greater sonic detail, you can download the actual MP3.

Make notes as you go and select only the tunes that you consider to be the best soul that you can find. As you find the best MP3s, make sure that you save their URL links as bookmarks or favourite places. You'll need them to set up the links from your page to the page where the MP3 resides.

Try The Right-Click Trick

When you have an MP3 that you want to download, you can simply click on the link with the right button on your mouse instead of the left button. A menu will appear from which you can choose to save the file the link points to. A dialogue box then appears from which you can easily select just the right location to place your MP3 file. Give it a try!

Make some notes about the artists and the tunes as you go, so you won't have to listen to the music all over again to remember why you liked them in the first place.

After you've collected the URLs to whatever number of hot MP3s you want to review, write a brief description of each of the artists and their tunes. Because you're writing about music that you love, try and state clearly what's so great about the music. Don't be fancy or overly inventive in your descriptions. Remember that your fans want to be guided to the best music more than they want to be impressed by your prose.

Yet Another Way To Make Money In The MP3 Business

As easy as setting up MP3-related Web pages is, many people don't want to take the time to learn how. A lot of musicians have heard about MP3s but they don't want to be bothered with learning how to encode MP3s, scan art, or any of the other tasks necessary to set up their band page on the Internet. Some musicians don't even have a computer!

You can help them for a fee! I suggest a minimum fee of £25 an hour but that's up to you. Make sure you ask for an hourly fee rather than a flat, one-time charge, so that you can make any changes and additions to their page without feeling like you've been underpaid.

Take out a small ad in the music section of your local newspaper and you'll be surprised about how many clients you'll get. You can also send flyers to all the recording studios in your town. You'll be an Internet music guru in no time!

Adding Photos And Artwork To Your Review Page

Add artwork to your review page to make it sparkle. You'll find cool art on most MP3 pages that has been provided by the artists themselves. Because some MP3 sites, such as mp3.com, have a space limitation regarding artwork and photos, you might also see if their page links to another site where you can find additional art. You can save the art to your own computer by right-clicking on the particular image that you want and then choosing the save option from the resulting pop-up menu.

Don't forget to ask the band or performer if it is okay to use the art as part of your review page. Most performers will be glad to give you permission because it will help you promote their music. Remember, if you tell a musician

Free Art! No Strings Attached!

There are many Web sites that provide free clip art to enhance your pages. You'll find a nice collection of images that you can use for your Web page at http://www.members.aye.net/~gharris/Groovy/grafix.htm.

159

that you are going to give their MP3 a glowing review, they will bend over backwards to help you set up your review page.

The Specialist Page: Some Hot Tips

Because you want people to return to your review page on a regular basis, try and feature a different song every day. You could call it 'Today's Top Tune' or something clever. But regardless of which type of review page you create, try to change your featured content on a daily or at least weekly basis.

Make sure that you check the links to the MP3s frequently as well. When a band retires their MP3s, the links no longer work. Make sure that you remove all links to retired songs every day. Otherwise, your users will quickly get frustrated and unhappy with your review page.

Add some new links to MP3s every day. Fresh content is the key to success for any review page. Your specialist page should also have something of interest other than MP3s. In this soul example, you could write an article about the history of soul. Later you could write articles about soul artists. With all speciality review pages you should easily be able to find interesting topics to write about, regardless of the genre you select.

MP3 Review Model Two: Be Comprehensive

This approach could be described as an 'MP3 Greatest Hits' sort of page. The secret here is to find cool music from several types of genres. The easiest way to do this is to peruse the music on peoplesound.com, mp3.com, or some other MP3 Internet site that you like. Try to stick to the most popular genres: soul, hip-hop, rap, electronic, techno, classical, rock, pop,blues, alternative rock and so on, at least at first. As your page grows, you can add more genres.

With a little work, you should be able to create an interesting series of links for songs that people might overlook. Don't forget to write up a brief review about each of the songs. Remember that you're the expert, so don't be afraid to act like one. If you select wisely, you will be able to create your own fan following and become an MP3 guru. Bands will crave your attention! Music lovers will look to you to point out great MP3s.

MP3 Review Model Three: Become A Local Expert

If you live in a large city, this approach might be your best bet. This page should concentrate on local artists that play live in your city. Do some research and find all the clubs in your town that support live music from local acts. If you call the clubs, they will probably be glad to provide you with a list of their upcoming shows.

You can also usually find a list of bands that play locally by looking in your newspaper. Most of these bands will be glad to put you on their mailing list (either email or snail mail) and you'll be constantly updated regarding their shows.

The best way to get revenue for this type of page is to charge something to the local clubs for a prominent listing on your Web page. You'll have to promote your page by spreading the word among bands, fans and clubs. You can do so by telephoning bands, handing out flyers at clubs and so on.

Have some business cards printed that list your name and your review site Web address. Business cards are an inexpensive form of advertising and you can design them yourself.

If you register with the various search engines, the following key phrases would no doubt serve you well: (Your City) Local Music Scene, (Your City) Live Music, (Your City) Concert Guide. Signing up at a search engine should help bring many readers to your Web page.

Make sure you write reviews regarding some concerts. Change your major content at least every week. You'll probably want to post new information on Monday so that people can get a head start on planning their weekend.

Link to MP3s recorded by the musicians in your town. That way, people can check out the band's music in advance.

How To Obtain Advertising Money For Your Site

Many companies offer money to Web page owners if you put banner ads on your site. It's best to do some investigation regarding these companies before you sign up. A good Internet spot for information regarding such advertising possibilities and other helpful Web page information and links can be found at `http://www.howtoweb.com/corner/advert.htm`.

Each company has different rules about how and when you'll get paid for these ads. Read their rules carefully before you agree to join up with them.

Amazon.com has a referral program where you get a percentage of book and CD sales if you send them customers. Because Amazon sells CDs, you can include a link to the CD containing the songs on your MP3 page. That way, your MP3s can spur a purchase of the CD!

Amazon calls this referral arrangement the 'Amazon.com Associates Program'. Through this program, you can offer links to books and CDs of your selection. Try to pick items that make sense for your Web site. If you are doing a speciality page, like one about soul, you could list both popular soul CDs and books about soul. You can also add a search link, which enables people to search Amazon's catalogue from your Web site and pay you if they order anything they find.

When you can, don't just list the books and CDs. Include honest reviews. Although the negative reviews may drive people away from certain items, it will get people to trust your positive reviews, making them much more likely to order those items.

If you have a general review page, list the top-selling CDs and general books on music so that you can make some additional money.

As for a local page, see if Amazon.com offers books about your town. If you live in a major city, you should be able to find plenty of books available. Don't forget to list CDs from famous bands that got their start in your city, too.

Go to Amazon.com for full details about the Associate Program. While you are there, order several extra copies of this book to give to your friends and family. They make wonderful gifts.

Earn Some Cosmic Credit

Amazon isn't the only site offering money for links to their site. CDNow offers something they call Cosmic Credit. You earn a commission of anything from 7% to 15% for each purchase made through your link to CDNow. Your Cosmic Credit can be used to purchase items from CDNow. Once you accumulate $100 of Cosmic Credit in your account, at the end of a calendar quarter you'll receive a cheque for that amount. Other online CD retailers offer similar schemes. Check out CDNow's scheme at: `http://cosmic.cdnow.com`.

The Least You Need To Know

➤ Selling MP3s that you don't own is illegal.

➤ MP3 review sites are a valuable service because people need extra help locating the best free music.

➤ There are several types of review sites to choose from.

➤ You earn money with a review site through various forms of advertising.

Chapter 12

Music Pirates

In This Chapter

➤ What is the Audio Home Recording Act?

➤ What is the Digital Millennium Copyright Act and how does it affect MP3s?

➤ What was the Diamond Rio dispute about?

➤ What if my own music gets pirated?

Who Stole The Music?

Who are the music pirates? For the most part, they are people that copy recorded music that they don't own and then sell the copies for a tidy profit. That really annoys the actual owners of the music because pirates usually forget to send the real owners a cheque when they burn off a few hundred bootleg copies of somebody's album. Pirates are absent-minded that way.

By strict definition, music pirates also include an awful lot of people who just want a copy of an album they can't find, don't feel like paying retail price for, or just want to listen to in the car, so they tape a friend's album for themselves. This places a lot of ordinary people in the position of technically breaking the law.

Audio Home Recording Act

Not liking commercial music pirates much and wanting also to take large groups of ordinary people out of the 'scofflaw' category, the lawmakers in the USA decided to fire a broadside at music piracy. To help out music copyright holders in their fight against these musical outlaws, they passed the Audio Home Recording Act (AHRA) in 1992. This law imposes a three percent surcharge on the sales of blank digital tape, discs and cartridges. Digital audio recording devices (such as DAT and Minidisc) have an added two percent to their price of sale.

This law also requires that certain digital music devices meant for personal use have a serial copy management system built in so that copies of copies of digital music cannot be made easily. The record companies want to make sure that if you're digitally copying an album, at least you're copying directly from the original, rather than copying from a copy of a copy of a copy. Some recording devices just won't let you copy a copy, while others copy it as an analogue rather than a digital track, reducing the quality of the recording.

So where does the money collected from the sale of the tapes and such go? It is gathered up and distributed to songwriters, record companies, publishers and so on. All people in America pay this surcharge. In the UK there is no such levy, while the situation in most of Europe is similar to that in America with differing rates per country. The reason there is no surcharge in the UK is that the relevant bodies feel that the blank tape levy discriminates against those of us who simply buy tapes to record our own music or to send audio letters to friends and relatives.

Who Gets the Audio Home Recording Act Money, Anyway?

The money collected in the USA goes to the Register of Copyrights and the Librarian of Congress. These are both US government agencies, of course. Two-thirds of the money goes to a Sound Recording Fund. Most of this money goes to record companies but 40% of this two-thirds goes to famous artists. A small bit of it goes to non-famous artists and backup musicians. The other third goes into a Musical Works Fund and is split evenly between songwriters and music publishers. Similar arangements are in place in the various European countries that collect a similar levy.

Some people think that this law might have come about because in the late 1980s, Sony (a major manufacturer of private recording equipment) purchased CBS Records (a major producer of commercially recorded music). Plus, Matsushita (another large manufacturer of private recording equipment) purchased MCA, another large record company. In the sunny days prior to the passing of the Audio Home Recording Act, Matsushita and Sony were against this type of law. After investing in the recording industry, they decided to support passing this interesting tax.

But perhaps that was a coincidence of some sort. (I'll pause for a moment while you put your jaw back in place. You don't think that big business would have us taxed for their own benefit do you?)

So, all Americans and most Europeans are picking up the tab for the pirates. In 1989, a study by the US Congress determined that there was no real evidence that home audio taping was reducing sales of pre-recorded, commercially released material. In fact, they concluded that home taping actually increased sales for the record companies. The law was passed anyway.

Copying Without Fear

There were two major benefits for consumers, however. After the AHRA was passed, manufacturers felt more comfortable making digital home music equipment. Now we could buy digital recording equipment that would perfectly duplicate music. More important than that was that we could now digitally copy pre-recorded music for our own personal, non-commercial use without fear of breaking any laws.

That's pretty good, too. It is perfectly okay to make your own CD of your favourite songs drawing from music in your own, purchased collection. Strictly speaking, making copies of something that was copyrighted wasn't necessarily something that you could do. Now you can. You pay for the privilege to do this via the surcharge added to your CD recorder and the blank CDs. But this law does not give you the right to start mass distribution of MP3s of your favourite songs.

The Digital Millennium Copyright Act

In 1990 Congress passed the Digital Millennium Copyright Act (DMCA). The purpose of the act was to help the Copyright law catch up with the reality of modern music technology.

If an Internet service provider, either intentionally or not, allowed users to keep illegal MP3s on its site, that storage of unauthorised, pirated MP3s could potentially cause them some legal problems. Or, even if an Internet service provider provides some helpful hyperlinks to surfers looking for pirated material, that could also cause the referring service some legal trouble, as well.

The Act Stinks

Rod Underhill, who wrote most of this chapter, isn't nasty enough towards the Audio Home Recording Act. This new tax (signed into law by Mr 'No New Taxes' himself, George Bush) has ugly causes and ugly effects:

➤ It is based on the assumption that some people were breaking the law (which is true) and that the proper thing to do is not to enforce the law but rather to treat everyone as if they had been breaking the law and had to pay for it.

➤ It weakens the control that copyright is supposed to provide, which was already weakened for musicians. Now, they don't have the right to say 'people at home can't make copies of my song and pass it around'. Instead, the musician has to accept it and hope he gets some cut of the money pile.

➤ It puts limits and added complications on information technology.

➤ The little guy is being taxed not to feed the poor or provide for our national defence but to pad the bank accounts of multinational media conglomerates.

➤ Buying a DAT recorder to make high-quality tapes of your cutting edge band that is nothing like that commercial music you so hate? Congratulations, you're supporting Capitol Records. Recording an audio letter to your mum on your Minidisc recorder? Well done, you're funding the Backstreet Boys.

New taxes, weaker copyright, crippled and expensive technology, all in the name of funding international multimedia conglomerates. This act is a loser all around.

The DMCA provides a safe harbour for these types of Internet-related businesses. You just can't get away from those nautical references when you're talking about piracy!

This issue concerns an Internet service provider giving someone space to store something that may be copyrighted when the copyright owner hasn't given permission for the duplication. For instance, if somebody puts up an MP3 version of a major hit record it could be embarrassing and could result in an unpleasant phone call from a lawyer.

In their wisdom, Congress passed a law that protects an ISP from being sued for copyright infringement when infringing material is on their Web site if certain conditions are met. The rules are fairly simple.

The ISP shouldn't be aware that the material is infringing. That simply means that if they know a song or composition is pirated or unauthorised, then they should promptly remove it from their site. So far, pretty easy, yes?

Making money from illegal MP3s will bar an ISP from the safe harbour. Put simply, the ISP shouldn't get paid by anyone who is accessing the infringing material. Making money from illegal MP3s, even if you don't know they are unauthorised, can potentially bar the ISP from the safe harbour.

After someone alerts the ISP of a copyright violation, the ISP should comply with certain reasonable 'notice and take down' procedures. The law provides a process that the ISP can safely follow in the event somebody complains about the copyright violation and the ISP is reasonably unsure of who actually owns the particular copyright. If you've been looking on the Web for MP3s, you may have seen notices that ISPs have removed MP3s from their site.

Lycos Moves Into Tricky Waters

Interested in the fad for MP3s, Lycos (the popular Internet search engine) established a special MP3 search engine, as mentioned in Chapter 11. People could pop over to Lycos on the Internet and easily find MP3s from all over the world. The International Federation of the Phonographic Industry (IFPI), located in London, decided to sue the Lycos partner company, which was involved with the actual search engine. That company, called FAST, is located in Norway. FAST was sued because the IFPI felt that the Lycos search engine amounted to a violation of copyright law because it contributed to copyright infringement by leading fans to unauthorised, pirated MP3s. Lycos will no doubt counter that they deserve the benefits of the safe harbour provided by the DMCA. At press time, the latest word was that Lycos and the IFPI had reached an understanding. Basically Lycos undertook to report any illegal activity uncovered by `http://mp3.lycos.com` to the IFPI .

167

Down To Rio

Diamond has this great little toy called a Rio (see p. 75 for a description). It fits easily into the palm of your hand, has no moving parts and plays MP3s. You can download MP3s to your computer and then transfer some of them to your Rio and then enjoy the music through a pair of headphones. It sounds pretty good, too. Trouble was, it also sounded sort of scary to the king of the anti-MP3 forces, the Recording Industry Association of America (RIAA), a group representing the record companies of the United States.

Prior to the Rio being released, the RIAA filed for an injunction in federal court to stop the sale of the Rio. They claimed that the device did not meet the specifications of the Audio Home Recording Act. That law, remember, requires money to be paid in the form of royalties and a serial copy management system to be placed in the device itself so that zillions of unauthorised copies can't be easily created with the device.

The Federal Court did issue a preliminary injunction that kept the Diamond Corporation from selling the Rio for a period of 10 days. However, after that 10-day period elapsed, the court ruled that there was no relationship between the Diamond Rio and unauthorised copying of MP3s. The Audio Home Recording Act was also not violated, according to the judge in the case, because there was no way of taking a copy of a song out of the Rio and thus it doesn't qualify as a copying device.

The Rio was set free, sort of. After some continued litigation, the Diamond Corporation agreed to produce the next generation of Rios with an added feature. They will play both MP3s, which can be easily duplicated and another format other than normal MP3s, which won't be able to be copied, due to encryption being added to the compressed sound file.

Although there are several types of handheld MP3 players available now, the Diamond Rio is quite popular and is a good example of how they work. They come in two editions, the first of which is the Rio PMP300. This cute little unit holds up to 30 minutes of digital-quality music and up to 12 hours of voice-quality audio. Plus, it has no moving parts and is about the same size as an audio cassette. You can also add on flash memory cards that give you room for several new songs per card and take the memory from the standard 32 MB up to 64 MB. As a rough guide, 1 MB is not quite a minute of music at the highest quality setting.

The Rio PMP300 'Special Edition' comes in a transparent teal case and has 64 MB of onboard memory straight out of the box. The memory can be increased with an add-on module to 96 MB.

Other companies that are putting out similar players include Creative Labs (the Nomad), ATLM Taiwan, Inc. (the Etman) and I-JAM MultiMedia Corp (the IJ-100). There are others, too. A summary of a selection of available players is given in Chapter 5. Have fun shopping!

Swindlers Lust: Stars And Their MP3s

In October and November 1998 The Beastie Boys posted an MP3 a week from their 1998 North American tour on their Web site for an exhilarating ten weeks until their label, Capitol, pulled the plug and the MP3s were replaced with Streaming Audio versions. While they were up there the MP3s were extremely popular and it was often impossible to download tracks as the demand on the server was so great.

On 1 December 1998, Public Enemy posted five MP3 tracks from *Bring the Noise 2000*, an album they claimed Def Jam Records refused to release, on the official Public Enemy Web site (`http://www.publicenemy.com`). Soon afterwards, Def Jam's parent company PolyGram forced the band to remove the tracks without an explanation. Ties between the label and the band were severed in the following weeks and Public Enemy went on to release their next album, *There's a Poison Goin' On*, in MP3 format through the Internet label Atomic Pop (`http://www.atomicpop.com`) before sending CDs to stores.

You can still download 'Swindlers Lust', a ditty about the rapaciousness of the record companies on the Public Enemy Web site.

In December of 1998, Billy Idol decided to give his fans an early holiday present. He released two new singles on mp3.com. The songs were free to all takers and turned out to be very popular. While it lasted, that is.

Idol's label, Capitol Records, evidently requested that the songs be removed from his mp3.com Web page only a few days after they were released, according to a press release posted on mp3.com at the time.

Other recording stars were quick to jump on the MP3 bandwagon, to the dismay of their record labels. Tom Petty released 'Free Girl Now', from his Echo CD, on the Internet as a free MP3. It didn't stay up for more than a day or so, either. One doesn't get the impression that the major record companies loved this sort of experimentation.

The Grateful Dead were pretty famous for letting fans tape their concerts, going so far as to designate a section of the venue just for tapers. But the Dead recently cracked down on MP3s of their music being distributed online. On the other hand, Julian Lennon and Cheap Trick both cheerfully distributed free MP3s on the Internet without any real problems.

MP3s are wildly popular and appear to be the grassroots' favourite format. Meanwhile, record companies and others are trying to supplant MP3s with various formats that cannot be easily copied. MP3s appear, given their support by fans, to be on solid ground. However, whether sites that contain MP3s can survive legal challenges remains to be seen.

The Mighty Six

There are really only six major record companies: Bertelsmann, EMI–Capitol, Universal, PolyGram, Sony Music and Warner Music. That's it. Between them they own the whole ball of wax.

They hate pirated music, too. But they only hand over to their bands about 50 pence for every £15 CD sold. They aren't giving much of a deal to the consumers, either. CDs are cheap to manufacture; yet prices keep going up and up (contrary to promises made when the format was introduced). US record companies alone made about three billion dollars in profits in 1998. That's a lot of money.

Pirates seem to think this is an excuse for stealing music. Of course, it isn't. But the music industry isn't helping with their high prices.

What If You Have Been Pirated?

If you're a musician, you might find out one day that your music has been placed on a Web site without your permission. There are two things that you can do.

You can just allow it to stay where it is. After all, it is free publicity for your act, right? Of course, you are going to want to make sure that the song is properly credited to you. You don't want other people taking your music and putting it up as an MP3 in their name.

Or, you might simply want to have the music removed from the unauthorised Internet site. If you do, let the managers of the Web page know by sending them an email. Most MP3-related music sites do not want to have unauthorised music on their pages and will swiftly move to remove music when they get a complaint.

Remember that the law establishes a responsibility for Internet service providers to respond to your reasonable request to have unauthorised MP3s removed. If there is a dispute as to whether you are the actual copyright holder of the song, they still have to respond to you so that you and your lawyer can attempt to resolve your complaint.

If you want to shut down an out-and-out pirate site using your music and you can't figure out how to locate its actual ISP, there are ways to track them down. You will find a wonderful article on how to accomplish this on mp3.com at `http://www.mp3.com/news/119.html`, written by MP3 guru Michael Robertson. Essentially, what you will learn is that you can find and verify unlicensed MP3s by using Internet search engines. You'll learn how to locate the server containing the suspect music and then how to identify the server owner or the ISP that the server uses. Finally, you will learn how to best make contact with the owner of the server so that you can have the offending music removed.

The Least You Need To Know

➤ The Audio Home Recording Act was introduced in America to allow people to make copies of commercial music for their own personal use. Similar laws exist throughout Europe but not the UK.

➤ People in the US and most of Europe pay for the right to make personal copies through higher costs for certain digital home stereo recording equipment and blank tapes and CDs.

➤ Internet service providers have certain responsibilities regarding housing unauthorised MP3s on their services.

➤ If your own music has been pirated, you have certain recourses to get the music removed from the offending site.

Chapter 13

Legal Rights

In This Chapter

➤ How do you get a copyright for your music?

➤ How do you get permission to release a cover version of a song you like?

➤ Why should you join the MCPS or the PRS and how do you do that?

➤ What are the rules about sampling music?

Instant Copyright

Feel like writing a tune? You're probably feeling quite creative about now, so go ahead.

Finished? Now record it. Sing or hum it into a cheap cassette recorder. It doesn't have to sound great.

All done? Great! Now you don't only have a song, you own a copyright. Copyright is a legal term. Having the song's copyright means that now nobody can record that song without your permission. Once a recording of that song is released, if anyone wants to sell recordings of his or her own version of that song, he or she has to pay you money. A copyright gives you music, control and money; what more could you want out of life?

Once you have written and recorded the song, even in a rough demo form, the copyright is established for you automatically, according to UK copyright law. It doesn't matter if you record a live version of it while you're playing a show, record a highly produced version at the best recording studio in the world, or sing by yourself into a Fisher-Price tape recorder – the copyright exists as soon as you've put the song on tape. Presto! It's legal magic.

There is another way you can establish your copyright. You can write the sheet music and lyrics on a piece of paper just as Wolfgang Amadeus Mozart did when he wrote his greatest hits. Doing so also establishes, or 'fixes' the copyright. You don't have to be able to write musical notation to get the job done – recording it in any fashion does the job just as well. If tape recorders had been around when Mozart was doing his musical thing, maybe he wouldn't have bothered to learn to read and write musical notation.

Registering Your Copyright

There are several ways you can make your copyright more tangible:

➤ The first option is to take a tape of the song you have written and then send it to yourself by registered post. When you receive the letter from the Post Office, keep the envelope sealed with the Post Office receipt attached and put it away in a safe place. When doing this it is essential that the Post Office stamp is across the seal of the envelope and that the date on it is legible. The envelope can be produced in court if you ever need to back up your claim to ownership of a work.

Keep A Record!

When registering copyright by post it is a very good idea to write the name of the songs on the outside of the envelope as you might find yourself repeating this exercise several times.

➤ The next option is to get a solicitor to sign and date your manuscript or tape. If you do this remember that in any court case you will need to be able to call on the person who has signed either to give evidence or make a sworn statement.

➤ Another alternative is to deposit a copy of the manuscript or tape with your bank.

➤ Finally the song can be registered with Stationers Hall, an independent copyright registry. The fee for the registration of a work or group of works is £30.00 plus VAT. This fee provides registration for seven years; thereafter re-registration for another seven years can be obtained by payment of a further fee. For more information please contact:

> The Registrar
> Stationers Hall
> Ave Maria Lane
> London EC4M 7DD
>
> Tel: 020 7248 2934
> Fax: 020 7489 1975

On A Legal Note

It should be noted that taking any of the measures described above will only establish the existence of a copyright from a particular date. They will not prove ownership of a copyright. If you've copied someone else's song, whether consciously or unconsciously (as happened to George Harrison with 'My Sweet Lord', which was deemed a copy of the old Chiffon's hit, 'She's So Fine'), you may still be liable to legal action.

Recording Other People's Songs

If you own the song, you can do anything you want with it. If you want to make an MP3 version of the song and put it up on a Web site, there's no one to stop you. (In fact, as you read in Chapter 9, 'Distributing Your MP3s', it's a good way to reach a wider audience.) So far so good. What if you didn't write the song? What if you want to record and release an MP3 of a song or musical composition that someone else wrote?

Remember, this is a different issue from ripping (that is, copying a song from) an MP3 from a commercial CD that you own. We covered that in a previous chapter, as you will recall.

Techno Talk

What Is A Cover Song?

A cover is nothing more than when you record your own version of a song that you didn't write yourself. If you decided to record your own version of your favourite Beatles song, you would be doing a cover of that song. Many famous recording artists have done their own covers of songs that they like, sometimes doing entire albums of cover songs. The upside of doing a cover song is that you don't have to write it and can select a song that might be familiar to the general public. The downside is that you have to pay for the right to use the song because you didn't write it and therefore don't own it.

Public Domain: Free Music For All My Friends

Copyright doesn't last forever. If you write an original tune you own it for the rest of your life. At that point your inheritors own it for another 70 years. That's it; nobody owns it anymore. Any fan of your work can record that song for free. 'In the public domain' is legalese for 'nobody owns the song anymore'.

There's a lot of music in the public domain. Much of it got there simply by being old. Other songs are in the public domain because their owners forgot to take some legal steps that were important under old copyright laws that don't apply to new music. Generally speaking, if a song is less than 70 years old, it probably isn't in the public domain, so you can't issue a CD of you whistling the Coronation Street theme without paying someone. If a song's more than 100 years old, it almost certainly is in the public domain, so feel free to do that rap version of 'Greensleeves'. (Don't, however, sample parts of someone else's version of 'Greensleeves' because that is invariably subject to a mechanical copyright which covers the arrangement and sound recording.)

If you are not certain whether a song is in the public domain, there are two organisations that specialise in licensing music rights that you can contact to find out. The Performing Right Society (PRS) can inform you of the right to broadcast a piece of music and can be reached at its World Wide Web site (`http://www.prs.co.uk`). Alternatively, the Mechanical Copyright Protection society (MCPS) can inform you of the copyright of a recorded piece of work. You can find their web site at `http://www.mcps.co.uk`.

Covering A Cover Song

You've decided you want to cover a new hit single. Because it's a brand-new song it's highly unlikely that it's in the public domain. You're snookered, right?

Wrong. You're welcome to record that song. In fact, the song owners even want you to do so. They hope that your own version hits the big time because they get to share in your success. How? You'll pay them a royalty for every copy of their song sold on a CD or cassette (a bit more if the song is more than five minutes long). That is a pretty good deal for you.

Is there a catch? Of course there's a catch. (After all, if it weren't a catchy tune, you wouldn't be covering it, would you?) The catch is that you have to obtain a licence for using the song and you must pay some money up front for the right to release it. The MCPS will be most pleased to give you all the forms that you need to obtain permission to do your favourite song.

The MCPS has been around since 1924 and represents more than 4000 British music publishers. Music publishers manage the various songs that they own. Some people, such as Sir Paul McCartney, have invested a great deal of money in buying the rights to famous songs. Sir Paul owns not only many of his own songs but also songs written by Buddy Holly and other famed artists, making him one of the most important music publishers in the world. The MCPS acts as a go-between between publishers such as McCartney's publishing company (MPL) and you, the aspiring musician. The MCPS makes it very easy to obtain the licence that you desire.

Let's Get Mechanical

The best way to contact the MCPS is via its Web site, at `http://www.mcps.co.uk` (shown in the next figure).

You can also contact the MCPS at the following street address:

> Mechanical Copyright Protection Society Ltd (MCPS)
> Elgar House
> 41 Streatham High Road
> London SW16 1ER

You can call the MCPS for licensing requests on 020 8769 4400, fax them on 020 8378 7300 or contact them by email at: info@mcps.co.uk.

Remember that this licence is for the use of the composition – that is, the right to record your own version of a song you like – or for the use of a sample from a commercial CD to incorporate in your own musical work. Don't call them for permission to rip an MP3 from your favourite CD for your own home use.

The Mechanical Copyright Protection Society is where you get mechanical licences so that you can record somebody else's song.

The Mechanical Licence

The mechanical licence is the permission you need to issue your cover song on CD, cassette or LP. Obtaining a mechanical licence is even easier than getting a driver's licence because there is no test. They don't even examine your vision. The MCPS Web site is easy to use and clearly explains the types of licences that are offered.

The Internet Licence

What if you don't want to sell CDs? That is, what if you don't want to put your cover song on a CD that you intend to sell but instead merely want your song to be available as a free MP3 from your Internet Web site? Do you need a licence for that? Or is it okay to give away a free MP3 of a cover song?

The MCPS knows what it wants you to do. It has a trial Internet licence that it wants you to buy from them. The MCPS also will set some sort of fee for the Internet licence from £50 to £1000 depending on the amount of music you intend to put on your site. Evidently, the entire concept of an Internet licence for cover songs is still under development.

Trans-Atlantic Alliance Aims To Set The Standard

As this book goes to press the boards of ASCAP (USA), BumaStemra (Netherlands) and the MCPS–PRS Alliance (UK) have agreed to create a shared service centre to handle music rights processing in the digital age. The project has yet to be officially named but carries the working title of International Music Joint Venture (IMJV). Its aim is to integrate the management of worldwide rights administration and set new standards for the future.

More information and contact details can be found at the web site `http://www.imjv.org`.

The Internet licence is not a new creation but one that is the subject of some debate. Is an MP3 a performance? Or a reproduction? Or neither? If it is a reproduction of a song, the Mechanical Copyright Protection Society would have jurisdiction. If an MP3 played on the Internet is actually a performance, the Performing Right Society would have jurisdiction.

Presently, it would seem that you should contact both the Mechanical Copyright Protection Society and the Performing Right Society regarding the song in question and see what their opinions are regarding Internet use of an MP3 version of a cover song that you have recorded.

At this point, peoplesound.com, mp3.com and the other major MP3 Internet sites each have house rules about cover songs. Some of them might not require you to have an Internet licence but you must have at least a mechanical licence for each. Check the FAQ (frequently asked questions) list on each site that you are interested in uploading your cover to. Remember, though, that just because the site lets you put the song up for download that doesn't mean that you are legally protected if any music publisher feels you are infringing on their copyright.

Please, don't release CDs or cassettes of a cover song without first obtaining the necessary licences. You might otherwise find yourself in serious trouble! Commercial use of somebody else's song without his or her written permission can bring you a lot of legal trouble. As much as you might love to do a mashed-up cover of a Smashing Pumpkins tune, it's not worth spending years breaking rocks for.

Covering A Song Your Sister Wrote

Your sister writes a catchy little ditty called 'My Family Sucks'. You want to record it. Of course you can – if she gives you permission.

As the songwriter, she should copyright the song before you release it via the Internet (or anywhere else, for that matter).

The creator of the song should also consider joining the Performing Right Society. That way, if your version of the song should ever become a smash hit on the radio, she'll get her well-earned performance royalties. If you are a songwriter or composer, you should join up, too. What if, after releasing your song on mp3.com or another Internet site, loads of traditional radio stations discover your musical genius and start playing it in major rotation? What if a thousand bands want to record cover songs of the song that you wrote? Don't you want to get rich?

Getting paid will be difficult if they don't know where to mail the cheque, which is where the PRS comes into the picture. The PRS is more than willing to collect the money that you are owed, deduct a small fee and forward the balance to you. It's a pretty good deal.

Joining The PRS

Becoming a member of the Performing Right Society is easy. The PRS lets you join as a writing member if someone has commercially recorded a musical composition of yours. If you haven't seen any of your music commercially released, don't panic. You can also join as an associate member if you have registered one musical work. You can read all about this and other great stuff about the PRS at `http://www.prs.co.uk`, shown below.

The PRS home page is packed with useful information for aspiring recording artists.

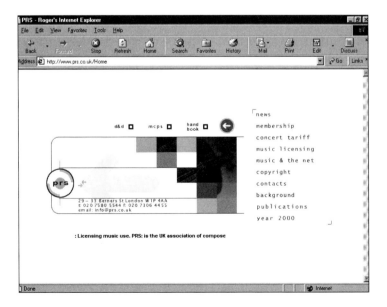

What About Sampling?

Sampling is the process of taking a piece of someone else's recording and making it part of your own. You might want to take a bit of the vocals from the Beatles' song 'Get Back', mix it with some of the guitar from Oasis's 'Don't Look Back In Anger' and round off your new creation with some of the drum loops of any one of a dozen tunes by your favourite dance project. Each bit that you copy and use from somebody else's sound recording is called a sample.

Sampling is somewhat easy to do and a lot of fun. Simply turn on the trusty MIDI-equipped computer or sampling keyboard, grab a commercially released CD and away you go. A lot of very creative music is done via sampling and as a form of musical expression, it is extremely popular.

However, sampling the music of another artist without permission is not only unfair but also illegal. A payment of a licence fee is usually required to get permission. Why? Because the songwriter owns the copyright to his or her music and you don't. Taking a bit of music from another song that you don't own and incorporating it into a new song that you've made up is usually forbidden. You won't go to jail for it but you'll find yourself facing a huge lawsuit.

If you like to use sampling in your own music, don't despair. You can get permission to use samples of songs that you don't own or otherwise have the right to use by contacting the Dance Division of the Mechanical Copyright Protection Society. Aren't they helpful?

For sample clearance issues contact Claims Team 2 Manager (0208 378 7441). Alternatively you can email your enquiry to dance.info@mcps.co.uk.

Look into this permission before you do your recording! Licensing the recorded music or sounds from a famous song can cost thousands of pounds. The safest route for a sampling musician is to use the sounds that you create on your own. You may come across samples on the Internet, on CD-ROMs, or other sources that you believe you might have the right to use in your own music. Owning a recording of a song does not automatically give you the right to sample it. Check carefully to see if you are allowed to use the samples in any way that you want. If you are not sure, don't use them in songs that you intend to release, as you may be engaging in a copyright infringement.

What About Fair Use?

'Fair use' refers to a section of the copyright laws that permits you to use 'reasonable' amounts from a copyrighted work without you having to first obtain a licence. What's 'reasonable'? Legally, reasonable requires that your sampling does not substantially impair the value of the original work.

This may sound simple but it isn't. Some people assume that a sampling artist can use 20 seconds or less of a copyrighted musical work without getting into trouble. This assumption simply isn't true.

There is no clear formula available to lead you along this slippery legal path. The rules in this area of the law are quite difficult for anyone to understand. Not even an experienced copyright lawyer can safely tell you how to be sure that fair use will protect you from a nasty copyright infringement suit. It would be nice to be able to tell you that you can safely use small bits of somebody else's recorded music but we can't. It is simply much safer for you to obtain a licence for the use of somebody else's recorded sounds and music.

European Contacts

Readers in other European countries should contact CISAC (the International Confederation of Societies of Authors and Composers) via their website at http://www.cisac.org for individual territory info. CISAC is the international umbrella organisation for author's rights societies and their site contains useful info plus links to all the member sites (which would include specific territorial information).

There are two specific pieces of European legislation coming up in 2000 that will affect all European Community artists who want to distribute their music via the internet – the Copyright Directive and the E-Commerce Directive. You can find the details on their website at http://europa.eu.int/comm/dg15.

The Least You Need To Know

➤ Copyright your original music before you release it on the Internet.

➤ If you haven't written the song you want to release, you must obtain a licence from the song publisher.

➤ You can freely use songs or music from the public domain.

➤ The Mechanical Copyright Protection Society is the place to get licences for cover songs.

➤ If you are a songwriter or composer, you should probably join the PRS.

➤ The safest thing is to avoid sampling the recorded music of another performer into your musical work unless you get written permission to do so.

Chapter 14

Compressed Successes

In This Chapter

➤ How can having an MP3 on the Internet promote my act?

➤ How are some MP3 bands managing to become opening acts for major performers?

➤ What types of extra promotion are available for my MP3s? Is it free?

➤ What about television, magazines and other non–Internet media? Are they interested in MP3 bands?

The Icing On The Cake

Dance music producer Danny J Lewis had enjoyed success on the dancefloor with his tunes but still found the process of getting his tunes out there frustrating. 'Over the years I've produced tracks that haven't slotted naturally into genres that record companies are keen to exploit,' explains Danny. 'I saw the Internet as a possible outlet for these tracks. peoplesound.com offered me a non-exclusive contract and the kind of big-budget marketing power that ensures my music reaches as wide an audience as possible.'

The exposure on peoplesound.com has already paid off for Danny with one of his tracks being picked by J.Walter Thompson for a Smirnoff Ice advert currently appearing on satellite and terrestrial TV in England and Ireland. The agency knew the sound they wanted but couldn't find an existing piece of music that fitted the brief. Then J. Walter Thompson discovered peoplesound.com.

After contacting peoplesound.com the agency ran a search for artists whose music matched the sound they wanted. 'After establishing that my music was the kind of sound they were after for the advert, J.Walter Thompson contacted me and gave me a brief to produce a custom-made piece of music,' says Danny. 'I delivered it a few days later and it was accepted'.

More Commercial Success!

Alan Bleay from the peoplesound.com band Ink also had success in this field. Following on from their good experience with Danny J Lewis, J. Walter Thompson came back to peoplesound.com to find music for their Persil commercials. Alan composed backing music for two separate adverts and was paid directly by the agency.

Such is the typical success story for many MP3 artists. They are finding a world wide audience by simply offering their music to the people of the world. They don't need an agent or a music lawyer. They don't require a contract with a recording company. MP3 has opened a very large door to a new world of musical freedom and thousands are stepping through.

But to what final success? To be fair, the MP3 movement is really still in its infancy. Will major stars spring from the world of free MP3s? Only time will tell, but every indication says 'yes'.

Meanwhile, other MP3 artists have obtained some notable successes.

Sign Me Up!

It's not only in the field of commissions to write advertising music that MP3 artists are finding success. peoplesound.com artist Jel signed to Blackcat records in January 2000 as a result of his exposure on the web and Kaja Wunder, another peoplesound.com artist, is in negotiation with a major label in Japan as we go to print.

Snowed Under

Deakin Scott, better known as Bullet Proof Sounds, is also the happy beneficiary of peoplesound.com's expertise in matching sounds to producers' needs. In his case the producers of Snow Odyssey, a movie about snowboarding, wanted a hard-hitting breakbeat track to use on the soundtrack. They contacted peoplesound.com who provided them with various examples in the style they described and they settled on Deakin's track 'Wireless and Miel' as being what they were after.

Deakin wasn't the only peoplesound.com artist to feature on Snow Odyssey; other peoplesound.com artists featured on the soundtrack include Alkahounds, The Preacher, Stoney Sleep, Saltgrass, Flexyman, Fantasmagroover and Kane.

Many such opportunities are striking MP3 bands all over the world. It is only a matter of time before a band 'breaks' via MP3s and hits the big time. We are living in the great golden age of MP3. Now is the time to get your music on the Internet and get discovered!

Check These Artists Out!

➤ You can find Danny J Lewis on the web at:
http://www.peoplesound.com/artist/dannyjlewis

➤ You can find more information about Bullet Proof Sounds at:
http://www.gerbilscratchings.co.uk

➤ Find out all about the Alkahounds at:
http://websites.ntl.com/~debaser/

➤ Check out The Preacher at:
http://www.dashdown.freeserve.co.uk/preacher/

➤ Stoney Sleep are wide awake on the Web at:
http://www.peoplesound.com/artist/stoneysleep/

➤ Saltgrass have their own Web site:
http://www.saltgrass.reeserve.co.uk

➤ Flexyman have their Web site at:
http://www.active-ingredient.co.uk/flexyman

➤ Fantasmagroover have a Web site at:
http://www.fantasmagroover.com

➤ Kane's details are on the Web at:
http://www.peoplesound.com/artist/kane/

➤ Read all about Ink at:
http://www.peoplesound.com/artist/Ink/

➤ Jel's info can be found on the Web at:
http://www.peoplesound.com/artist/jel/

➤ Kaja Wunder's details are on the Web at:
http://www.peoplesound.com/artist/misskajawunder/

Your Songs Featured On Promotional Albums

Fifty peoplesound.com artists were selected for a musical CD-ROM entitled '50 Great Tracks'. peoplesound.com printed 50 000 copies and distributed them for free with Pine Electronic's Dmusic MP3 players worldwide.

The CD-ROM was also given out at the Music Live 99 exhibition in Birmingham to over 3000 attendees and cover mounted with 30 000 issues of PC Pro's DVD special in January 2000.

Not a bad way for an artist to get some promotion. Unlike similar promotional CDs designed to bring attention to unsigned bands that you might have come across in the traditional or non-MP3 field of music promotion, not one artist paid a cent to be on this promotional album.

peoplesound.com also feature a free audio CD of tracks from 14 peoplesound.com artists that is given away free from their website at http://www.peoplesound.com. Once again, that's pretty good publicity for free. *Computer Music* and *.net* magazines have also featured peoplesound.com artists on their cover CDs after hearing about the great sounds on peoplesound.com.

Radio Plugs The MP3 Star

Fantasmagroover's 'Modelling Must Play Well' received airplay on Radio One FM which actually led to a recording for a John Peel session.

Meanwhile the band Stumble are currently being fought over by A&R men as their track 'How Many Times Do I Have To Kill You Before You Die?' has been highly acclaimed by the music press. Following on from a rave review in NME, John Peel has been playing it on his Radio One show, saying that it is only available through peoplesound.com.

peoplesound.com artists Toyskin, with their 'Prize Every Time', and Twinkie, with 'TK-1', have also been played on Radio One's evening session.

Judge Jules Passes Sentence

Top dance DJ Judge Jules gives his opinion on a selection of dance tracks on peoplesound.com every week at http://www.peoplesound.com/jjules/. Not every dance act can claim to have such illustrious judgement passed on their tracks!

More and more MP3 acts are getting press, radio play and even record contracts. Expect to see many new acts 'breaking' via MP3s in the not too distant future.

How To Get Special Attention For Your MP3s

Most bands want to get Song of the Day or other feature spots. There isn't any sure-fire way to obtain such extra promotion from an MP3 site but it can't hurt to send review copies of your CDs, press clippings and newsletters to the MP3 Internet provider of your choice. Remember that they are hunting for great artists and are usually happy to hear about a great artist, even if the tip is coming directly from the artist.

Reality Check

Everything in this chapter is true. However, these are all just possibilities. Remember this:

➤ If you upload a song, people *might* download it.

➤ If they download it, they *might* listen to it.

➤ If they listen to it, they *might* like it.

➤ If they like it, you *might* build a reputation.

➤ If you build a reputation, you *might* get media and record label attention.

➤ If you get attention, you *might* end up with hit music and financial success.

But that's a lot of maybes. The real truth is that only a small percentage of the thousands of musicians making MP3s (like most of those not making MP3s) will ever make a substantial portion of their living from their music. Only a very small proportion of these will ever have a hit song and most of those will be flashes in the pan. If you're making music because you want to be a superstar, you'll likely be crushed. If you're making music because you love making music, however, you're already a success.

The Least You Need To Know

➤ Having a popular MP3 band can lead to many types of media attention including radio, magazine and television exposure.

➤ You may want to mail promotional materials to mp3.com or other MP3 sites in an attempt to call attention to your band.

➤ Not every band will get selected for some major, extra promotion but more opportunities are coming up all the time.

➤ The business of making music is a difficult fight full of longshots. The art of making music, however, can be a lifelong source of joy.

Guide To The Music And Artists On The CD-ROM

In This Appendix

➤ Listen to MP3s from some of the best artists on the Internet.

➤ Read their opinions about what MP3s have done for them.

➤ Learn from fellow musicians how you can best promote your music with MP3s.

To close our look at music on the Internet with MP3, we'll turn the spotlight on some outstanding artists who have achieved some measure of fame by distributing their music electronically. We're helping them out by providing their MP3 files on the CD-ROM that accompanies this book.

We've broken this appendix down by genre; hopefully, everyone will find something they like by an artist they might not have known about before.

Electronica

Danny J Lewis

Artist information: Danny J Lewis has been producing house music for nigh on a decade now and has built up a strong following among clubbers and DJs. He enjoyed a top 30 chart success with summer 1998's 'Spend the Night' and recently composed the music for the cool Smirnoff TV advertising campaign. If you like your house with a deeper jazzy feel then Dan's your man!

Album available: *Danny J Lewis*

Song on the CD: 'Show Me'

About the song: A more traditionally US-based sound for Danny J Lewis than his speed garage fans may expect. This mix is a predominantly instrumental dub in a minor key.

Song file location on the CD-ROM: electronica\Danny J Lewis – Show me.mp3

About the MP3 experience: 'I make music because I love creating it, and quite often the tracks that I produce don't fit into the "conventional" blueprint that record labels are interested in. MP3 frees my creativity, I can record what I want, whenever I want and release it out into the world with no risk. I want people to hear my music and digital distribution via a site like peoplesound.com suits me fine.'

Danny J Lewis info on the Web: http://www.peoplesound.com/artist/dannyjlewis/

Danny J Lewis contact info: danny_j.lewis@virgin.net

Danny J Lewis in full acid-burn effect!

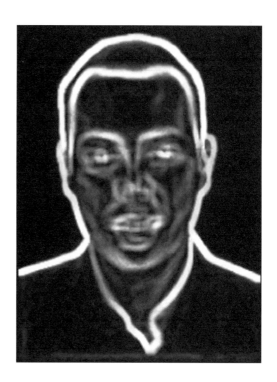

D.O.S.E

Artist information: D.O.S.E formed in 1995 when asked to write a 'dance tune' for vocalist Mark E Smith on PWL offshoot label Coliseum. The result, 'Plug Myself In' was released in March 1996 to widespread critical acclaim. Following further remixes they signed to Mercury Records releasing the awesome, deranged *Crack Man In Bat Den Sex Shock* EP again to widespread praise yet popular indifference. When cruelly dropped from the corporate bosom and left to languish in bleakest Manchester out of nowhere came 'Inch', yet again featuring Mark E Smith, a masterpiece of neo-Beefheart surrealist chaos.

Album available: *D.O.S.E*

Song on the CD: 'Crazy Monkeys'

About the song: Warped electronica wearing its Fall and Beefheart influences on its sleeve, 'Crazy Monkeys' may be a sign of the direction electronica is heading in. If it isn't it should be.

Song file location on the CD-ROM: electronica\D.O.S.E – Crazy Monkeys.mp3

D.O.S.E info on the Web: http://www.peoplesound.com/artist/dose/

The Full D.O.S.E.

Paranoia

Artist information: Paranoia are collectively a South African–Anglo beat pop combo comprising multi-instrumentalists Lorenzo Livingstone and Brad Groblar, veterans of over 40 musical projects and planning complete global domination (it sez 'ere).

Album available: *The Hysteria EP*

Song on the CD: 'The Summer (Club Extended Mix)'

About the song: For those who like their house deep and beaty, 'The Summer' sounds like one of those tunes you'll hear in Ibiza next, er, summer.

Song file location on the CD-ROM: electronica\Paranoia – The Summer (Club Extended Mix).mp3

Paranoia info on the Web: http://www.peoplesound.com/artist/paranoia/

Paranoia.

Nihilist

Album available: *Phrenitis*

Song on the CD: 'Blueback'

About the song: Taking us into the techno void the Nihilist makes a statement with his brand of amphetamine techno given the liberal 303 treatment. It may be that Nietzsche was wrong, God may not be dead; he might just have changed his name to Roland.

Song file location on the CD-ROM: electronica\Nihilist – Blueback.mp3

Nihilist info on the Web: http://www.peoplesound.com/artist/nihilist/

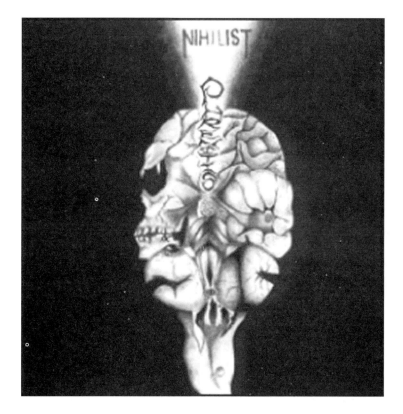

Nihilist – Phrentitis.

Floyd Dice

Artist information: Floyd is probably best known for inventing Baby D and writing/producing the No. 1 hit 'Let Me Be Your Fantasy' and No.4 album *Deliverance*. He was also known as part of The Housecrew & Brothers Grimm from the hardcore days.

Album available: *Floyd Dice*

Song on the CD: 'Bad Day'

About the song: Floyd has been on the scene for a long time and his experience shines through in the style and production of this track. A cool and jazzy slice of drum'n'bass, 'Bad Day' certainly has the potential to chill you out after a bad one.

Song file location on the CD-ROM: electronica\Floyd Dice – Bad Day.mp3

Floyd Dice info on the Web: http://www.peoplesound.com/artist/floyddice/

Floyd Dice.

The Preacher

Artist information: Influenced not so much by other artists as by the genre of film, The Preacher's name was inspired by the fifties movie 'Night Of The Hunter' starring Hollywood tough guy, Robert Mitcham. The Preacher's music is a dizzy haze of dance, hip-hop, big beat, techno-jazz and filmatic atmospheres. Go to The Preacher's official Web site, and check out the new album, *Spreading The Word*, released early in 2000.

Album available: *Of Gods and Monsters*

Song on the CD: 'Here's the Preacher'

About the song: Today's sermon concerns the danger that mediocre music harbours for the soul. Thankfully The Preacher is here to ensure that we find salvation via a healthy diet of breakbeats, jazz and cinematic sounds. Hallelujah!

Song file location on the CD-ROM: electronica\The Preacher – Here's the Preacher.mp3

About the MP3 experience: 'As well as being a musician I am just completing my third year as a media student and will soon be seeking work in the multimedia industry (Web sites and hopefully music in media). MP3, therefore, particularly interests me and has meant a huge amount to me. What peoplesound.com and other such companies have allowed myself and others to do is (to coin one of my many used phrases and also the title of my next album due out in January 2000) 'spread the word' of our music. It is a daunting task for unknown musicians to get themselves heard at the best of times. peoplesound.com and MP3 brings the listeners to the musicians instead of trying to get the musicians to the listener.

'I have no idea how many people have listened to my tracks but I can guarantee that a lot more people have heard my material because of peoplesound.com than would have otherwise. I believe that the way the music industry controls what people can hear in terms of style, etc. is preventing people from listening to alternative music and stunting creativity and character. It's like being in a sweet shop but only being allowed to buy certain varieties. All the other types of sweets are hidden under the counter. MP3 is giving musicians the opportunity, the chance to get discovered when disillusioned by record companies who try to pigeonhole music and listeners the chance to hear otherwise unavailable material. Who will be the next big discovery or what will be the sound of 2000? MP3 sites could well hold the answer instead of silly little A&R men in suits who wouldn't know good music if it jumped up and bit them.'

The Preacher info on the Web: `http://www.dashdown.freeserve.co.uk/preacher/`

Get a gob full of The Preacher.

Traversal

Artist information: Traversal's sound includes numerous tough tracks for the dedicated clubber. A big influence on their sound has been the Trade club style pioneered by the late great Tony De Vit, who played out thumping sets, and the British progressive sound of Paul Oakenfold.

Album available: *Hard House and Trance* EP

Song on the CD: 'Feel For Me'

About the song: A thumping tune, 'Feel For Me' is certainly the kind of thing that goes down a storm at Trade with its big kick and electronic vocal hook.

Song file location on the CD-ROM: electronica\Traversal – Feel For Me.mp3

Traversal info on the Web: http://www.peoplesound.com/artist/traversal/

Traversal's Hard Trance and House *EP.*

PallMall

Artist information: PallMall is the name of an eclectic rock/pop sample-based project by Samantha Kassus and Paddy Sturrock. Based in North London they have been working on material for the past year using analogue synths, tape loops and samples as well as 'real' instruments.

Album available: *PallMall*

Song on the CD: 'Is She All You Want'

About the song: Pop on a trip hop vibe with the melodic hooks and heart rending vocal of 'Is She All You Want'.

Song file location on the CD-ROM: electronica\PallMall – Is She All You Want.mp3

PallMall info on the Web: http://www.peoplesound.com/artist/pallmall/

Bullet Proof Sounds

Artist information: 'I started doing music at the age of 14 originally with a keyboard and a Tascam PortaStudio. This gave me a real feel of how music was produced in studios and so on.

'At the age of 15, I started sending out demos, which in a way might have seemed really stupid, as the music was never really all that good, but it got me some good contacts because of my age and ambition. It got me a mention on a single called 'My Time' by Souvlaki which felt amazing at the time. I also got replies on my demos from people like Sister Bliss, Robert Miles, and Paul Oakenfold.

'At 16, I got a PC with some music software, and realised this was gonna be my next big step. Through the process of sending out my demos, I got a phone call from the magazine *Computer Music*. They wanted to put a track from the demo in the magazine and give the song away on the cover mount CD, which was amazing for someone like me, as I was still at school at the time. During, this same year, I also got work experience at Roll-Over Studios, which was mainly down to knowing the group Arkarna, as they have a big part in working there. It was a superb time to be there then as Leftfield were also there producing their second album, so when someone like that's working there, you know the studio has got to be a big name.

'Now I'm 17, I've started a site on the Web called Gerbil Scratchings, which is a site to help me, and a few other artists get established. I've also had a song on a movie called 'Snow Odyssey', which was down to peoplesound.com who sent my track off to the producers who were looking for music for the production. I've also been looking 'round trying to get remixes. Pitchshifter and Cooler have agreed to give me a shot at remixing. Pitchshifter have given me a go on the basis of hearing the track 'Disturbed England' and they sent me a letter personally saying they liked it. A band called Roc who used to be signed to Virgin have accepted a remix I did of their single 'Soviva',

197

and said they will release it on a future release. Patrick Nicholson in Roc has given me much encouragement towards the building of my song structures too, which has helped a lot.

'All in all, I think things are happening a lot more than ever now, but I am still hoping a record deal of some sort will be offered to me soon, so if you like the music, please get in touch.'

Album available: *Bullet Proof Sounds*

Song on the CD: 'Disturbed England'

About the song: If The Prodigy appeal to you then 'Disturbed England' will be right up your (sub)urban alleyway. A big breakbeat slice of punk and funk, this tune rocks!

*Bullet Proof Sounds'
Deakin Scott in cartoon
effect.*

Song file location on the CD-ROM: electronica\Bullet Proof Sounds – Disturbed England.mp3

Bonus song (only available with this book): 'I Don't Know Why…' Featuring guitar from Fabian Lomas and vocals by Deakin Scott, 'I Don't Know Why…' demonstrates Bullet Proof Sounds' eclecticism.

Bonus song file location on the CD-ROM: electronica\Bullet Proof Sounds – I Don't Know Why.mp3

About the MP3 experience: 'I think MP3 is one of the best things that has ever happened to the Net and who ever created the compression, hats off to them. It's helped me and over a million others upload songs to the Net quick and fast and it's also been the start to a vast majority of companies starting businesses on the Net, peoplesound.com being the most obvious choice.

'There is still the issue of illegal MP3s on the Net though and that's never gonna stop, so I suppose MP3s are only really bad, if you're a bit uptight about the situation. You have to remember, there are some bands that aren't too bothered about it and can face up to the fact, that it's gonna happen, whether they like it or not. As Nostradamus predicted, the world is gonna change as we know IT. I believe 'IT' could be interpreted as information technology.'

Bullet Proof Sounds info on the Web: http://www.gerbilscratchings.co.uk/bulletproofsounds/

Bullet Proof Sounds contact info: deakin@gerbilscratchings.co.uk

Marshall & Oakley

Artist information: Mike Marshall and Lawrence Oakley, both classically-trained musicians, had been working on various musical projects before they met in late 1997; Mike with Beat Foundation, Distant Drum, Steelfish Records and Skinny Malinky Records and Lawrence in film, TV and advertising music. In 1998 they teamed up with distributor intergroove and formed their own record label, MM Records.

You can buy MM Vinyl on the net at http://www.recordstore.co.uk and MP3 and CD products at http://www.peoplesound.com

Album available: *Marshall & Oakley*

Song on the CD: 'Eclipse'

About the song: A trancey break-it-down-and-build-it-up tune that will have any bedroom, boudoir or dance-floor buzzing. Lovers of lush trancey strings and melancholic moments will be in their element.

Song file location on the CD-ROM: electronica\Marshall&Oakley – Eclipse.mp3

Marshall & Oakley's label, MM Records.

About the MP3 experience: 'We'd already got our vinyl distribution deal sorted out,' Mike explains, 'but we wanted to be right in the thick of it when Internet distribution started to kick off. MP3 simply means that we can get our music to more people – and faster.'

Marshall & Oakley info on the Web: http://www.peoplesound.com/artist/ marshalloakley/

Indie

Fantasmagroover

Artist information: Named after the prototype fighter plane developed by the Americans in the '60s, Fantasmagroover originally hail from the glamorous area of Macclesfield, Manchester.

The band are:

➤ Matt Babbs – vocals, guitar

➤ John McMenemie – bass

➤ George Double – drums, vocals

'Modelling Must Pay Well', featured on the Fierce Panda EP *The Joy Of Plecs* alongside songs by Cay, The Monsoon Bassoon, The Samurai Seven and Chicks, only 1000 copies were pressed (vinyl only) and it sold out in the first week. Good airplay from Radio One FM led to a session recorded for John Peel broadcast early last year; a new one is out in March. Also available on Fantasmagroover's own Spangle label are the singles 'Buzz Aldrin' and 'Bag of Spanners'.

Fantasmagroover released 'Bag of Spanners' produced by Paul Tipler (Placebo, Idlewild) on 24 January, 2000 and plan to release 'Butch Reads a Pamphlet' in March/April of the same year.

Album available: *Fantasmagroover*

Song on the CD: 'Modelling Must Pay Well'

Fantasmagroover in moody publicity mode.

About the song: 'Modelling Must Pay Well' was written as a tongue-in-cheek romantic view of the pleasures of pornography. The sample at the start is taken from the classic '60s porn flick 'Black Buggery'.

Song file location on the CD-ROM: indie\Fantasmagroover – Modelling Must Pay Well.mp3

About the MP3 experience: 'We've been offered various deals but a priority for us at the moment is being in control', notes Matt, 'Things like peoplesound.com give us a chance to get our music to a wider audience without having to charge for it. We want people to hear our music, that's why we do it!

'In five years time MP3 players will be as commonplace as Walkmans are now, I just hope that the technology won't mean a million shit music sites. You're always going to need some sort of quality control, not everyone can be a famous rock star.'

Fantasmagroover info on the Web: http://www.fantasmagroover.com

Stumble

Artist information:

➤ Steven Battelle – Vocals, Guitar

➤ Child – Bass, Vocals

➤ Mark Gibson – Drums

➤ Simon Jablonski – Guitar

Stumble are four teenagers from Derby releasing their third single after the last gained excellent reviews in the national press and numerous plays by Mary Anne Hobbs and on Steve Lamacq's Evening Session.

Emma B, John Peel and Steve Lamacq at Radio One have already played the new single. As well as being playlisted by XFM and GLR it has also received the number one position on Radio One's Buzz Chart, voted for by the general public, beating the likes of the Beastie Boys and the Super Furry Animals to the top slot.

Album available: *How Many Times Do I Have To Kill You Before You Die?*

Song on the CD: 'How Many Times Do I Have To Kill You Before You Die?'

About the song: A frantic Foo Fighters-inspired melodic punk anthem, 'How Many Times Do I Have To Kill You Before You Die?' takes a stab at the heart of pop punk.

Song file location on the CD-ROM: indie\Stumble – How Many Times.mp3

About the MP3 experience: 'The Internet and the MP3 isn't going to knock record companies out of the picture. They'll embrace it. Record stores will have computers in their stores where you can download tracks.' – Steven Battelle

Stumble info on the Web: http://listen.to/stumble

Stumble contact info: Stumble, PO Box 5048, Derby DE1 9YT, UK

Email: stumble@sumoconstruction.ndo.co.uk

Sumo Construction (management) – Neil Cooper +44(0) 973 102527

Stumble with attitude.

The Dukes of Hang-Gliding

Artist information: As the band's name suggests the Dukes take a less than conventional approach to their music. Catchy tunes and eclectic backing complement witty, intelligent lyrics. Their EP is a great introduction to the band and one that deserves to spread their popularity far and wide.

Album available: *The Dukes of Hang-Gliding*

Song on the CD: 'The Murder Song'

About the song: The Dukes indulge themselves in a cup of musical hysteria with this taste of their lyrically bizarre yet melodically smooth tunes.

Song file location on the CD-ROM: indie\The Dukes Of Hang-Gliding – The Murder Song.mp3

The Dukes of Hang-gliding info on the Web: http://www.peoplesound.com/ artist/thedukesofhanggliding/

Elegant, eclectic, elegaic, The Dukes of Hang-gliding.

Gas Solari

Album available: *Space Psyche Trance*

Song on the CD: 'Ambition'

About the song: A melodic dirge reminiscent of early Velvet Underground, 'Ambition' is as fine a slice of white noise angst as you've heard for a long time.

Song file location on the CD-ROM: indie\Gas Solari – Ambition.mp3

Gas Solari info on the Web: http://www.peoplesound.com/artist/gassolari/

Gas Solari standing by the wall.

Toyskin

Artist information: Originally formed at school as a three-piece noise outfit, Toyskin soon discovered that their hearts were set in writing and recording music that was slightly avant garde. By July 1998 the band was a four piece and put out their first release, a self penned 7″ single entitled 'Prize Every Time' (which went on to receive Radio One air time). With the fifth member joining in 1999 the debut album *I Want to Turn Left* was finished. The record concentrated on the live band, using all manner of time signatures alongside traditional catchy melodies.

The second album surfaced in August 1999 entitled *5 Days in a Renault 5* taking the band in a totally different direction. The 11 tracks cover '80s pop, ambient drum 'n' bass, mainstream, noisy lo-fi, rock and the acoustic piano ballad. At this point Toyskin decided that live performance was not a viable option any more, the equipment required to perform such self-indulgent monstrosities was too expensive for an unsigned band such as themselves. December 1999/January 2000 was spent recording their third album *Lucy Button LP* (minus some of the original members), which has taken them in a chilled-out but more normal direction. Toyskin are using a lot more programming and sequencing as their know-how and equipment develops.

Album available: *5 Days In A Renault 5*

Song on the CD: 'Pretending to be a Dog'

About the song: 'For the life of me I can't remember why we gave the track this appalling title, but it's too late to alter it now.

'"Dog" is a bit of an oddity really, the whole idea with the *5 Days* record was to see how many different genres we could cover using the various "skills(?)" we all possessed. "Pretending to be a Dog" was our attempt at mainstream. It's pretty simple, the whole song is hinged around one simple riff, which in turn is coated in '70s wah

wah guitar (the only live instrument in the song, very unusual for us). We laid a computerised voice over the top, this rattles away quoting various phrases that have been used by MCs on dance radio programs at one point or another. And that's about it, we deliberately kept it simple to contrast with some of the other nonsense on the record.

'The recording equipment used for "Dog" was pretty basic, a home PC and a few cheap mics. It took about 12 hours to complete in two separate sessions and, as with all of our material, was recorded at home.'

Song file location on the CD-ROM: indie\Toyskin – Pretend To Be A Dog.mp3

About the MP3 Experience: 'Downloading MP3s from the Net is certainly an interesting idea that seems to be taking off. Obviously for people like myself, it makes my music available all over the globe, but people in China aren't really likely to stumble on the Toyskin site. But as the Internet becomes more popular, and better software becomes available to the home publisher, one day the record-buying public might visit my site, hear a free MP3 and order a record direct from me.

'Many people say that it will eventually eliminate record companies. But the next step will be the new breed of Internet record companies such as peoplesound.com and mp3.com. Give away some of your music for free, if someone likes it then sell them a CDR of the act and cream the profits.'

Toy Skin info on the Web: `http://www.toyskin.fsnet.co.uk`

Toyskin – a load of rubbish sucks.

Monc

Artist information: If James Bond were a young man in 1999 Monc would be on his stereo. Monc's sound draws on early '60s chic and late '60s psychedelia with a wonderful twist reminiscent of Portishead or Massive Attack. This is lounge club music for the twenty-first century, managing to be mellow, funky and uplifting all at once.

Album available: *Monc*

Song on the CD: 'Away'

About the song: 'Away' sounds like psychedelic-era Beatles or a tune from The Monkees movie 'Head' with enough originality to transcend mere nostalgia and make it a candidate for the soundtrack of the next Austin Powers movie.

Song file location on the CD-ROM: indie\Monc – Away.mp3

Monc info on the Web: http://www.monc.net

Monc, truly bizarre.

Babel Tree

Artist information: Formed in 1997 Babel Tree consists of three individuals named Mano, Ben and John. In the same year they recorded their debut album on a Pentium 133, the sound distinctive and professional. During 1998 they played several live dates in the UK. In August 1999 Babel Tree launched their Web site offering free singles and a 'slick, colourful and user friendly cerebral experience', according to *City Life*. The Web site was named Channel 5's 'web site of the week'.

Album available: *Babel Tree*

Song on the CD: 'Gee Bees'

About the song: Lazy but never laid-back, Babel Tree play with a nonchalance born of consummate confidence. 'Gee Bees' is a classic indie–blues track that Gomez would give their favourite anoraks for. Catch them before they explode.

Song file location on the CD-ROM: indie\Babel Tree – GeeBees.mp3

Babel Tree info on the Web: http://www.babeltree.ndo.co.uk/

Babel Tree, three guys named Mano, Ben, and John.

Saltgrass

Artist information: 1998 saw the unearthing of Saltgrass. Hailing from north London this four piece have been busy recording and producing new songs on an eight track, in the smallest home studio in the world (probably) 1999 was definitely not a space oddity for Saltgrass; it's just a matter of time before touchdown! ... tick, tick, tick.

'Inspiration wise I think we've got quite a crazy background: there's everything from Captain Beefheart, Nick Drake, The Beastie Boys, Neil Young, Mc5, Ry Cooder, Aphex Twin, Robert Johnson, Buffalo Springfield, the list goes on and on... We have a lot of records even some criminal ones!'

Album available: *Songs From the Saltmine*

Song on the CD: 'Not The One'

About the song: '"Not The One" was written about the feeling you get when travelling, all the thoughts that go through your head when going through customs, borders, airports etc., the paranoia that we put ourselves through every day, and for what! It's also about being herded around Disneyland fashion, being drawn in by the shine then realising it's 'Stepford Wives' territory and trying to "not be the one they're looking for"...'

Song file location on the CD-ROM: indie\Saltgrass – Not The One.mp3

Saltgrass's album Songs From the Saltmine.

About the MP3 experience: 'I was quite amazed at MP3s when the guy who designed our Web site introduced me to them, primarily the amount of information you can get in such a short space of time. We transferred three tracks and were quite surprised at the quality. The data compression seems to work pretty well, we had a couple of tracks used on a snow boarding video that were MP3 format. We went to the screening at the cinema and it came across really well. I think MP3 has really opened people's eyes as to what can be done over the Internet and stirred up the music industry, which isn't such a bad thing really is it!'

Saltgrass info on the Web: http://www.saltgrass.freeserve.co.uk

Saltgrass contact info: feedback@saltgrass.freeserve.co.uk

Twinkie

Artist information: NME and Radio One Evening Session favourites, Twinkie present their new material on peoplesound.com. Also available on vinyl on November 1 the four piece, fronted by Moo, will be appearing at a club near you soon.

Album available: *Twinkie*

Song on the CD: 'TK-1'

About the song: Twinkie play a perfect piece of indie pop on 'TK-1' that will either have you bouncing around the room or off the walls.

Song file location on the CD-ROM: indie\Twinkie – TK-1.mp3

Twinkie info on the Web: http://www.peoplesound.com/artist/twinkie/

Twinkie take the biscuit.

Alkahounds

Artist information:

➤ Jim Cuzen – Guitar, Vocals

➤ Suzy Johnston – Guitar, Vocals

➤ Dez Holland – Bass

➤ Paul Bridges – Drums

Jim started Alkahounds around 1993, having been playing and writing his own material since 1989. The band (Jim and Dez) applied and received a grant for £200 from The Prince's Trust in Glasgow to record their first demo, recruiting new drummer, Paul Bridges, and finally a female guitarist in 1995 – enter Suzy Johnston.

They have played at all the top rock venues in Glasgow (King Tuts, Arena, Nice and Sleezy, 13th Note, Venue and the University circuit.) Throughout the summer of 1995, Jim and Suzy worked together continually, and from Jim's 80-plus songs they settled on a strong collection of 20 odd. Jim and Suzy started to work off one another to produce the original sound of the Alkahounds.

Now filled with confidence, they embarked on a self-produced three-song demo which more truly reflected the Alkahounds' true calling. Their combined influences include The Pixies, Breeders, The Amps, The Beatles and '80s/'90s US punk. The band and their sound, although encapsulating these influences, simultaneously transcend them, cutting a very individual figure within the Glasgow music scene. The demo was well received and incited interest from various sectors of the industry.

Notwithstanding their strong and loyal following the Alkahounds have successfully sought after and attracted newcomers to the Hounds fan base.

The band has their feet firmly on the ground when it comes to ambition. Their main objective is to secure a recording deal which will allow them the opportunity to invest all their time and effort into writing and recording new and better material.

More recently Alkahounds have completed their most impressive demo to date, recorded and mixed at Riverside Studios in Glasgow and produced by Duncan Cameron (Teenage Fan Club, Bmx Bandits and the Supernatural). The band has had some airplay in America, and are also registered with peoplesound.com who are using some of their tracks for the forthcoming video and soundtrack CD *Snow Odyssey*. They are also members of NeMIS (New Music In Scotland).

Album available: *Alkahounds*

Song on the CD: 'Noah'

About the song: Erring on to the heavier side of the indie music canon, Alkahounds combine punk, metal and eclectic indie to worthy effect. If those three styles don't appeal to you then you should look elsewhere; if they do then dive in, you'll lap this up!

Song file location on the CD-ROM: indie\Alkahounds – Noah.mp3

About the MP3 experience: 'About three years ago Alkahounds went into the recording studio to lay down a four-song demo. When completed we decided that the most economical way to get the demo out to record companies and publishers was to have a master CD made then record them to tape on a single tape deck in real time. This was a painstaking procedure and involved hours upon hours of attention and time.

'Upon completion of mind-numbing, time-eating CD-to-tape copying, it was time to target the record companies and publishers most suited to our style of music. Where do you start? Is it worth sending to this company or that publisher? Are they still in existence? Do they still accept demos? Will the tape ever arrive? Will the A&R listen to it? Do they only accept demos from their own country? Are they a real company? How many jiffy bags do I need to buy? How many can I afford to send every week? All of these thoughts cross your mind when working to a tight budget and I'm sure there are several more that I have overlooked. Once sent, you have the disappointment of no reply, the company no longer exists or no thank you letters because you sent to an inappropriate company. No wonder so many up-and-coming bands have short life spans, they give up disheartened.

'Three years on and things have changed and oh how they have changed. The Internet monster is growing at a phenomenal rate. New users world wide daily. Then along comes the scourge of the music industry and the saviour of up-and-coming bands in the form of MP3s. Web sites offering free hosting to unsigned bands, putting their biographies, photos, contact information and your songs in the revolutionary MP3 file format. This allows the ordinary Internet user access to your music, where they can download songs you have selected and if they like it they can either contact you or buy the EP or full length CD. This helps when building a fan base and people from every corner of the globe have an opportunity to sample your music. Without the Internet and MP3 this would have been unthinkable.

Alkahounds on the way up.

'The down side for record companies is the ease at which their artists can be pirated. The upside though is they can also visit the MP3 sites to investigate potential artists to sign. They can find the genre most suited to them and listen to the MP3 file and if they like it they can contact you. You can email record companies, give them the address for the site and they can go for a listen. This is just too good to be true if you are working to a tight budget, but it is starting to pay off for cyber bands and to sum it up, remember three years ago!'

Alkahounds info on the Web: http://websites.ntl.com/~debaser/

Pop

Zee

Album available: *Right About Time*

Song on the CD: 'Never In A Million Years'

About the song: Those of you who are prone to a bit of clubbing but don't like your music to be too deep or too banging will lap this up. Zee's tracks are extremely accessible, combining pop tunes with dance beats and a great vocal. It's a bit like Steps for grown-ups without the cheesy connotations, and I mean that in the nicest possible way.

Song file location on the CD-ROM: pop\Zee – Never In A Million Years.mp3

Zee info on the Web: http://www.peoplesound.com/artist/zee/

Zee.

Wave

Artist information: Wave is the partnership of songwriter Justin Gibson and the techno wizardry of producer John Fortis. They are inspired by the explosion of electronica into the popular music scene of the 1980s and beyond. They have already been likened to a fresh-sounding Pet Shop Boys as well as being original in their own right.

Album available: *Wave*

Song on the CD: 'Try A Little Harder'

About the song: Straight out of the eighties in pure electro-pop mode, 'Try A Little Harder' is a bouncy tune that is hard to resist with an infectious chorus.

Song file location on the CD-ROM: pop\Wave – Try A Little Harder.mp3

About the MP3 Experience: 'We feel that the rate that the Internet is evolving will see a society governed completely by e-commerce. This is a very exciting time with far-reaching consequences. As far as music on the Net is concerned never has there been a time where the potential to reach a global market can be masterminded from one's own home – modem + ingenuity = total world domination! The future of music? Everything, nothing and anything can and will happen with a Luddite revolution thrown in for good measure.'

Wave info on the Web: `http://www.peoplesound.com/artist/wave/`

Wave contact info: wave@mod-art.demon.co.uk

Justin, or half a Wave.

Prince Albert

Artist information: Prince Albert are a trio of musicians who have worked as session musicians for various artists over a number of years, recording, playing and producing various styles of music. After seeing successful results through working for other artists and bands, they decided to put their own ideas into a project named Prince Albert. Although as a trio they write the music, they also collaborate with vocalists that they have worked with to sing on chosen tracks. Up until now they have been self-financed which enables them to produce and write their own style of music without external influences.

Album available: *Lollipop*

Song on the CD: 'Lollipop'

About the song: An eclectic mix of drum'n'bass, indie and girlie vocals, 'Lollipop' is one of those 'love it or hate it' tracks that will probably appeal more to pop and indie fans than drum 'n' bass fanatics.

Song file location on the CD-ROM: pop\Prince Albert – Lollipop.mp3

Prince Albert info on the Web: http://www.peoplesound.com/artist/princealbert/

Prince Albert's 'Lollipop'.

Maroon Town

Artist information: Maroon Town are a vital and exiting nine piece band that combines breakbeat, ska, rap and dub in a high-energy musical fusion. The band's name is taken from a remote upland community in Jamaica, formed by runaway slaves.

This nine-piece multiracial Brixton band would be more at home on Trojan records than on Two Tone. The band is incredibly tight and their sound is an exciting fusion of ska, reggae, dub and a host of other styles. They have successfully toured around the globe and it is testament to their talent that they received the highest sponsorship ever for an unsigned band in a $100 000 deal with Dr Marten.

Album available: *Maroon Town*

Song on the CD: 'Are You Ready?'

About the song: 'Are you Ready?' is an uplifting ska tune from Maroon Town with Spaghetti Western overtones, I kid you not!

Song file location on the CD-ROM: pop\Maroon Town – Are You Ready.mp3

About the MP3 experience: 'For an independent band like us often embroiled in the hassle of looking out for distribution, MP3 is going to open up a whole different universe of getting our music out. It's direct to our fans/customers, cuts out record company sheep-like mentality and leaves it down to pure marketing to advertise our site and our product. Marketing is the key now and good ideas go a long way. As for sending demos out – that's ancient history now!'

Maroon Town.

Maroon Town info on the Web: `http://www.peoplesound.com/artist/maroontown/`

Maroon Town contact info: freedom@maroontown.co.uk

Trippa

Artist information: Delivering their own brand of edgy industrial pop combined with soaring orchestral arrangements, which has led some people to describe the band as the new Eurythmics, Trippa are set to be the next in a long line of Welsh pop successes.

Album available: *The Trippa EP*

Song on the CD: 'Where Are You?'

About the song: 'Where Are You?' is one of those power pop ballads you either love or hate with a strong vocal performance.

Song file location on the CD-ROM: pop\Trippa – Where Are You.mp3

Trippa info on the Web: `http://www.peoplesound.com/artist/trippa/`

Trippa.

217

Ki-Aura

Artist information: Ki-Aura was formed early 1999 and consists of two band members: Billy Attridge and Phillip Coady. Their main influences are the sound of Euro dance and commercial house. They've been working together since 1985 with Steppin' Out records as Outside World. They are looking for a record deal and have done a lot of remix work with Event One Music and in particular a dance act called The Slaves of Kane. In the five years that Billy and Phill have been working together they have worked on many different styles of music and look forward to continuing to do so.

Album available: *Miles From Above*

Song on the CD: 'Always There (Radio Edit)'

About the song: '"Always There" reflects the style of music Ki-Aura are trying to create, geared toward the crossover charts and mainstream dance clubs. The track itself was an experiment to see how elements of gospel music would fit into a commercial dance track.'

Song file location on the CD-ROM: pop\Ki-Aura – Always There (Radio Edit).mp3

About the MP3 experience: 'Both of us think that MP3 allows artists such as ourselves to compete on a level playing field with the big established record labels. It allows us to potentially have our music heard by anyone in the world without the need to unduly worry about distribution. As artists, having experienced how records companies operate and the length of time it takes them to get a record contract signed, sealed and delivered, it allows us to get our music out there while it's still fresh.'

Ki-Aura info on the Web: http://www.ki-aura.co.uk/

Ki-Aura – juicy!

Simulate

Simulate at their desk job.

Artist information: Simulate is a production-orientated dance act with two core members, Max Preece and Simon Lockyer. Vocalists are featured as required by the song and hired in. Two additional works on the Internet album *Stimulasm* were collaborations with Nick Harvey (the cyber-punk on Radio One's Chris Moyales UK PLAY show, who also wrote the music for the Chinese government for the Hong Kong handover) and Kevin Charge who, among tours and sessions, played for Oddessy. Max Preece is the owner of Max Studios where he and Simon have recorded much of Simon May's TV music and the album *Boy I Miss You* for BMG in the Far East.

'Enjoy' and 'Secret' are the free download tracks on peoplesound.com. 'Enjoy' was a four year old demo and 'Secret' an Ibiza house track which has sold well over 100 000 copies on four UK dance albums. Max is currently co-writing with Andy Hill and Simon is finishing a second album with Simon May for the library music company KPM.

Between themselves and the artists they produce and manage they have had 13 songs on eight albums in the last 18 months, not including any of the TV themes or incidental music.

Previous near misses in the early nineties include a film theme for Hollywood Pictures and track 'Tempted' on 10 other US movies including Coneheads, Assault with a Deadly Weapon and Milk Money.

Album available: *Stimulasm*

Song on the CD: 'Secret'

About the song: 'Secret' is one of those Ibizan summer tunes that conjures up memories of the magic isle.

Song file location on the CD-ROM: pop\Simulate – Secret.mp3

About the MP3 experience: 'Simulate now see the future of music distribution as digital and online (particularly as now major broadcasters are accepting MP3 as a legitimate submission and transmission format). Apart from a few reservations regarding royalty collection procedures [they are both directors of a Denmark Street music publisher] and anti-piracy precautions, are happy to exploit and be exploited by this new technology.

Initially there will be an explosion of rubbish on the Net but, as in any field, the good material and talent will surface. The companies that exercise caution and rigorous quality control, similar to top A&R now, will undoubtedly become wealthy market leaders. It remains to be seen whether the major labels can move swiftly enough to maintain both their younger customer base and market position.'

Simulate info on the Web: http://www.peoplesound.com/artist/simulate/

Kaja Wunder

Artist information: Kaja, an Estonian-born poet who speaks seven languages, came to London two years ago in search of musical collaborations. After hooking up with various co-writers she found her style which she describes as a cross between Enya, Dubstar and the Cranberries.

Kaja Wunder.

Album available: *Kaja Wunder*

Song on the CD: 'Pure'

About the song: Kaja Wunder will find it difficult to avoid comparisons to The Corrs, just as a year or two ago she would have been compared to The Cranberries in mellow moments or Mary Black. This track certainly wouldn't be out of place on one of those Celtic Heart-type compilations.

Song file location on the CD-ROM: pop\Kaja Wunder – Pure.mp3

Kaja Wunder info on the Web: http://www.peoplesound.com/artist/misskajawunder/

Charlie Waterford

Artist information: During her two years in the business Charlie has performed self-contained on the club circuit and has had TV appearances with Vanessa Feltz on BBC1 and with Michael Barrymore on 'My Kind Of People'.

Album available: *Charlie Waterford*

Song on the CD: 'Instead Of This'

Charlie Waterford.

About the song: If you had to write the book on how to achieve pop success in our times then sounding like Britney Spears would be high on that list. Unfortunately for Charlie Waterford, Britney Spears has already filled that particular vacancy. Still, if you are a fan of Ms Spears, and there are quite a few of you out there, you'll lap this up. Expect good things from Charlie though, she has more strings to her bow and clearly has the talent to find her own niche, and her four-track EP showcases them well.

Song file location on the CD-ROM: pop\Charlie Waterford – Instead Of This.mp3

Charlie Waterford info on the Web: `http://www.peoplesound.com/artist/` `charliewaterford/`

ZOEe

Artist information: ZOEe is 17, and has considerable vocal talents that she has inherited from her professional singing mother. ZOEe dances and has a healthy attitude towards hard work. She is currently doing live club work and is also rehearsing with her dancers for showcase slots.

Song on the CD: 'Dedicated'

About the song: Another piece of perfect pop dance, 'Dedicated' bounces along in that light 'n' breezy girlie vocalist style that you will either love or hate.

Song file location on the CD-ROM: pop\ZOEe – Dedicated.mp3

About the MP3 experience: 'I've been getting into MP3 as an instant way of hearing what's going on. Its got to be the way forward as it brings communication and music together in one easy package. The quality's great as well.'

ZOEe info on the Web: `http://www.peoplesound.com/artist/zoee/`

ZOEe.

Rock

Stony Sleep

Artist information: Hailing from North London, Stony Sleep formed in the bedroom of one (young) Ben Smith with brother Christian and friend William. 'This Kitten Is Clean' was their debut single for Big Cat Records, whilst their debut album *Music For Chameleons* finally hit the streets in the UK in July 1997 to a mass of critical acclaim throughout the music press.

Album available: *A Slack Romance*

Song on the CD: 'Khartoum'

About the song: No leather jacket required: this is rock for everyone. This has the energy, the quality and the tunefulness to appeal equally to metalheads, skaters and indie kids. Stony Sleep are set to awake and when they do the world will know about it. Outstanding.

Song file location on the CD-ROM: rock\Stony Sleep – Khartoum.mp3

Stony Sleep info on the Web: http://www.peoplesound.com/artist/stonysleep/

Stony Sleep look up.

Lazydog

Artist information: Lazydog are comprised of ex-Redwood (Almo Sounds) musician–songwriters, Ali Cowan (bass, vocals 'n' stuff) and Rob Blackham (guitar, computers 'n' stuff).

After becoming discontented with the late '90s Britrock scene, the two got together with Massive Attack producer Neil Davidge and came up with something new and exciting. Songs, soul and melody remained key elements, with an acoustic vibe forming the backbone of the sound – this being inevitable with such influences as Nick Drake and Tim Buckley. Couple this with a progressive vibe, a soulful groove, and a willingness to embrace technology, and you have the Lazydog sound.

Album available: *Sampler*

Song on the CD: 'Summer Dream'

About the song: 'The track "Summer Dream" is a song about stoners, and the apathy associated with people who "live for a toke" – people who can just about be arsed to "get up and make the tea". Drifting, sliding, and drowning in a hazy summer dream is where a lot of people find themselves, and observance to a certain extent, participation, gave rise to the song. In essence, it's chilled, lazy and dreamy.'

Song file location on the CD-ROM: rock\Lazy Dog – Summer Dream.mp3

Lazydog.

About the MP3 experience: 'MP3 has allowed the music of Lazydog to be accessed by anyone, anywhere around the world. The potential is there, and the Internet is bound to play a large part in the future of the music industry. As far as Ali and Rob are concerned, the technology is there to be used – whatever it takes to allow them to put out the songs they write will be utilised. In the end, what counts is the music, and anything that serves as a vehicle for this is a good thing.'

Lazydog info on the Web: http://www.redwood.org.uk

Lazydog contact info: mail@redwood.org.uk

Kane

Artist information: London-based trio; rolling, throbbing, bass-driven, industrial strength songs tuned down with a fully expanded, spliffed-out stoner rock edge. Blistering guitar riffs over ferocious bass lines cut with hostility and feedback. That's Kane.

Album available: *Kane*

Song on the CD: 'Get Up 52'

About the song: Spliffed out and full of feedback, 'Get Up 52' sounds just like one of those tracks Beavis and Butthead are always shaking their heads to. A bloody good tune then!

Song file location on the CD-ROM: rock\Kane – Get Up 52.mp3

Kane info on the Web: http://www.peoplesound.com/artist/kane/

Kane.

The Agents

Artist information: The Agents formed in London 1995. The line up has settled on Carl Dinesen (bass), Greg Darling (lead guitar), Nick Collings (drums) and Malcolm Litson (guitar, vocals). Their shared common thread is Anglo/American alternative music. Influences include The Clash, Joy Division, Pixies, Nirvana, Leftfield, Bowie, The Fall, Fugazi. The attitude is punk. They call it speed-beat. The future is still open.

Album available: *The Agents*

Song on the CD: 'Big Sting'

About the song: '"Big Sting" is a song about consumption. The machine keeps eating and no-one knows when it is going to stop. It is about money, freedom and control. Play it loud.'

Song file location on the CD-ROM: rock\The Agents – Big Sting.mp3

About the MP3 experience: 'We have always felt our music was as good as, if not better than, some of the rubbish that gets released through the usual channels. The industry is not inclined to take risks. Some music defines fashion as opposed to repeating a pale version of what has gone before. So far our output has been self-funded and generated with the help of friends. This includes recording, performance, photography, artwork, a video and even a projection on to the Houses of Parliament. If "They" won't help you then you do it yourself.

The Houses of MP3 – a projection by The Agents. (Photograph: Alex Estrella.)

'MP3 has now offered us an outlet to homes, offices and people's heads that has unlimited potential. This is great for off-centre bands like ourselves, although we still have to make outstanding music, more so than ever. MP3 is a democratic medium. Our sounds are a speck in a universe of information that keeps expanding. Andy Warhol's prediction is coming true, except everyone's fame may now be less than five minutes.

'To develop we still need people to get on board. Bands don't survive unless they find an audience that matches their belief. MP3 may help us find this audience. It has injected The Agents undiluted into a mainstream vein that was previously unavailable and that is a good thing. It gets us out there.'

The Agents info on the Web: http://www.geocities.com/theagentsfeedback

The Agents contact info: agentfeedback@hotmail.com

Psycho-Dynamics

Artist information: Psycho-Dynamics are a band that has the potential for great things. From claustrophobic verses into huge crashing choruses, the radio-friendly sound of their music is complimented by their live performance. On stage, they strip down to two guitars, drums, bass and a vocal to plough through a set of hit songs, bringing more of an edge to their sound.

Album available: *Psycho-Dynamics*

Song on the CD: '3 Words'

Psycho-Dynamics.

About the song: Don't let the scary front man scare you away kids! Psycho-Dynamics play very approachable indie–pop which should find favour with all indie lovers and a fair section of pop addicts. They describe their songs as 'radio-friendly', which is as good a summation as any for their affable sound.

Song file location on the CD-ROM: rock\Psycho-Dynamics – 3 Words.mp3

Psycho-Dynamics info on the Web: http://www.peoplesound.com/artist/
psychodynamics/

Ian Habgood

Artist information: Ian's professional career in music began while he studied performing and composition at Newcastle University. During this period he played on trumpet alongside acclaimed jazz artists such as Andy Sheppard, Georgie Fame, and Jarmuz. The music he creates is extremely varied and ranges from full classical arrangements to modern chilled grooves and from wacky children's songs to bossa nova sounds. Artist influences include Donald Byrd, Stevie Wonder, John Barry, Burt Bacharach and Brian Eno.

Album available: *Composer-Producer-Instrumentalist*

Song on the CD: 'Pray'

About the song: A blues-driven ballad with intense vocals, this tune is as strange and eclectic as Ian's repertoire. In his own words, '"Pray" was an experiment. The idea was to turn a simply produced folk song into something bigger and stranger.'

Song file location on the CD-ROM: rock\Ian Habgood – Pray.mp3

About the MP3 experience: 'I think MP3 is a good thing because with an MP3 player you can make your own compilation for the day. As an artist it's great because it allows you to get your music out there where people can hear it.'

Ian Habgood.

Ian Habgood info on the Web: http://www.peoplesound.com/artist/ianhabgood/

Ian Habgood contact info: +44 (0)7931 707 696, +44 (0)1202 571 667

Scud

Artist information: Scud have been around for a few years now since their first release, 'Po-Face', on Sycophant Records in 1994. This was followed by the single 'The Edwin Incident' and the album *Bullgator* on BGR Records of Nottingham, both of which gained favourable reviews In *Kerrang!*, *Metal Hammer* and *Terrorizer*.

Album available: *Guapo's Day Job*

Song on the CD: 'Appease'

About the song: Are you ready to rock? If you're not don't listen to this track then as it rocks as loudly and heavily as it can. If you are, then you'll love this.

Song file location on the CD-ROM: rock\Scud – Appease.mp3

Scud info on the Web: http://www.peoplesound.com/artist/scud/

Scud – Guapo's Day Job.

Ban Jyang

Artist information: 'Jyang is an invention of my own mind, a character in a story that has never been physically written down or recorded in any way, except through verbal explanation. As a kid, I fancied myself as a bit of budding author, and one of the many ideas banging around my head at the time was this oriental folklore style tragedy. Who knows where it came from? The closest I'd ever been to the orient was going down the Co-Op and buying a packet of Mr Ben's Savoury Rice! "Ban" is a courtesy or title, like "Mr".

'I decided to design a Web site to promote BJ that you can visit at `http://www.banjyang.com`. There are areas still under construction that I keep tinkering with when I get the time and I've got plans to build an online shop for merchandise and alike. In fact the idea is to move a lot of energies into finalising the Web site and creating a central nervous system, if you like. I plan to make everything "Ban Jyang" available from this central pool. Everything from CDs to T-shirts to posters, even a download area where you can sample old and new material in MP3 format.'

Album available: *Religious Love Hater*

Song on the CD: 'Sect'

About the song: I get the impression that Ban Jyang aren't in regular attendance at the local Sunday school. They cover a range of metal styles; 'Sect' even has hip hop influences. A powerful voice, heartfelt lyrics (it's the parents I blame) and tight tunes should see Ban Jyang score big with the *Kerrang!* crowd.

Song file location on the CD-ROM: rock\Ban Jyang – Sect.mp3

About the MP3 experience: 'I'm a bit of a beginner with the format but the potential is enormous. For me it means I can get my music files down to a manageable file size, it also means I can get my music heard via the Internet, which has got to be the biggest shop window on the planet. MP3 means I can record an album straight on to my hard disk, compress the damned thing into a gnat's arse, bang it up to the Web site and make it available for download to anyone who's got a computer, and guess what? No record label screwing me out of my hard earned! Now that can't be bad. The thing is, I can't afford to pay studio rates and mass CD manufacturing.

'I'm not signed to a major label so I'm forced to find another way. MP3 has opened up that door. I can sit at home and record whatever I feel like using my PC, and have it sitting on my site for all to enjoy in a couple of minutes. Now you can buy next-generation portable digital audio players like the Nomad II, another exciting innovation. Things are looking bright for us DIY musos. It's got to be good for the consumer too. I mean if people can buy the albums online and direct from the band at perhaps half the cost that you see in the high street, what are you gonna do? I can't talk about your superstars of course but for the likes of me, it's a Godsend.

'From a personal point of view I want to get my music played to as many people as possible, which is where the Internet comes into it's own. If people like it enough to buy, they can simply download an entire album's worth of MP3's or even one track at a time. It's the consumers' choice and no-one gets ripped off and everyone is happy.'

Banjyang info on the Web: `http://www.shinyhead.freeserve.co.uk/` and `http://www.banjyang.com`

Ban Jyang contact info: mark@shinyhead.freeserve.co.uk

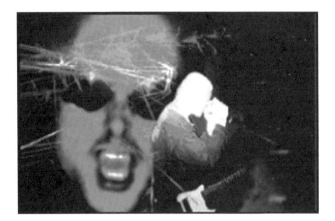

Ban Jyang.

Asterix

Asterix.

Artist information: Asterix are a four piece from Co. Derry. They began their lives as killing, joke-loving, thrash pop merchants, and have played together in various incarnations since 1984. Maturity and trips abroad encouraged them to mellow out

231

and Donal, Vincent, Frankie and Darren regrouped as four vocally-driven, melancholic pop craftsmen, producing work of great beauty and emotional intensity

Albums available: *I Know Your Soul, Somewhere in Bhutan*

Song on the CD: 'Somewhere In Bhutan'

About the song: Melancholic, harmonic pop that can't disguise its thrash rock past, this has more hooks than a coat rack.

Song file location on the CD-ROM: rock\Asterix – Somewhere In Bhutan.mp3

Asterix info on the Web: http://www.peoplesound.com/artist/asterix/

Freeloader

Artist information: A refreshing, yet intense, punk/hardcore crew blending sheets of white noise with melodic suss, Freeloader carve out a racket that is unmistakable and inescapable. With a maniac frontman busting all known blood vessels, dragging his troops towards riot ensuing intensity. Hop on, stage-dive left, get in a fight – let's pogo.

Album available: *Back Room Sessions EP*

Song on the CD: 'Denial'

About the song: Punky pop with manic overtones, 'Denial' isn't in it, thank goodness!

Song file location on the CD-ROM: rock\Freeloader – Denial.mp3

Freeloader info on the Web: http://www.peoplesound.com/artist/freeloader/

Freeloader.

Others

Darius

Artist information: Darius is a 23-year-old singer–songwriter and multi-instrumentalist who lives between London and New York. Influenced by Prince, George Michael and Seal, he has written and recorded with Jimmy Harry (Kylie Minogue, RuPaul), Ronald Bell (Kool and The Gang, The Fugees) and most recently worked with Rachid on several tracks for his debut album, *Prototype* (MCA/Universal).

Album available: *Give It 2 U*

Song on the CD: 'Give It To You'

About the song: '"Give It To You' is a feel-good song that thumps as much as it soothes.'

Song file location on the CD-ROM: others\Darius – Give It To You.mp3

About the MP3 experience: 'MP3 meant a lot of exposure as an unsigned artist. It's been nice to take some form of control over getting my music out to people without the usual industry hassle. Today's music business seems to be less and less about music; the MP3 experience is hopefully bringing the music back again.'

Darius info on the Web: www.mp3.com/darius/

Darius contact info: dnasty@talk21.com

Darius.

Flexyman

Artist information: Flexyman is a reggae artist who has been in the music business for the last 15 years. In that time he has released two singles which were distributed by Jet Star. A qualified music facilitator working at schools, colleges and workshops, the previous band he sang with won a Battle of the Bands competition in the East Midland area. His album is now finished and ready for world-wide distribution by Man-na Hearts Promotion.

His live work includes appearances on cable television taped during the Hyson Green festival in Nottingham, a performance at the Derby Motor Show, a small tour of Jamaica and a UK tour with Culture from Jamaica.

Album available: *Money Talking*

Song on the CD: 'On The Road'

About the song: A superb serving of accessible reggae that will find favour across the spectrum. 'On The Road' is a classic piece of pop-reggae.

Song file location on the CD-ROM: others\Flexyman – On The Road.mp3

Flexyman info on the Web: http://www.active-ingredient.co.uk/flexyman

Flexyman – Money Talking.

Last Men Standing

Artist information: The group came together in 1998, and consists of three members: Koaste on vocals, Genesis on production and DJ Enema on the cut. The group had one basic intention. With the constant mediocrity of most hip-hop acts nowadays, they wanted to produce tracks that more actually reflected their realities and environment.

Album available: *Call To Arms EP*

Song on the CD: 'Call To Arms'

About the song: UK hip-hop with style from Last Men Standing. The group have a stated mission to raise the standing of British hip-hop world wide, something they will surely achieve if they can maintain output of this calibre. This is one for the clubs and the charts.

Song file location on the CD-ROM: others\Last Men Standing – Call To Arms.mp3

Last Men Standing info on the Web: http://www.peoplesound.com/artist/lastmenstanding/

Zohar

Zohar.

Artist information: Zohar combines spiritual Middle-Eastern chants with experimental beats, drum and bass textures, and deep ambient grooves, to create a powerfully hypnotic cinematic score of sounds and rhythms – a deconstruction of ancient and modern. Festival appearances have included The Lizzard Eclipse Festival, Homelands, Knebworth and Glastonbury.

Albums available: *One; Three; Seven, Elokainu*

Song on the CD: 'Angel'

About the song: Combining the best of world music with ambient, dub and trip-hop 'Angel' is one of those grooves that chills as it entrances.

Song file location on the CD-ROM: others\Zohar – Angel.mp3

Zohar info on the Web: `http://www.peoplesound.com/artist/zohar/`

Stylle Freee

Artist information: Stylle Freee (pronounced 'style free') consists of the musical talents of Roger D.Morrison and Judith Ferguson. The duo have been collaborating for over five years and have written and produced a vast array of original material covering all popular styles of music.

With their substantial experience in writing and producing, the duo have been involved with several independent record labels. Roger has written and arranged songs for three record companies and has had a solo album of original material released entitled *Pictures In My Mind* (which had favourable reviews in *Blues & Soul* and *The Voice*). Judith has had several releases as a featured vocalist on a popular dance independent with one track resulting in a promotional video that had extensive TV coverage.

Their most experience has been on live circuit, where they have been consistently showcasing their repertoire of original songs and groovy covers. The Stylle Freee band consists of Markus Anderson on bass, Paul McCarney on drums and Marveline G. on backing vocals. They have also worked with some of the capital's finest session musicians and singers. Their gigs have taken them all over the UK over a five-year period and they have developed a strong polished show.

Stylle Freee are also an aspiring writing–production team with their own home studio providing original material for up-and-coming artists and passing on all their relevant experience. Ultimately they would also like to write for more established artists.

The duo, in association with Groove Brew Records (a small independent label based in South London), have produced a Mega EP special available now on promo. They are currently seeking the right recording/publishing deal to further promote their talents and would be very interested in some form of licensing deal for their product.

'Our influences are as diverse as our tastes but on the whole we are about real songs with imaginative lyrics and strong melodies. Qualities which are typical of such artists as Stevie Wonder, Aretha Franklin and Prince, who as well as great writing abilities possess excellent vocal prowess and live musical ability. This is not to say we are against sample-based releases, but we feel a good marriage between the technology and real musicianship always has something more special and we try to achieve this in our writing and producing.

Stylle Freee, so you don't have to be!

'There are some great innovators who are always pushing the boundaries, not always feeling they have to fit in and be pigeon-holed. We can relate to this and although we always try to cater to the more popular market, we always try to offer something a little different with our own music and the artists we write and produce for.'

Album available: *The Future Looks Bright*

Song on the CD: 'Back Where U Oughtta Be'

About the song: 'This track was first written about 18 months ago and we went for a more modern R&B production with live guitar. The software we use is Cubase VST and all the parts were fully programmed with the exception of a hip-hop-style drum loop in the midsection.

'We've always preferred a fat vocal sound so I tracked up Judith's vocals quite a few times on the choruses. The whole track was completed within two-and-a-half days and was mixed in our own home studio. The track was mastered at a friend's studio in South London. As this track has been so well received (it is currently available on a compilation in Japan) we have completed several remixes.'

Song file location on the CD-ROM: others\Stylle Freee – Back Where You Ought To Be.mp3

About the MP3 Experience: 'Like so many artists with a certain amount of talent and musical skill, we are constantly frustrated by what we consider to be a decline in the signing and exposure of new artists by the industry – with the exception of certain types of acts that are fashionable at the time.

'We have been aware of the need for other ways of promoting our work to as wide a market as possible and now with the power of the Internet and the World Wide Web this dream can be realised. Having spent many months learning all your music software, how to manipulate your samples, not to mention keeping the creative juices flowing, the thought of mastering the Net and all the associated software was more than a little bit daunting.

'So after discovering peoplesound.com and understanding a little bit about different audio file formats we were pleased to hear about the arrival of MP3 and the fact that you can compress a standard CD-quality audio file to about a tenth of its size and retain its quality. This is still relatively new to us but we are obviously excited by the possibilities and we will be exploiting this format as much as possible with our ever-growing knowledge of the Net. We look forward to some international musical interactions.'

Stylle Freee info on the Web: `http://www.peoplesound.com/styllefreee/`

Stylle Freee contact info: Tel: +44 (0)208 376 3589 or +44 (0)378 407708

Ian Habgood

Artist information: See entry on p. 236.

Album available: *Composer-Producer-Instrumentalist*

Song on the CD: 'The B Theme (Featuring Vibes)'

About the song: The jazz groove is evident in this filmic instrumental that demonstrates this artist's musical proficiency. 'I wanted to write something that sounded old and yet new at the same time, It has subtle jazz influences, from sixties and seventies loungecore.'

Song file location on the CD-ROM: others\Ian Habgood – The B Theme (Featuring Vibes).mp3

Ian Habgood info on the Web: `http://www.peoplesound.com/artist/ianhabgood/`

Ian Habgood contact info: +44 (0)7931 707 696, +44 (0)1202 571 667

Jozef Olechowski

Artist information: Descendant of a family with a strong musical tradition, Jozef Olechowski started his piano studies with his father. He carried them further in Krakow and Katowice, major centres of piano studies in Europe. His liking of the European romantic repertoire together with his close links with Mexico have determined Jozef Olechowski's encounter with Mexican romantic music.

Album available: *Almay Corazon – Ernesto Elorduy, Nostalgia Por Mexico* (with Elena Duran)

Song on the CD: 'Melodia – L.G Jorda'

About the song: One for the classical fans, this piece is a sensitive piece of playing that brings out all the lyricism of the original composition.

Song file location on the CD-ROM: others\Jozef Olechowski – Melodia – L.G Jorda.mp3

Jozef Olechowski info on the Web: http://www.peoplesound.com/artist/ jozefolechowski/

Jozef Olechowski.

Nat Birchall

Artist information: Nat Birchall embodies the past, the present and the future of jazz. Deeply rooted in the heady ambience of the '60s and classic labels such as Impulse, Blue Note and Prestige, Nat possesses an attitude of reality and integrity that he couples with the imaginativeness of original compositions that stretch the mind and swing the soul.

Album available: *Sixth Sense*

Song on the CD: 'Helix Nebula'

About the song: Smokey, bluesy jazz that is drenched in atmosphere, 'Helix Nebula' benefits from a strong composition and expressive playing.

Song file location on the CD-ROM: others\Nat Birchall – Helix Nebula.mp3

Nat Birchall info on the Web: http://www.peoplesound.com/artist/
natbirchall/

Nat Birchall.

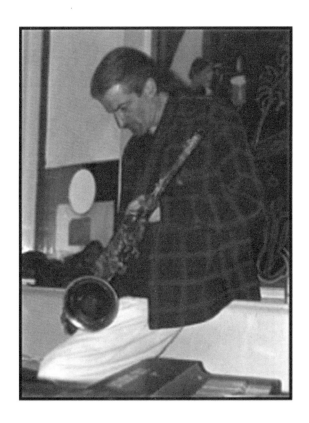

Iris

Artist information: Iris have no biography, blurb or bullshit to share with you. They simply request the pleasure of your ears. Download their music into the well and swell of your psyche and let them take you beyond strawberry fields. 'I find our music incredibly hard to describe because as soon as I put it into words it all sounds so regurgitated and intellectual. When I'm singing, each song becomes a theatrical performance for me and I have a vivid imagination of where I am and all the sensory things that surround me.' – Joanna Swan, singer from Iris.

Album available: *Comfort And Destiny*

Song on the CD: 'Too Much Of You'

About the song: 'When recording "Too Much Of You", I became a jaded torch singer of the 1950s who, in an old back-street jazz club at three in the morning, sings her cracked and bitter ballad of a failed love affair. There is always a very surreal dream state to the pictures in my mind and our music, the enigmatic piano loop, clapped out drums and 007 Bond-like trumpet add to that quality.'

Song file location on the CD-ROM: others\Iris – Too Much Of You.mp3

About the MP3 Experience: 'What would you prefer, A: To know that the album you poured your passion and creativity into sits in a hundred A&R offices throughout England gathering coke-infested dust. Or B: to know that within a couple of months, thousands of people all over the world have listened to, and downloaded, two of your favourite tracks from the above album? To make money would be fantastic but I am just so happy to be heard!'

Iris info on the web: http://www.peoplesound.com/artist/iris/

Iris' lead singer Joanna Swan.

Hi-Life Maha

Artist information: Born in Ghana, West Africa, Love Isaacs grew up in a community of highlife music and dedicated himself since the age of 10 to playing drums and singing. He left Ghana for Britain to continue his musical career and also to study studio engineering. Love created his band in 1992; the name Maha is a word which has connotations of giving enjoyment.

Album available: *Fre Me*

Song on the CD: 'Fre Me'

About the song: Electronic Hi-Life music with pop and reggae influences, 'Fre Me' is a soulful yet joyous tune that lives up to Maha's promise.

Song file location on the CD-ROM: others\Hi-Life Maha – Fre Me.mp3

About the MP3 experience: 'MP3 is a help to musicians in getting songs heard by people who may not have had the chance to hear them otherwise.'

Hi-Life Maha info on the Web: http://www.maha-music-productions.com

Love Isaacs contact info: bands@maha-music-productions.com, and acts@african-caribbean-ents.com

Love Issacs.

The Least You Need to Know

➤ A wide variety of musicians are using MP3s on the Internet to promote their music.

➤ They are reaching new fans from all over the world.

➤ You are now ready to join the MP3 movement!

Afterword

The digital compressed audio revolution is raging even as you read this page. And it truly is a battle; the music manufacturing industry is fighting hard to put a rein on it, even as individual record companies and artists are plotting ways to make money in the compressed digital world.

Predicting the future even in the best of situations is a chancy situation. After all, if we lived in the twenty-first century that the science fiction writers predicted 50 years ago, we wouldn't have digital music but we would all have flying cars in our garages.

So we can't pinpoint the future but, with a little thought, we can focus on some important and likely directions it may take.

The Digital Music May Not Be MP3

The revolution is compressed digital music. MP3 just happens to be the popular format. Assuming that it's going to continue to reign is like someone in 1910 assuming that because a lot of people were buying Model T Fords, in the future everyone would own a Model T.

Many companies are working on competing standards and not just minor companies, either. IBM, Microsoft and Lucent Technologies are all pitching their own audio compression schemes because there is big money to be had in developing the scheme that becomes popular. All these new schemes include systems to copy-protect the files so that record companies would be able to sell you compressed music that would work on your player but would not work on someone else's player.

Compression schemes are also competing on quality and getting the same quality audio into less space or better-quality sound out of the same space. Although there is only so much compression can improve, every little bit helps.

Big Companies Won't Give It Away

There is one quality to look for that the big–company standards won't offer: free access to the standard. One of the irritants about MP3 is that someone holds a patent on it and aims to collect money from everyone making encoders. This licence fee adds substantial costs to many MP3 efforts. A quality compression standard that was free for all to use would likely be embraced by many. If such a thing is likely to arise, it will probably come either from academia or from a pro-fessional consortium... and even then, it will have to compete in the marketplace of concepts with formats that have financial backing behind them.

Still, all this doesn't mean that MP3 will be wiped out. Some of the attempts at new formats are really just improved versions of MP3. These use the basics of MP3 com-pression but add copy-protection information or added compression features. Compare that with the way that home video tape has evolved. VHS tape has been around for decades now and at the beginning it didn't have the best video quality and it didn't have copy protection. Now there is Super-VHS and copy-protection schemes but the players will still play the same old VHS tapes recorded in the 1970s. Back then, there weren't tapes that would store up to nine hours, or little VHS-C tapes for handheld camcorders, but these features have been integrated into VHS, rather than eliminating it.

The Web Appears To Be Taking Over

Currently, the Internet is something that everyone is talking about and many people have access to. In fact, if you live in some communities, it is easy to assume that everyone has Internet access. Alas, that is not yet the case, particularly in our poorer communities.

However, it may well be true in the days to come. The Web, phone and TV seem to be converging into what will end up being a single data tube that will be able to receive and send all sorts of signals. If that happens, that will change the way we access many things that are essentially data, music included.

Hardware Will Become Cheaper

It's hardly a new observation that what was impossible yesterday is available today and cheap tomorrow. The first digital watches cost hundreds of pounds; now you can find them for a fiver. The price of a portable CD player is less than one tenth of what the first ones cost. In the last 20 years, the price of computer memory per byte has dropped over 99.99%. And it's faster, more compact and more reliable to boot.

The price of compressed music hardware is likely to drop harshly and the capability is likely to swell. A £150 portable player that carries a half-hour's worth of music is going to be seen by many people as an expensive novelty item. A £40 player that has 80 hours of music, on the other hand, can be the main device in your mobile sound arsenal. (And wouldn't it be cool if you could just plug that player into a special interface in your car dashboard and take those same songs on the road?)

Physical Music Media May Die

Once the big music owners see that everyone is hooked to the Internet and are likely to be able to play compressed music, there is a lot of incentive to sell everything via download, rather than having you buy CDs and compress them yourself. If they sell you the compressed file, they can make sure that the copy protection is in place so that you can't go around sharing the file with others. Better still, they are spared the cost of actually having to manufacture the CD and they keep from having to share the cost with the CD stores.

For the customer, it saves the trip to the CD store. It's particularly good if your tastes go beyond the currently popular recordings. Even a good record store is only going to carry a fraction of what's available, which is itself a small portion of everything that has ever been released. Online, however, everything is available and there's little reason for anything to ever be deleted.

Don't expect this to happen without a fight. There are too many pounds tied up in selling you physical CDs. All those CD store chains aren't going to give up without a struggle; expect them to try both to win you over and to erect legal blockage to this move toward all-electronic music distribution. They won't be the only ones facing this sort of concern because video rental stores are likely to face similar problems with Internet distribution of movies. Even the record labels are likely to keep in the fight because switching the customers to downloadable music means they no longer have control over distribution. It's just about as easy to find a small music label's Web site as that of a big label.

No Storage Needed At Home

If you have a CD collection, you know that the longer you have it, the more space it takes up. It's easy to expect that your home stereo MP3 player will need an ever-increasing amount of storage space – bigger and bigger hard disks to be filled with downloads over that ultra-high-speed Internet connection (even though the disk itself takes up little physical space). Just the opposite may be true – if the MP3 player is hooked up at a reasonably high speed, you really don't need to store the music at all!

Instead, every time you want to hear a song, it could be sent at lightning speed over the Internet. This would not only keep the cost and complexity of your player down, it would also make it easier for the music owner to make sure that you aren't copying the tune. The music company might charge you a very small amount for each time you play a song or it might keep track of which tunes you've paid for and are allowed to play.

Subscribe To Music

Once you're set up to download each song as you listen to it at home, the entire model for how you pay for music may change. Consider the way you pay for basic cable: a fixed monthly charge, no matter how much or how little you watch, no matter which of the basic cable channels you choose to enjoy. In the downloadable music equivalent, for some per-month price (say, £10), you could listen to any song you want, whenever you want, on your home stereo. No need to 'own' any music, since you can always hear it. Some central tracking company would see how often people listened to each song and split the artists' portion of the money appropriately. Sound strange? It's actually a lot like the way that radio stations pay for music. You may even be able to reduce your monthly fee if you let advertisers throw in occasional ads.

Of course, you could still play your own playlists but this would also open up the new job of playlist jockey. Some big band fan could program up good big band selections. Doctor Demento could offer a good mix of novelty and comedy recordings 24 hours per day. Chuck D. could offer a special program of his favourite old school tunes. Some hip street kid could offer up playlists of the newest sounds in whatever the currently popular genre is. When you choose to listen to someone's playlist, they'd get a small cut of your subscription fee.

Digital Music May Take To The Air

There are already various forms of digital broadcast going on. Soon, TV broadcasting will be switching over to HDTV, with digital compressed video and audio. Once people are listening to portable devices that have both decompression and radio tuning already built in, it won't be much of a change for the players to start decoding radio signals.

What would be gained from this? On the one hand, it could be used to improve the audio quality of radio, putting a high-quality compressed signal in the same bandwidth that an analogue radio system used to take up. On the other hand, several lower-quality signals could be compressed on to the same channel, allowing a wider range of listening options.

Music Will Still Be Music

All of this won't change the fact that it's not the technology that gives us joy. Little bundles of electronics may make the sound sharper, cheaper or more portable but they're still doing the same basic job as the old Edison cylinders: allowing us to enjoy the tunes created by talented music makers.

Glossary

AAC   An audio compression system that gives better compression rates than MP3. It is short for advanced audio coding.

analogue   Used to refer to sound that has not been turned into numbers. An analogue sound wave can be infinitely variable, as opposed to digitised sound, which is limited to discrete values.

ASFS   An encoded compressed music file format supported by Virtuosa Gold.

Audio Home Recording Act   A US law passed in 1992 that increased home music copying freedom while placing restrictions on audio players and taxes on players and recording media.

auxiliary   Refers to a socket on your sound card that you can connect other audio playing devices to; also called line in.

bit rate   The amount of data used to hold a given length of music; measured in kilobits per second or Kbps.

CBR   Short for constant bit rate, this term describes MP3 files where each second of the music is compressed to the same size.

CDA   Refers to the uncompressed encoding method used to store audio on a standard CD; short for compact disc audio.

CDDB   An online database of CD album information.

CD-R   Drives and media that let you make your own CD-ROMs and audio CDs with your computer; short for compact disc-recordable.

CD-RW   Drives and reusable media that let you store data in a CD-like format; short for compact disc-rewritable. Although CD-RW media cannot be read by normal CD players or CD-ROM drives, most CD-RW drives can also write to CD-R media, which does not have that limitation.

CISAC   Confédération Internationale des Sociétés d'Auteurs et Compositeurs (International Confederation of Societies of Authors and Composers).

codec   Any system to store data in less space; short for compressor/decompressor.

compress   To store a set of data using less space while retaining necessary information.

constant bit rate   *See* CBR.

copyright   Legal right to control the reproduction of writing, music, photos, artwork or film.

DAE   The ability of a CD-ROM drive to transfer the digital audio information from an audio CD to the computer; short for digital audio extraction.

decode   To convert an encoded audio file into uncompressed, unencoded digital audio information.

decompress   To convert a compressed audio file into an uncompressed one.

digital audio   A recording of sound stored as a series of numbers.

digital audio extraction   *See* DAE.

digitise   To convert analogue audio into digital audio by repeatedly measuring (also called sampling) the sound wave.

docking station   A holder used to store a portable MP3 player. This holder is connected to the PC, and is used to transfer data to the player from the PC. Some holders are also used to recharge the player's batteries.

encode   To convert data into a specific file format.

encrypted   Refers to data files that are stored so that they cannot be properly read without a password or key of some sort. This process is used to create audio files that will run on your player but not on anyone else's.

fair use   A legal concept describing certain legitimate cases for reproducing copyrighted material without a licence.

flash memory   Computer memory that does not lose stored data when the power is turned off.

hardware   Physical portions of computer equipment (compare **software**, which includes programs, files and so on).

ID3   A format for including informational tags in an MP3 file, allowing many players to display information about the song.

Internet radio   Streaming digital audio transmissions over the Internet that can be listened to by anyone with the compatible receiving program.

ISO   Short for International Standards Organization, a group that sets standards for various engineering and design concerns.

jack   A connector that receives another connector into it. Also called a socket.

Kbps   Short for kilobits per second, a measurement of the amount of data it takes to make a second of music in an MP3 file.

kilobit   1024 bits. A bit is the smallest unit of computer data storage.

line in   Refers to a socket on your sound card that you can connect other audio playing devices to; also called auxiliary.

lossless   Refers to compression methods in which the compressed file could be decompressed into an exact replica of the original uncompressed file. Also refers to reproduction methods in which the copy is an exact match of the original.

lossy   Refers to compression methods in which the compressed file cannot be decompressed into an exact replica of the original uncompressed file. Also refers to reproduction methods in which the copy is not an exact match of the original.

MCPS   *See* Mechanical Copyright Protection Society.

Mechanical Copyright Protection Society   A recording rights service that you can contact to secure permission to cover a song.

mechanical licence   A form of permission granted allowing you to cover a given song and release it on record, tape or CD.

mic in   The socket on a sound card designed to have a microphone connected to it.

microdrive   A form of very small hard drive that can be used in place of flash memory in some instances.

MIDI   Short for musical instrument digital interface, this refers to a standard for connecting electronic instruments and computers. Also refers to a file format used to store the computer equivalent of sheet music, with a list of which notes are being played and what instruments are playing them.

miniplug   The sort of plug used on the end of headphones for portable tape or CD players.

MP3   Short for MPEG-1 Layer 3, this term refers to a standard of audio compression originally designed for inclusion with compressed video.

MP4   A term that has been used to refer to various audio compression schemes that are deemed to be better than MP3, including AAC among others.

MPEG   Short for the Moving Pictures Expert Group, a committee within the ISO that designs standards related to digitised video. Their various standards are labelled MPEG-1, MPEG-2, and so on.

MPMan   A series of portable MP3 players manufactured by Saehan and released in the UK by G2E.

MusicMatch Jukebox   A Windows-based MP3 player, encoder and manager that can also deal with CDs, WAV files, and other digital audio formats.

patch   A small program used to change or update another program.

Performing Right Society

player   A device or program that decodes and plays digital audio files.

playlist   A file with a list of songs for a player to play or select from.

plug   A connector that gets inserted into a socket.

plug-in   A small program that another program can run, adding functions to the larger program.

PRS   *See* Performing Right Society.

public domain   A legal term referring to works that are not covered by copyright (either due to age, to not having their copyright maintained, or to having material deliberately put into the public domain by its creator) and thus can be copied or used freely.

RCA plug   A standard style of connector usually used for connecting audio and video components.

RealAudio   A popular standard for streaming audio.

RIAA   The Recording Industry Association of America, a group that acts as advocate for the interests of a number of CD and cassette publishers.

Rio   A popular portable MP3 player made by Diamond Multimedia.

rip   To copy the digital audio information from an audio CD on to a computer.

sample   This term refers to a single digital measurement of a sound wave, with a series of samples being used to make digital audio recording. The term is also used to refer to segments of existing recorded works being included in a new work, as is often done with dance and hip-hop music.

SanDisc   A compact brand of flash memory storage.

SDMI   Short for secure digital music initiative, an attempt to create a digital audio file format that will be acceptable to the recording industry by alleviating their concerns about uncontrolled digital copying and reuse.

shareware   Programs that are distributed at no charge by the publisher, but with the expectation that the user will try them and then pay for them if they find the program is of use.

Shoutcast   A popular streaming audio solution supported by Winamp, often used for Internet radio stations.

skin   A file or group of files that creates an alternative look for a program without really changing its function.

SmartMedia   A popular standard for flash memory cards, used by MP3 players, digital cameras, and other portable devices.

socket   A connector that one inserts another connector into; also called a jack.

software   The programs and information that a computer uses (compare to hardware, which are the more physical portions of a computer; for example, a CD-ROM is hardware, but the data stored on the CD-ROM is software).

Sonique   A program used for playing MP3s and other digital audio.

sound card   An internal computer device used to turn computer data into output for speakers, and to digitise audio from outside the computer.

streaming audio   Digitised sound that you listen to at roughly the same time as it is being sent over the Internet.

tag   A piece of descriptive text embedded into an MP3 system.

tethered system   A hardware MP3 playing device designed to remain connected to your computer.

theme   An alternative design for a program's appearance, similar to a skin.

Usenet   A system of online message boards available through the Internet.

variable bit rate   A system of MP3 encoding that does not record every segment of the music at the same bit rate.

255

VBR   *See* variable bit rate.

WAV   A format for uncompressed digital audio files.

Winamp   A popular player program for MP3s and other digital audio formats.

Index

Licensing Agreement

By opening this package, you are agreeing to be bound by the following:

The software contained on this CD is, in many cases, copyrighted, and all rights are reserved by the individual software developer and/or publisher. You are bound by the individual licensing agreements associated with each piece of software contained on the CD. THIS SOFTWARE IS PROVIDED FREE OF CHARGE, AS IS, AND WITHOUT WARRANTY OF ANY KIND, EITHER EXPRESSED OR IMPLIED, INCLUDING BUT NOT LIMITED TO THE IMPLIED WARRANTIES OF MERCHANTABILITY AND FITNESS FOR A PARTICULAR PURPOSE. Neither the book publisher nor its dealers and distributors assumes any liability for any alleged or actual damages arising from the use of this software.